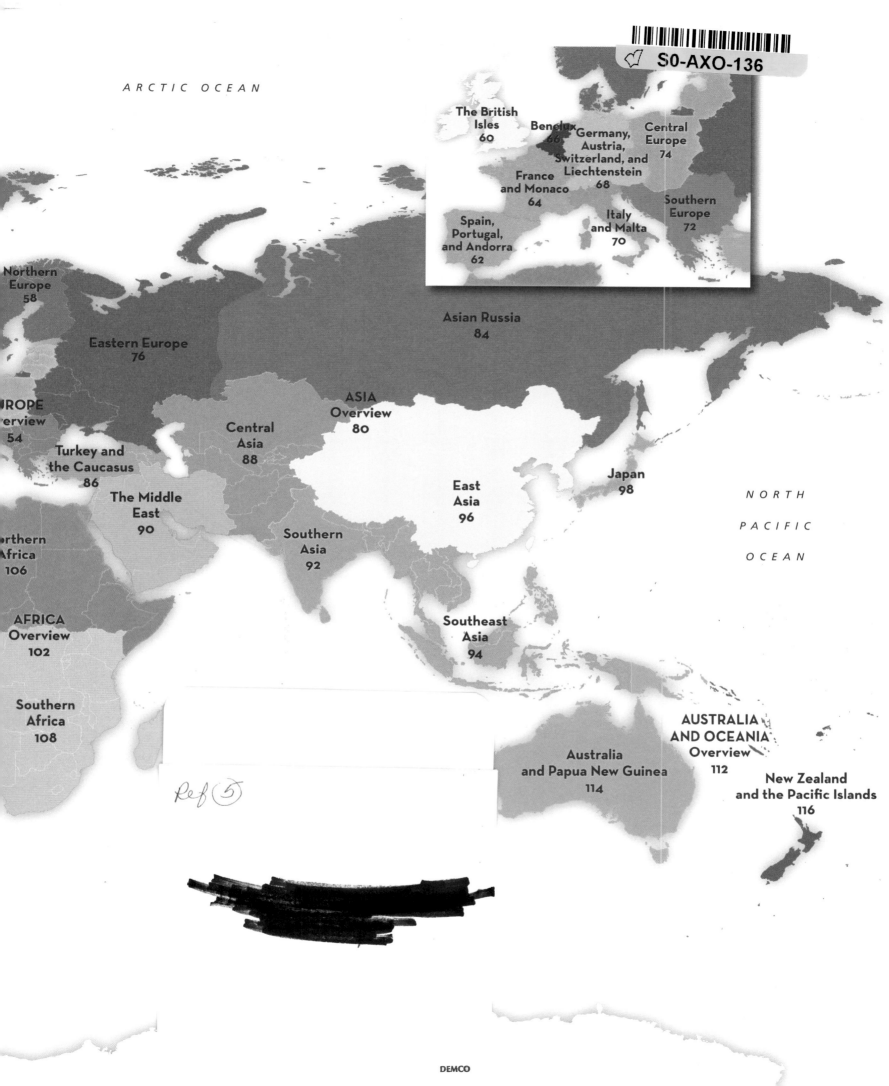

ARCTIC OCEAN

S0-AXO-136

NORTH

PACIFIC

OCEAN

Ref 5

DEMCO

HAMMOND

CHILDREN'S
WORLD
ATLAS

Published in North America by HAMMOND WORLD ATLAS
CORPORATION, part of the Langenscheidt Publishing Group
36-36 33rd Street, Long Island City, NY, 11106

Executive Director, Publishing Karen Prince

Produced for HAMMOND WORLD ATLAS CORPORATION by

McRae Books Srl
Via del Salviatino, 1 - 50016 Fiesole (Florence), Italy
info@mcraebooks.com
www.mcraebooks.com
Publishers: Anne McRae, Marco Nardi
Text: James Harrison, Anne Mcrae
Statistics: for the political spreads, CIA Factbook 2008; for the
introduction: United Nations
Maps: Laurie Whiddon, Map Illustrations
Design project: Marco Nardi
Design: Marco Nardi
Editing: Anne McRae
Illustrations: Manuela Cappon, Lorenzo Cecchi, Matteo Chesi,
Ferruccio Cucchiarini, Fiammetta Dogi, Gian Paolo Faleschini,
GB Project, Paola Holguin, Sabrina Marconi, Federico Micheli,
Antonella Pastorelli, Studio Stalio (Alessandro Cantucci,
Fabiano Fabbrucci, Andrea Morandi, Ivan Stalio), Paola Ravaglia,
Andrea Ricciardi di Gaudesi
Photographs: 13 (top right), 23 (top left), 29 (top center and right):
NASA; 28 (bottom): A detail of a Map of New Amsterdam, 1660 "The
Castello Plan", Museum of the City of New York, The J. Clarence
Davies Collection, 29.100.709; 29 (center right): New York City
subway map © Metropolitan Transportation Authority. Used with
permission

Printed and bound in Italy

ISBN-13: 978-08437-0972-8

HAMMOND

CHILDREN'S
WORLD
ATLAS

Contents

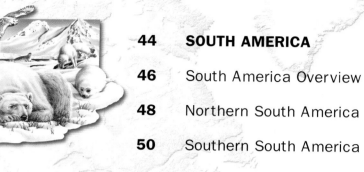

Introduction

At the end of the first decade of the 21st century we can begin to see the major new trends that will shape the century to come. Several key themes emerge, including globalization, the communications boom, and the fast pace of economic growth in emerging economies. Countries such as China, India, and Brazil will overtake the current large economies of North America and Europe by mid-century and perhaps re-shape global power maps by the end of the century. Population growth and decline are also key trends as they relate to mass migration of people from poorer regions who seek better lives in wealthier nations. Mass tourism broadens horizons everywhere as more and more people travel to increase their knowledge and experience. Traditional peoples and lifestyles are increasingly threatened in a fast-paced, globally connected world, while the natural environment registers the toll of population increase, pollution, and the lack of planning for sustainable growth.

Below: View of Hong Kong Harbor. Hong Kong became one of the world's leading financial centers in the final decades of the 20th century. It was returned to China in 1997 and is now a special administrative region within China.

■ REGIONAL POPULATION GROWTH

GROWTH RATE*

- −0%
- 0–1%
- 1%
- 2%
- 3%

*2006 estimate.

Above: The population is growing at different rates around the world. The biggest increase is in Africa and parts of Asia. In some, mainly northern, regions the population is actually declining. The countries with the highest population growth rates tend to be among the poorest, and have the fewest jobs to offer their new citizens.

ENVIRONMENTAL ISSUES

Many scientists believe that climate change caused by global warming is the most serious challenge we will face this century. The clearing of rain forest for timber and farmland, pollution caused by industry, cars, airplanes, and industrial accidents (including leakage of radioactive substances and poisons, or oil spills), among other things, are all major concerns. In recent years environmental groups, governments, and concerned individuals have tried to educate people about how to live in more environment-friendly ways. (See pages 22–23 for more information on climate change and the environment.)

Left: Common household appliances such as refrigerators and air conditioners are often powered by electricity generated by the burning of fossil fuels. This releases greenhouse gases and increases global warming.

POPULATION GROWTH AND DECLINE

The world's population is projected to reach nine billion by the year 2050. Scientists worry that there won't be enough food and clean freshwater to support such a large number of people. It is especially worrying that the population is growing fastest in many of the poorest nations. In many parts of Europe the population has stopped growing and is now shrinking.

Below: Wild animals often pay the price of human population growth as their habitats are occupied by farmers. Red wolves became extinct in the wild in the United States. They have since been reintroduced into North Carolina.

THE FASTEST-GROWING ECONOMIES TODAY

Between them, China and India have a population of almost 2.5 billion people; that's about 40 percent of the population of the world. China has the fastest-growing large economy in the world today, with India running a close second. Russia and Brazil are two other large economies that are growing very quickly. Today economists refer to these four countries as the BRICs (Brazil, Russia, India, China) and explain that if they continue to grow at present rates by 2050 they will become the dominant world economies. In 2007 economists at the Goldman Sachs investment bank in the United States predicted that the Indian economy would surpass that of the US by 2043.

Above: This statue shows Krishna, one of the most popular Hindu gods in India. The largest democracy in the world, India is a kaleidoscopic mixture of religious beliefs, languages, and cultures. While more than a quarter of Indians continue to live below the poverty line, recent economic growth has made many others much wealthier.

GLOBALIZATION

Countries around the world are ever more closely linked by the exchange of goods, services, and culture (music, television, film, advertising), and the trade organizations and treaties that seek to encourage globalization. Closely related to this is the communications boom—the huge increase in the use of the internet and other electronic devices that people use to stay in touch. Tourism and migration are also opening doors between peoples and cultures.

Above: A call center in India where operators answer questions from all over the world. With its large English-speaking population, India has absorbed a large amout of outsourced work from developed nations.

Above: Our word "nomad" comes from the Greek word nemein, which means "roving for pasture." Most nomads are herders of sheep, cattle, horses, or reindeer, and spend their lives moving in cyclic patterns in search of the best grazing for their livestock.

TRADITIONAL LIFESTYLES

Indigenous peoples around the world are threatened by discrimination and prejudice. Often their beliefs, languages, and ways of life are outlawed or simply ignored so that they lose a sense of themselves and their cultural identity. The economic livelihoods of some traditional peoples are also endangered, for example when farmers take over land previously occupied by nomadic herders or when wars or political disputes redraw borders, preventing movement to and from pastures.

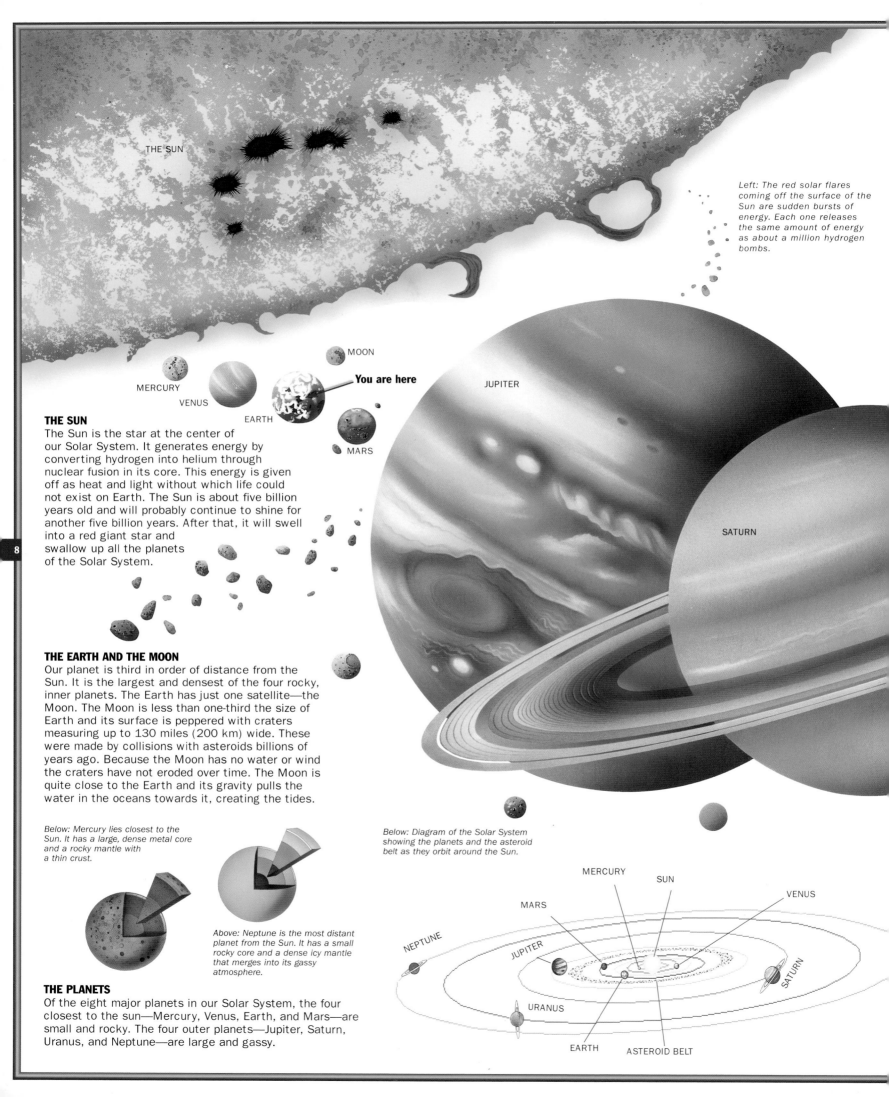

THE SUN

Left: The red solar flares coming off the surface of the Sun are sudden bursts of energy. Each one releases the same amount of energy as about a million hydrogen bombs.

MOON

MERCURY

VENUS

You are here

EARTH

MARS

JUPITER

SATURN

THE SUN

The Sun is the star at the center of our Solar System. It generates energy by converting hydrogen into helium through nuclear fusion in its core. This energy is given off as heat and light without which life could not exist on Earth. The Sun is about five billion years old and will probably continue to shine for another five billion years. After that, it will swell into a red giant star and swallow up all the planets of the Solar System.

THE EARTH AND THE MOON

Our planet is third in order of distance from the Sun. It is the largest and densest of the four rocky, inner planets. The Earth has just one satellite—the Moon. The Moon is less than one-third the size of Earth and its surface is peppered with craters measuring up to 130 miles (200 km) wide. These were made by collisions with asteroids billions of years ago. Because the Moon has no water or wind the craters have not eroded over time. The Moon is quite close to the Earth and its gravity pulls the water in the oceans towards it, creating the tides.

Below: Mercury lies closest to the Sun. It has a large, dense metal core and a rocky mantle with a thin crust.

Above: Neptune is the most distant planet from the Sun. It has a small rocky core and a dense icy mantle that merges into its gassy atmosphere.

Below: Diagram of the Solar System showing the planets and the asteroid belt as they orbit around the Sun.

MERCURY

SUN

MARS

VENUS

NEPTUNE

JUPITER

SATURN

URANUS

EARTH

ASTEROID BELT

THE PLANETS

Of the eight major planets in our Solar System, the four closest to the sun—Mercury, Venus, Earth, and Mars—are small and rocky. The four outer planets—Jupiter, Saturn, Uranus, and Neptune—are large and gassy.

8

Our Place in Space

For thousands of years people believed that the Earth was the center of the Universe, with the Sun, the stars, and everything else revolving around it. When, in 270 BCE, a Greek philosopher called Anaxagoras suggested that the Earth moved around the Sun, he was ridiculed. More than 1,800 years would pass before astronomers such as Copernicus and Galileo proved beyond all doubt that the Sun lay at the center of the Solar System with the Earth and the other planets orbiting around it. Later astronomers showed that the Universe has no center, that the Sun is merely one of billions of stars in our galaxy, and that the galaxy itself is just one among billions of others. Our Solar System was formed from a vast cloud of whirling dust and gas leftover from the Big Bang that occurred at the beginning of the Universe. As far as we know, Planet Earth is the only place in the Universe where life exists.

You are here

Above: Our galaxy, which is called the Milky Way, is shaped like a spiral. It contains about 200 billion stars like our Sun.

THE UNIVERSE

Most scientists now believe that the Universe began about 15 billion years ago with a gigantic explosion known as the Big Bang. At that time all the matter in the Universe—previously squashed into a small, dense ball—exploded and began to expend. As it expanded, galaxies and stars were formed from the matter within it. The Universe is still expanding and may continue to do so for another 10 billion years, or even forever. The Big Bang was the beginning of time. We do not know what existed before then.

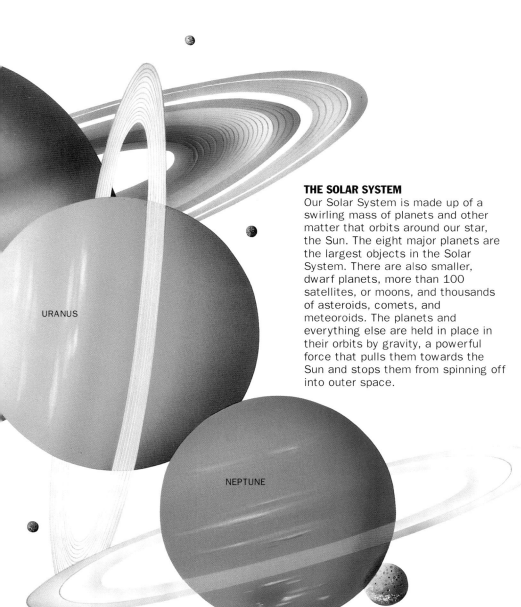

URANUS

NEPTUNE

THE SOLAR SYSTEM

Our Solar System is made up of a swirling mass of planets and other matter that orbits around our star, the Sun. The eight major planets are the largest objects in the Solar System. There are also smaller, dwarf planets, more than 100 satellites, or moons, and thousands of asteroids, comets, and meteoroids. The planets and everything else are held in place in their orbits by gravity, a powerful force that pulls them towards the Sun and stops them from spinning off into outer space.

SUN

Daytime in the Americas. Nighttime in Africa and Europe.

PLANET EARTH

DAY AND NIGHT

A day is the time it takes the Earth to rotate (spin) once on its axis. Daytime happens on the side of the Earth that is facing the Sun. When it is nighttime, that side of the Earth is facing away from the Sun. It takes 24 hours for the Earth to rotate once, so that one day includes daytime and nighttime.

SOLAR ECLIPSE

Sometimes the Moon blocks the light from the Sun, throwing a shadow on the Earth; this is called a solar eclipse. In a total solar eclipse the Moon blots out the Sun entirely for about seven minutes. In a partial eclipse the Moon only partly covers the Sun. There are between two and five solar eclipses every year, but total solar eclipses are quite rare.

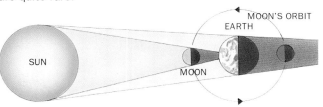

MOON'S ORBIT
EARTH
SUN
MOON

Planet Earth

Our planet was formed along with the rest of the Solar System about 4.6 billion years ago. When it had just formed, the Earth was a red-hot, semi-molten ball. Heavier materials in the semi-molten planet sank towards the center. Lighter materials stayed near the surface, where they cooled and started to turn solid. In this way they formed the Earth's crust, which was covered with volcanoes. These spewed out gases, dust, and molten rock. The gases formed an atmosphere, where steam condensed into water that fell as rain and created a vast ocean. Many millions of years later life began in the seas. Today, the Earth is about 7,950 miles (12,750 km) in diameter. From space, it looks like a perfect sphere, but it is actually slightly flatter at the North and South Poles and bulges out at the Equator. Geologists call this shape a geoide.

Above: About 200 million years ago all the continents were joined together in a single supercontinent that we call Pangaea. By 100 million years ago they were breaking into separate continents. Some recognizable shapes are already identifiable. The continents continue to move and the shape and position of our planet's landmasses will keep on changing.

DRIFTING CONTINENTS

Continental drift refers to the way the continents on Earth move in relation to each other. In 1912 the German scientist Alfred Wegener observed that if all the continents were pushed together their outlines would fit almost exactly into each other. He developed the theory that millions of years ago a single enormous landmass called "Pangaea" gradually broke up and the different parts of the Earth's crust carrying the continents slowly drifted away from each other. This theory is supported by the fact that the same kinds of rocks and fossils have been discovered on the coasts of different continents at the points where they would meet if their edges were placed side by side.

THE INSIDE STORY

Our planet (right) is made up of three main layers—the crust, the mantle, and the core. The mantle is the thickest layer, making up more than 80 percent of the volume of the planet. It is 1,800 miles (2,880 km) deep and made of molten rock (magma). The core is so hot that it reaches temperatures of 12,000°F (6,600°C). The core is really made of two layers of iron. The outer section is molten (liquid) iron, but there is so much pressure in the center of the Earth that the inner core is solid.

TRUE NORTH

Because the Earth's core is mainly made out of iron, it generates magnetic currents. As the Earth rotates, the liquid outer core spins and creates the Earth's magnetic field. This is very important for human navigation around the globe, as the needle of a compass always points to magnetic north. The interior of the Earth is like a huge magnet, pulling everything towards the center: this is called gravity and it is the reason why we don't fall off the planet!

INNER CORE

A GIANT JIGSAW

The Earth's rigid outer layer, or crust, is broken into about 30 massive slabs of rock, floating on the denser mantle; these are called tectonic plates. The plates are constantly on the move, riding like rafts on the softer rock of the Earth's mantle and carrying the continents and islands with them as they drift. Most move about 4 inches (10 cm) a year. The plates are not always moving in the same direction, however, and as they shift around they can move apart, bump edges, or slide past each other. The edges of the plates are often visible on the Earth's surface in the form of rifts and fault lines, as well as valleys and mountains.

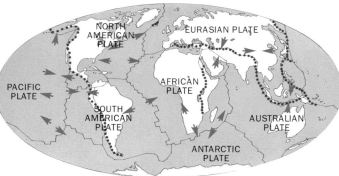

NORTH AMERICAN PLATE
EURASIAN PLATE
PACIFIC PLATE
AFRICAN PLATE
SOUTH AMERICAN PLATE
AUSTRALIAN PLATE
ANTARCTIC PLATE

Left: The map shows some of the major tectonic plates. The red dotted lines show some of the places where the plates are colliding.

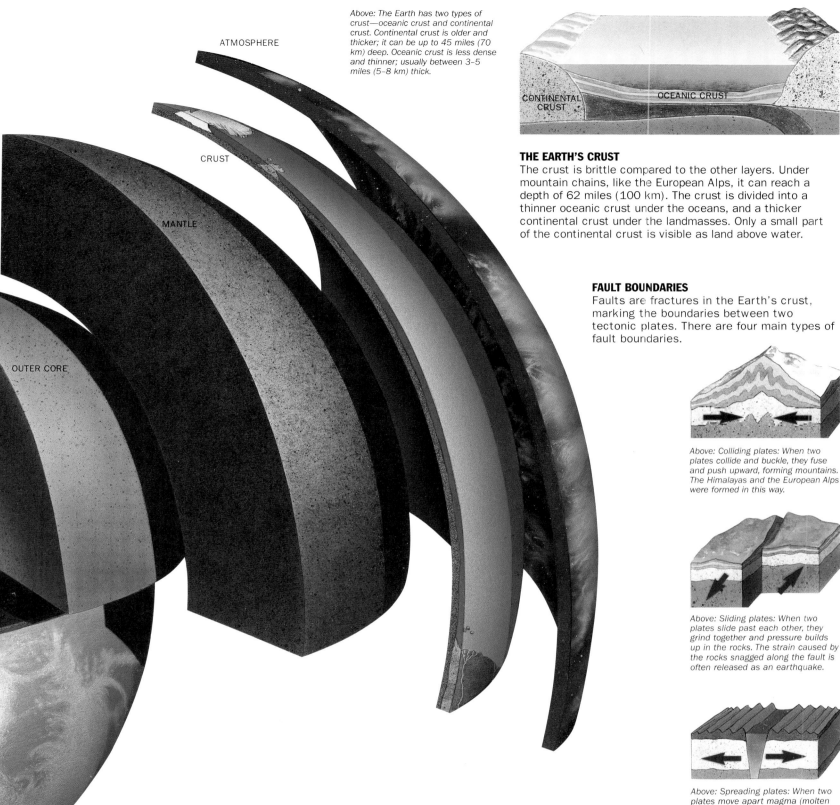

ATMOSPHERE

CRUST

MANTLE

OUTER CORE

Above: The Earth has two types of crust—oceanic crust and continental crust. Continental crust is older and thicker; it can be up to 45 miles (70 km) deep. Oceanic crust is less dense and thinner; usually between 3–5 miles (5–8 km) thick.

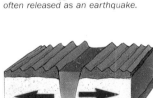

CONTINENTAL CRUST

OCEANIC CRUST

THE EARTH'S CRUST

The crust is brittle compared to the other layers. Under mountain chains, like the European Alps, it can reach a depth of 62 miles (100 km). The crust is divided into a thinner oceanic crust under the oceans, and a thicker continental crust under the landmasses. Only a small part of the continental crust is visible as land above water.

FAULT BOUNDARIES

Faults are fractures in the Earth's crust, marking the boundaries between two tectonic plates. There are four main types of fault boundaries.

Above: Colliding plates: When two plates collide and buckle, they fuse and push upward, forming mountains. The Himalayas and the European Alps were formed in this way.

Above: Sliding plates: When two plates slide past each other, they grind together and pressure builds up in the rocks. The strain caused by the rocks snagged along the fault is often released as an earthquake.

Above: Spreading plates: When two plates move apart magma (molten rock) surges up and cools, forming a new crust. Spreading plates are mostly found under the oceans.

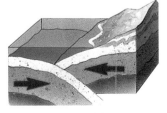

Above: Diving plates: When two ocean plates or an ocean plate and a land plate collide, the denser plate dives underneath the other, plunging into the Earth's mantle

VOLCANOS

Volcanos are openings in the Earth's crust from which molten rock and steam flow or erupt. Many volcanos are cone-shaped mountains built up by repeated eruptions. Others, known as fissure volcanos, are vents which occur along fractures in the Earth's crust. Some fissure volcanos are several miles long. Undersea fissure volcanos occur along ridges in the ocean floor. They pour out lava which becomes the new ocean floor.

Right: Cutaway diagram of an exploding volcano.

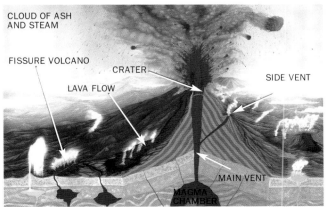

CLOUD OF ASH AND STEAM

FISSURE VOLCANO

CRATER

LAVA FLOW

SIDE VENT

MAIN VENT

MAGMA CHAMBER

Weather and Climate

Weather and climate are not the same thing. Weather changes from day to day and according to the season. Climate is the pattern of weather in a given region over a long period of time. The various regions of the Earth have different climates, depending on their latitude (distance from the equator), altitude (height above sea level), distance from the sea, and winds. In places that are at high latitudes, such as the polar regions, the Sun's rays fall at low angles because of the tilting of the Earth's axis. They pass through a thick layer of the Earth's atmosphere and much of their heat is absorbed. This makes the climate in these regions cold. Near the equator, the Sun's rays fall from directly overhead. This causes a constantly warm climate throughout the year. In between the polar regions and the equator, at mid-latitudes, are the temperate regions. They have warm summers and cool winters. Altitude affects climate because as you go higher the atmosphere becomes thinner and retains less heat. This is why mountainous regions are colder than lowlands. Places that are near the sea generally have warmer climates because ocean currents and sea breezes stop the weather from becoming too hot or too cold.

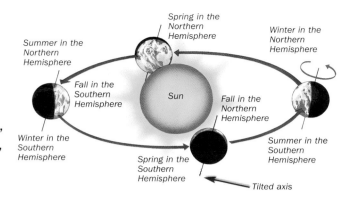

THE SEASONS

The temperate and polar regions of the Earth experience four distinct seasons—winter, spring, summer, and fall—because the axis of the Earth is tilted. As the Earth orbits around the Sun, the people in the hemisphere tilted toward it see the Sun higher in the sky and have longer days; this is summer. While it is summer in the Northern Hemisphere, it is winter in the Southern Hemisphere, and vice versa. There is much less seasonal variation near the equator because the tilting of the Earth does not affect the amount of sunlight. In these regions the days are about the same length all year round. Seasons in the tropics are dominated by the tropical rain belt, which creates wet and dry seasons.

■ WORLD CLIMATE ZONES AND OCEAN CURRENTS

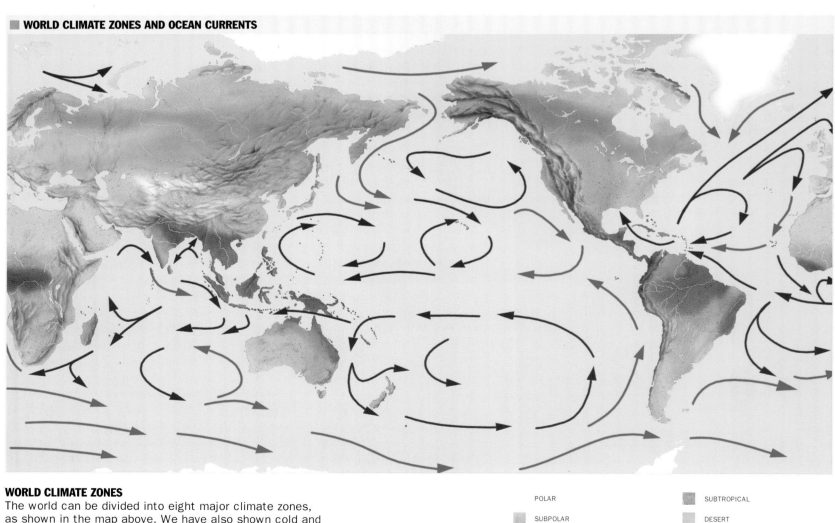

WORLD CLIMATE ZONES

The world can be divided into eight major climate zones, as shown in the map above. We have also shown cold and warm ocean currents which affect the world's climate. Warm ocean currents near land at high latitudes can bring warmer weather than might be expected while cold currents can bring cooler weather.

POLAR

SUBPOLAR

COLD TEMPERATE

MOUNTAIN

TEMPERATE

TROPICAL

SUBTROPICAL

DESERT

→ COLD OCEAN CURRENTS

→ WARM OCEAN CURRENTS

WEATHER FORECASTING

Modern weather forecasting uses advanced technology to collect and make sense of information received from weather satellites, manned and automatic weather stations, weather balloons, and many other sources. Knowing what the weather will do next is not only useful to tell us whether to take our umbrella to school but can also help save lives.

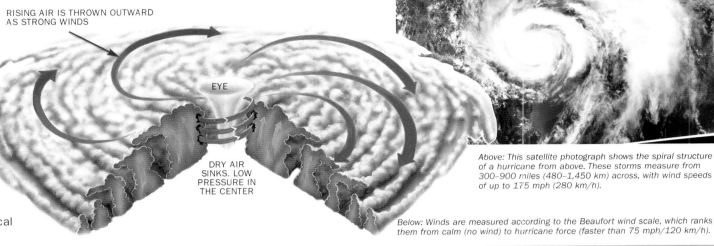

RISING AIR IS THROWN OUTWARD AS STRONG WINDS

Right: Hurricanes form when hot, moist air rises from warm oceans then condenses to form clouds. Air rushes in at the surface to replace the rising air. As the storm strengthens it begins to swirl around a central eye and fast-rising air is thrown outward.

EYE

DRY AIR SINKS. LOW PRESSURE IN THE CENTER

Above: This satellite photograph shows the spiral structure of a hurricane from above. These storms measure from 300–900 miles (480–1,450 km) across, with wind speeds of up to 175 mph (280 km/h).

HURRICANES

Hurricanes are tropical storms that develop over warm oceans during the hottest months of the year. Once formed, they drift westward with the trade winds and then turn toward mid-latitudes as they lose strength. Hurricanes go by different names according to where they occur. In the Indian Ocean and north Australia they are called cyclones. In the northwest Pacific Ocean, near Asia, they are called typhoons after Tai Fung, which is Chinese for "great wind." They are called hurricanes in North America after Hunraken, the Maya god of the winds.

TORNADOS

Tornados are violent, twisting funnels of air, usually about 500 feet (150 m) across that normally stay on the ground for about five miles (8 km). They move in a straight line and often cause terrible destruction. Most tornados have wind speeds of about 40 mph (64 km/h), but in the most deadly can reach 300 mph (480 km/h).

Below: A dark, funnel-shaped tornado moves across the landscape. Tornados occur on every continent except Antarctica, but they are most common in North America.

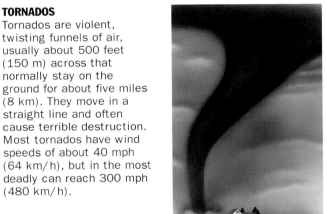

FLOODING

Flooding occurs when more rain falls than can be contained in the rivers and lakes that normally hold the water. In developed countries rivers, lakes, and coastal areas are managed by building levees, sea walls, and other barriers that are meant to stop and direct rising waters.

Below: Winds are measured according to the Beaufort wind scale, which ranks them from calm (no wind) to hurricane force (faster than 75 mph/120 km/h).

WINDS

Winds occur all over the world and are caused by air being heated by the Sun and rising. Cool air rushes in to take up the space, creating a wind. There are many different types of wind, from global winds, such as the trade winds that blow constantly away from the equator, upper-level winds, called jet streams, and many local winds and breezes too.

Right: Regions that are flooded frequently often have very fertile soils. For this reason they are usually densely populated. When floods occur the devastation and loss of life can be huge.

FIRES

Many fires are started by arsonists (people who deliberately light fires), but a lot are also started by natural causes. Regions that suffer from droughts are especially vulnerable because vegetation from wetter times dries out and can easily be ignited by lightning. However, fires are not always bad. Sometimes the flames burn up dead vegetation, making way for renewed growth. In areas like Australia, where fires are common, the local vegetation has evolved to cope with regular burn offs and recovery and regrowth is fast. Australia is the most fire-prone country in the world, with more than 15,000 fires raging every year.

BLIZZARDS

Snowstorms are winter storms where large amounts of snow fall. A massive snowstorm with high winds and very cold temperatures is known as a blizzard. Blizzards occur in temperate zones and while they are less fierce than tropical hurricanes, they often cover huge areas, with diameters of over 1,000 miles (1,600 km).

13

The Natural World

Over the course of the Earth's long history, plants and animals have colonized almost every corner of the planet. The Earth can be divided into ten or more different areas, called biomes, where various species of plants and animals co-exist. Each biome has specific climatic conditions and the animals and plants that live there have special adaptations to help them survive and make the best of those conditions. Recent human activity—such as clearing forests for timber or farmland, and pollution—has changed many biomes for the worse.

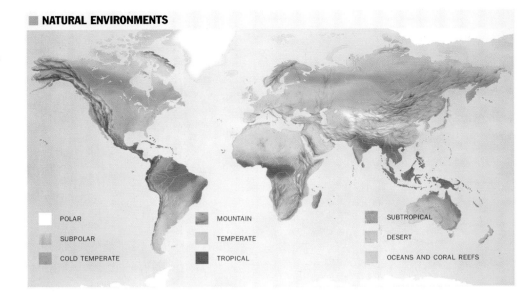

NATURAL ENVIRONMENTS

POLAR

SUBPOLAR

COLD TEMPERATE

MOUNTAIN

TEMPERATE

TROPICAL

SUBTROPICAL

DESERT

OCEANS AND CORAL REEFS

GRASSLANDS

There are two types of grasslands: savannas, or tropical grasslands, which occur in warm zones close to the equator, and temperate grasslands, also known as steppes, prairies, or pampas, which flourish in cooler areas. Savannas have two distinct seasons: the wet season and the dry season, and are dotted with trees and shrubs. Temperate grasslands have no trees.

MEDITERRANEAN

The Mediterranean, or chaparral, biome is named for the area around the Mediterranean Sea that separates Europe and Africa. These areas have hot, dry summers and short, mild winters. They are covered with hardy, evergreen shrubs and woodland. Drought and fire are common hazards here.

OCEANS AND CORAL REEFS

The marine, or ocean biome, covers more than two-thirds of the planet. There are more species of plants and animals in the oceans than on land. Coral reefs are among the most densely populated ocean areas. They occur in warm, shallow waters, usually near land in tropical seas. The reefs are formed from coral polyps, tiny animals that live in large colonies; when the coral polyps die, their hard limestone skeletons pile up to make a compact reef.

FRESHWATER

Lakes, rivers, ponds, bogs, swamps, ditches, and canals are all part of the freshwater biome. Most of the plants and animals that stay here live near the shore or on the surface of the water. The area where freshwater meets salt water is called an an estuary.

THE POLAR REGIONS
The polar regions extend around the extreme northern and southern tips of the planet. Both seas and land are covered by a permanent layer of ice. The few plants and animals that live here have special adaptations, such as thick fur or blubber beneath their skins, to survive in the very harsh conditions.

CONIFER FORESTS
A broad belt of conifer forests runs across Europe, Asia, and North America in the northern hemisphere. This area, known as the boreal forest or taiga, has long, cold winters and short summers. The trees are cone-shaped so that snow slides off easily, and dark green year-round to help absorb the Sun's heat more quickly.

MOUNTAINS
The mountain, or alpine, biome occurs on mountains all over the world, beginning at about 10,000 feet (3000 m) but below the permanent snowline. Cold, windy, and often snow-covered, it is a harsh environment. Alpine animals have larger lungs and more blood cells to make up for the lack of oxygen.

DESERTS
Deserts have very low rainfall. They can be hot or cold. Hot deserts occur in the tropics. Cold deserts are further from the equator and usually also far from the sea. Not many plants and animals live in the desert; the ones that do have special adaptations for conserving water.

TROPICAL RAIN FORESTS
Hot, humid rain forests occur in tropical areas near the equator. Rain forests are densely populated with plants and animals. The thick vegetation is thought to produce 40 percent of the Earth's oxygen.

WOODLANDS
Deciduous forests occur in temperate regions. There are four distinct seasons in these areas, and most trees lose their leaves in the fall and winter. Woodlands are home to a variety of plants and animals; they are able to change their habits to suit the changing seasons. A lot of deciduous forest has been cut down for timber and cleared for farmland.

15

A World of People

The world's population today is almost 6.7 billion—that's 6,700,000,000 (6,700 million) people. Each year the figure increases, currently by an extra 80 million people a year, or 200,000 people every day. At this rate it will double again in 50 years—in other words, within your lifetime. That means twice as many mouths to feed and twice the number of jobs to create and houses to build. Experts reckon it will continue to grow at least until the year 2050, although the rate of growth is slowing down. Figures show that mothers in rich countries tend to have fewer children than those in less developed countries, so the best hope for world population numbers is that the rate of growth will fall as the world becomes wealthier. In some European countries there are even worries about falling population numbers. Thanks to improved healthcare and better nutrition, more people are living longer than in the past. Pregnant women are also better cared for now and fewer babies die at birth or in infancy. The good news is that more people around the world can expect to lead long, healthy lives.

LANGUAGE

More than 6,500 languages are spoken in the world today. Linguists divide them into families (see map, right). In countries where a number of languages are spoken, one or more are chosen as "official" languages and are used in schools, on television, and by the government. Chinese has the largest number of native speakers. English is the most widely spoken official language.

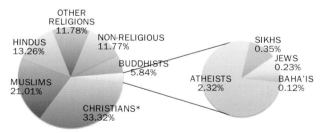

Above: Religion around the world. *Includes Roman Catholics 16.99% Protestants 5.78%, Orthodox 3.53%, Anglicans 1.25%

RELIGIONS

Every human society has some kind of religion where supernatural powers in the form of gods or spirits are recognized and worshiped. As the pie chart above shows, Christianity, Islam, and Hinduism are the most widespread religions today. Atheists are people who do not believe in gods or supernatural powers of any kind.

Above: Chinese diviners consult the I Ching, a key Confucian text.

URBANIZATION

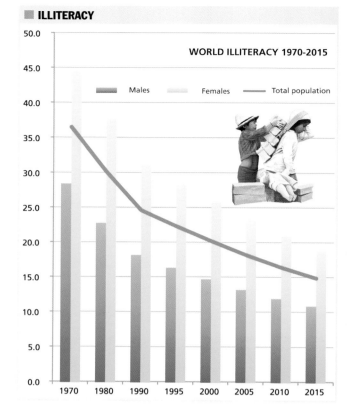

Source: United Nations, Department of Economic and Social Affairs, Population Division (2006).

URBANIZATION

In 2005, almost half of the world's population lived in cities, up from just 13 percent 100 years ago. That figure is likely to rise to 60 percent by 2030. People move to cities to find jobs and to make better lives for themselves and their children.

ILLITERACY

WORLD ILLITERACY 1970–2015

Males   Females   Total population

Above: More than two-thirds of the world's 785 million illiterate adults are found in only eight countries (India, China, Bangladesh, Pakistan, Nigeria, Ethiopia, Indonesia, and Egypt). Of all the illiterate adults in the world, two-thirds are women. Extremely low literacy rates are concentrated in three regions—South and West Asia, Sub-Saharan Africa, and the Arab states, where around one-third of the men and half of all women are illiterate (2005 est.)

WORLD LANGUAGE FAMILIES

- INDO-EUROPEAN
- CAUCASIAN
- AFRO-ASIATIC
- KHOISAN
- NIGER-CONGO
- NILO-SAHARAN
- URALIC
- ALTAIC
- SINO-TIBETAN
- TAI
- AUSTRO-ASIATIC
- DRAVIDIAN
- AUSTRONESIAN
- OTHER

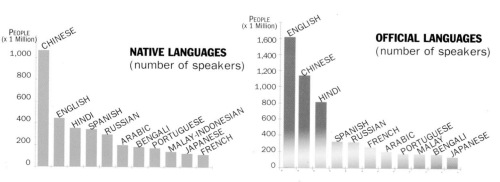

NATIVE LANGUAGES (number of speakers)

OFFICIAL LANGUAGES (number of speakers)

WORLD POPULATION GROWTH 2010–2050

ASIA
60.32% — 59.95% — 59.28% — 58.34% — 57.29%

B
2010-2050 POPULATION TRENDS IN SELECTED COUNTRIES

NIGERIA +82.36%

INDIA +35.90%
USA +27.88%
AUSTRALIA +31.27%

CHINA +4.24%
GERMANY -10.05%

C
WORLD POPULATION DENSITY PER SQUARE KILOMETER 1950-2050

People per sq km

1950 — 19 people / sq km
2000 — 45 people / sq km
2050 — 68 people / sq km

AFRICA
14.94% — 16.57% — 18.25% — 20.01% — 21.74%

EUROPE
10.58% — 9.42% — 8.50% — 7.79% — 7.23%

SOUTHERN AMERICA

NORTHERN AND CENTRAL AMERICA

OCEANIA

2010 — 2020 — 2030 — 2040 — 2050

Left: The large graph shows how population growth will continue to soar in Africa until 2050. During the same period it will begin to slow in Asia while remaining constant in the Americas and Oceania. In Europe, population growth will decline. Values are given as percentages of the World total population.

Left: Graph B shows population trends in selected countries between 2010–2050. Nigeria, like many other countries in Africa, will have very high growth. In Germany the population will decrease by more than ten percent.

Left: Graph C shows world population density in 1950 and 2000, and projected density in 2050. As you can see, there are more and more people to squeeze into the same space.

AGING POPULATIONS

New problems are emerging in countries where population growth is stable or declining. In many parts of Europe governments pay pensions to older people after they stop working. With fewer young people to contribute to pension schemes, and many more elderly people to be paid, no one quite knows where the extra money will come from. In some countries governments are raising the minimum retirement age so that people will stay at work for more years.

17

Above: A road sign on the Mexican–US border warns families that they may not enter the United States without permission.

IMMIGRATION

Huge numbers of people around the world are moving within their own country, as well as to different ones. Most travel from villages to the cities, where there are more jobs to be found. When they move abroad, some migrants are treated unfairly by people in the host country. They may be accused of taking work from people born in that country, or of forcing down wages by accepting low pay. Some people in host countries worry that too many immigrants will change their culture and language, or fear overcrowding. Yet immigrants are vital to the economies of most developed countries. They do the jobs other people don't want, and provide some of the basic services on which society depends.

Below: French police detain illegal immigrants. Many countries are now debating how many newcomers to allow in, and how best to integrate them into the host society.

UNWILLING HOSTS?

Some countries are more willing than others to accept immigrants. No state in the world currently allows unrestricted movement across its borders. In general, those with free-market economies and democratic governments are most welcoming to immigrants. Yet even those nations sometimes restrict the number allowed in per year or use other means to limit the number of people who can settle there. Once admitted, immigrants may have to take language tests or complete community service programs before they can become full citizens.

The Planet Provides

Planet Earth has vast stores of natural resources of many different kinds. Natural resources are usually divided into two distinct groups—renewable and nonrenewable. Renewable resources include the air, soils, sunlight, and fresh water which enable plants to grow. Plants absorb carbon dioxide during photosynthesis and release the oxygen we need to breathe. Since plants can make their own food, they form the basis of the food chain. People and other animals either feed directly on plants or feed on the animals that feed on plants. Plants also provide timber, fuel, and textiles, such as linen and cotton. If carefully managed, renewable resources can replenish themselves and last forever. Nonrenewable resources include minerals, natural gas, oil, and coal. These substances were formed over millions of years and we cannot wait for them to renew themselves. Oil, gas, and coal provide most of the energy we use in industry, for transportation, and many other aspects of daily life. Scientists are working hard to find alternatives to these resources before they run out.

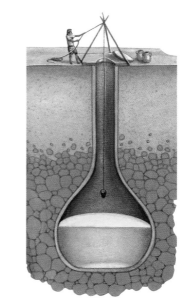

WATER IN THE GROUND

Where rocks and soils are suitable, rainwater often trickles through the surface layers of the Earth and collects deep underground. These buried lakes are called "aquifers." In many dry lands, where rains often fail, aquifers provide a vital water supply. People dig down deep to find underground water (left) and use buckets or pumps to raise it to the surface.

Right: This diagram shows environmentally friendly methods of farming. Different crops are grown to keep the soil fertile, and animal manure is used instead of fertilizer. Tiny insects called aphids, which damage crops, are eaten by ladybugs instead of being killed with pesticides. Cattle can graze on fresh grass instead of being fed artificial food pellets. The food grows and ripens naturally, and is sold at local markets.

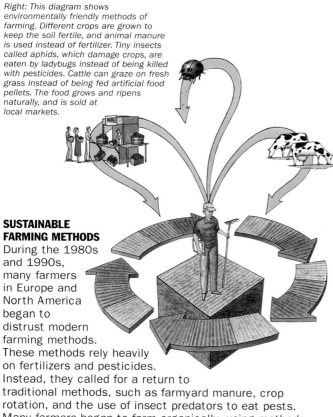

CARRIED FOR MILES

Clean water is a vital and increasingly scarce resource. In many parts of Africa, Asia, and South America, getting water from rivers or wells is a tiring, time-consuming task. Millions of women, like these (right) in Africa, have to walk miles each day to bring water to their families.

THE FIRST FOOD CROPS AND FARMING

The plants and animals that are farmed today all existed in the wild until the first farmers learned how to domesticate them. The map below shows where plants and animals were first domesticated. From their original locations, many have spread around the globe. The first domestic plants would have been much smaller and with much lower yields than the ones we know today. Early farmers, like modern ones, managed the reproduction of their plants to increase yields by selecting the largest and best strains for seeding.

SUSTAINABLE FARMING METHODS

During the 1980s and 1990s, many farmers in Europe and North America began to distrust modern farming methods. These methods rely heavily on fertilizers and pesticides. Instead, they called for a return to traditional methods, such as farmyard manure, crop rotation, and the use of insect predators to eat pests. Many farmers began to farm organically, using methods that were sustainable. Their produce was popular with shoppers, and sold for high prices.

◼ DOMESTICATION OF PLANTS AND ANIMALS

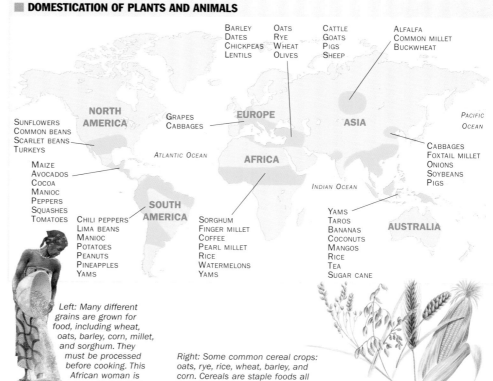

NORTH AMERICA

SUNFLOWERS
COMMON BEANS
SCARLET BEANS
TURKEYS

MAIZE
AVOCADOS
COCOA
MANIOC
PEPPERS
SQUASHES
TOMATOES

SOUTH AMERICA

CHILI PEPPERS
LIMA BEANS
MANIOC
POTATOES
PEANUTS
PINEAPPLES
YAMS

GRAPES
CABBAGES

EUROPE

BARLEY   OATS   CATTLE
DATES   RYE   GOATS
CHICKPEAS WHEAT PIGS
LENTILS OLIVES SHEEP

ALFALFA
COMMON MILLET
BUCKWHEAT

ASIA

AFRICA

SORGHUM
FINGER MILLET
COFFEE
PEARL MILLET
RICE
WATERMELONS
YAMS

YAMS
TAROS
BANANAS
COCONUTS
MANGOS
RICE
TEA
SUGAR CANE

PACIFIC OCEAN

CABBAGES
FOXTAIL MILLET
ONIONS
SOYBEANS
PIGS

AUSTRALIA

ATLANTIC OCEAN

INDIAN OCEAN

Right: These farmworkers are carefully packing lettuces into boxes on a farm in California. The lettuces may be shipped to markets all over North America, but when using sustainable methods farmers prefer to deliver to local markets where the produce arrives fresh.

Left: Many different grains are grown for food, including wheat, oats, barley, corn, millet, and sorghum. They must be processed before cooking. This African woman is separating grain from the chaff.

Right: Some common cereal crops: oats, rye, rice, wheat, barley, and corn. Cereals are staple foods all over the world.

HARNESSING THE WIND

Winds blow constantly all over the Earth. Wind turbines are used to harness their energy to produce electricity. This is a clean, renewable energy source and some countries have invested heavily in it. In Denmark, 19 percent of electricity is produced in this way.

Above: Three-bladed wind turbines are placed in locations with plenty of wind and close to transmission lines.

Left: In 2006 India signed a co-operation pact with the USA, guaranteeing India access to US nuclear technology and fuel so that it can meet its energy needs.

THE NUCLEAR OPTION

More than 15 percent of the world's electricity is produced using nuclear technology. There are 440 nuclear power plants operating in 31 countries. The US, France, and Japan are world leaders in nuclear power production. France produces almost 80 percent of its electricity in this way. Many people oppose nuclear power because of the danger of accidents, possible terrorist attacks on nuclear plants, and the nuclear waste leftover from power production.

WATER IS ENERGY

Hydroelectricity is the most widely used form of renewable energy. About 20 percent of the world's electricity is produced by harnessing the power of falling water. It is a very clean way of gathering energy which produces no waste or greenhouse gases. There is some environmental damage when terrain is flooded to create reservoirs for dams.

MINERALS

Minerals, such as copper, gold, silver, zinc, and aluminum, are nonrenewable resources. They have a wide range of uses, especially in industry. Minerals are extracted from the ground and then processed for use, usually by smelting. Both mining and smelting are often hazardous for the natural environment.

BIOFUELS

Biofuels are solid, liquid, or gas fuels derived from recently dead biological material. This distinguishes them from fossil fuels, such as oil and natural gas, which are derived from long dead biological material. Biofuels can be produced from most plants. They offer the possibility of producing energy without increasing the amount of carbon in the atmosphere, unlike fossil fuels which return carbon that was stored beneath the Earth's surface for millions of years.

Above: Timber, beets, and palms are three important sources of biofuels.

THE PLANET'S "LUNGS"

Rain forests are the "lungs" of our planet. They absorb large quantities of carbon dioxide and release oxygen. The widespread practice of burning off or cutting down the forests releases even more carbon dioxide into the atmosphere. Increasing amounts of carbon dioxide are responsible for higher temperatures and global warming.

Right: The largest rain forest on Earth grows in the Amazon Basin, in South America. It covers an area about the size of Australia.

FOSSIL FUELS

Fossil fuels such as oil, natural gas, and coal, are burnt to produce about 85 percent of the energy used on the planet. However, fossil fuels are nonrenewable resources (and running out) and they release large amounts of harmful carbon dioxide into the atmosphere. Recent, steep increases in oil prices may finally make biofuels and other renewable energy sources viable options.

Left: Drilling for oil.

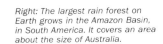

The World in Contact

The final decades of the 20th century were marked by huge increases in the amount and speed of global contact. A revolution in technology led to a boom in the use of electronic post (email) and internet use around the world. International trade increased as many trade barriers were abolished or modified and multinational companies became more widespread. International institutions, like the World Bank, the World Trade Organization (WTO) and the United Nations (UN), became increasingly active in resolving disputes and trying to solve economic and health problems. Travel for business and pleasure grew steadily as new low-cost airlines reduced airfares and online booking and ticketing made travel simpler. Together, all these changes are described as "globalization." The world is now more in touch than it has ever been before.

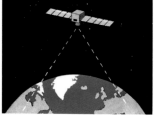

Above: Satellites orbiting the Earth have many different uses. Some are for telecommunications and broadcasting. Others monitor the planet and send the information back to Earth.

Right: The new Airbus A380 made its first commercial flight for Singapore Airlines on October 27, 2007. With space for up to 853 passengers, it is the largest passenger jet ever.

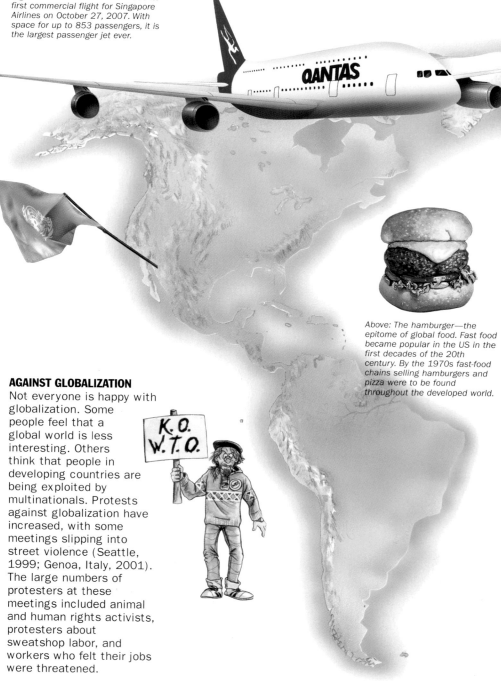

THE UNITED NATIONS

The UN was founded after the Second World War with the aim of maintaining world peace by encouraging international co-operation to resolve social, cultural, economic, and humanitarian problems that might otherwise lead to war. Through its various agencies, it also encourages the development of education, protects refugees, encourages international trade and economic growth in developing countries, protects the environment, provides aid in emergencies, and promotes better health through the World Health Organization (WHO.)

AID ORGANIZATIONS

There are many different aid organizations operating in the world. UNICEF and UNESCO, both run by the UN, are among the largest organizations. They are both actively involved in promoting health and education in developing countries (among other things). British-based OXFAM is one of many that provides food and clothing in emergencies. It also runs long term projects to help people become self-sufficient. Amnesty International helps political prisoners throughout the world, while the International Red Cross (Red Crescent in Muslim lands) provides doctors and health care.

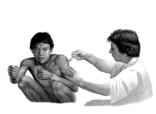

Above: Some diseases have been eradicated by inoculation.

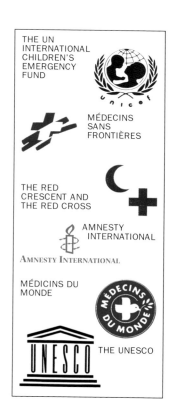

THE UN INTERNATIONAL CHILDREN'S EMERGENCY FUND

MÉDECINS SANS FRONTIÈRES

THE RED CRESCENT AND THE RED CROSS

AMNESTY INTERNATIONAL

MÉDICINS DU MONDE

THE UNESCO

Above: Logos of some of the most important international organizations that try to reduce poverty and improve peoples' lives.

WORKING TOGETHER

Poverty, disease, and illiteracy continue in many parts of the world. However, much has been achieved in the last 50 years: infant mortality has been halved; the number of children starting school in the developing world has risen to 75 percent; and average life expectancy has risen by one-third. Many of these achievements are due to international organizations, such as the United Nations, working with local governments.

AGAINST GLOBALIZATION

Not everyone is happy with globalization. Some people feel that a global world is less interesting. Others think that people in developing countries are being exploited by multinationals. Protests against globalization have increased, with some meetings slipping into street violence (Seattle, 1999; Genoa, Italy, 2001). The large numbers of protesters at these meetings included animal and human rights activists, protesters about sweatshop labor, and workers who felt their jobs were threatened.

Above: The hamburger—the epitome of global food. Fast food became popular in the US in the first decades of the 20th century. By the 1970s fast-food chains selling hamburgers and pizza were to be found throughout the developed world.

THE INFORMATION REVOLUTION

In the wake of the agricultural and industrial revolutions, the world is now facing a third historic change: the Information Revolution. New digitized media, conveyed through computers over the internet, have transformed how we think, study, work, and have fun. The revolution is still in its early days, and no-one knows exactly how it will shape up. If all goes well, people will be better informed, better educated, and better entertained.

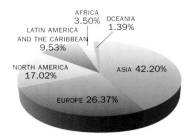

AFRICA 3.50%   OCEANIA 1.39%
LATIN AMERICA AND THE CARIBBEAN 9.53%
NORTH AMERICA 17.02%
ASIA 42.20%
EUROPE 26.37%

Left: This pie chart shows the geographical location of internet users around the world.

INTERNET USE

About 1.5 billion people now use the internet on a regular basis. People use the internet for practical purposes, like researching school projects or booking vacations, but they also use it as a chance to meet and socialize with new people—without ever leaving home. Social networking services like Facebook and Friendster put people in touch across the globe.

Below: Logos from the most popular online social networking services.

Blogger   facebook   FOTOLOG
bebo   friendster   LIVEJOURNAL
StudiVZ   hi5   CYWORLD
SKYROCK   myspace.com   orkut

Right: Tourists waiting to visit the Louvre in Paris. France received more than 80 million foreign tourists in 2007.

TOURISM

Tourism has become a global industry with more and more people traveling every year. In 2007 over 900 million people traveled outside their countries for leisure. The top four international destinations are France, Spain, the US, and China (in that order). More than 50 million people visited each of these countries in 2007. People travel for many different reasons, and the travel market is becoming more sophisticated with niche offers, like cooking-school vacations or spa holidays.

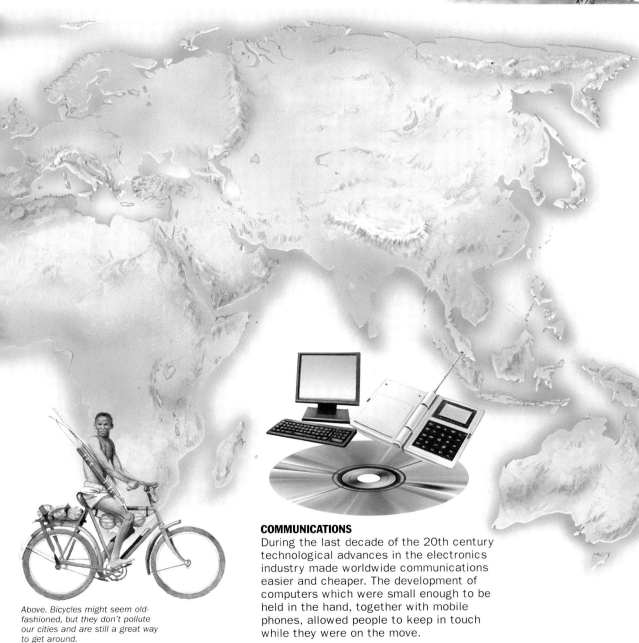

WORLD SPORTING EVENTS

World sporting events attract competitors and spectators from all around the world, as well as massive television audiences. One of the most important is the Olympic Games, whose symbol of five rings (above) represents the five major continents. The Olympic Games are held every four years and have both summer and winter competitions.

Above. Bicycles might seem old-fashioned, but they don't pollute our cities and are still a great way to get around.

COMMUNICATIONS

During the last decade of the 20th century technological advances in the electronics industry made worldwide communications easier and cheaper. The development of computers which were small enough to be held in the hand, together with mobile phones, allowed people to keep in touch while they were on the move.

Challenges

The Earth reuses and recycles everything. All our natural resources, including water, air, the soils, plants, and animals are part of endless natural cycles that allow life to exist. But over the past 200 years, rapid population growth, the spread of industry, and many different human activities have begun to interfere with the Earth's natural environment. Some nonrenewable resources, such as oil and natural gas are running out. Resources that can replenish themselves are not being given the chance to do so; our seas are overfished, our soils are overfarmed, and our forests are rapidly being cut down. The climate is also being affected—it is getting warmer at a dangerously fast pace. According to scientists, human activities are at least partly to blame. Unless action is taken, the results are likely to include more extreme weather conditions that will affect much of the globe, expand deserts, and cause sea levels to rise as the polar ice cap melts.

POLLUTION

Factories and cars can fill the air with grime and poisonous gases. But they need not do so; strict laws governing factory wastes and car emissions have been shown to lessen air and water pollution. You can help by using public transport or traveling by bicycle or on foot over short distances (this is also good for your health).

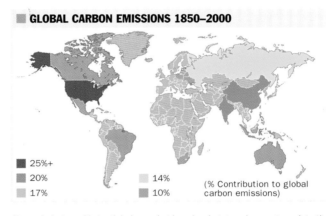

GLOBAL CARBON EMISSIONS 1850–2000

- 25%+
- 20%
- 17%
- 14%
- 10%

(% Contribution to global carbon emissions)

Above: Industry adds to global warming by releasing greenhouse gases into the atmosphere. This map of the main sources of emissions shows that the heaviest polluter is the United States. Africa and Oceania, which pollute the least, are the places most at risk from climate change.

THE NATURAL WORLD AT RISK

As people spread across the globe, moving into the last wilderness areas and cultivating ever more land, the space available for animals is shrinking. Forests are cut down, the seas are fished on an industrial scale, and previously marginal lands are used for farming. The result is a growing threat to biodiversity—the huge variety of life forms living on the planet. In future years, climate change may provide a new threat by disturbing traditional patterns of birth, growth, and feeding.

Above: Tigers are among the many animals that may become extinct because of human activities. Of the eight tiger species, only five remain.

REDUCING CARBON EMISSIONS

Carbon dioxide (CO_2) is released into the atmosphere by human activities, and this is a major cause of global warming. CO_2 and other "greenhouse gases" hold heat in the atmosphere that would otherwise vanish into space. To curb global warming, people need to reduce the amount of CO_2 that they release —their "carbon footprint." CO_2 that has already been released can be captured and stored deep in the Earth or under the sea.

RECYCLING WASTE

Obtaining the raw materials needed to manufacture goods uses up energy that adds to global warming. Recycling waste can help to reduce the amount of energy we use. Some materials are easier to reuse than others—aluminum, used to make cans, is particularly effective, plastics generally less so. Everyone can help by using recycling facilities and taking glass to bottle banks—always provided that the journey to the recycling center does not use up more energy than it saves.

Right: Aluminium cans are 100 percent recyclable. Each one recycled saves enough energy to power a television set for three hours.

SAVING OZONE LAYER

A layer of ozone in the upper atmosphere filters out damaging radiation from the Sun. CFCs (chlorofluorocarbons) released by refrigerators, air conditioners, and aerosols, among other things, are gradually destroying the ozone layer. This may lead to increases in skin cancer and harmful effects on crops. You can help by buying CFC-free products.

DESERT EXPANSION

Global warming may cause less rainfall in some areas already prone to drought. Regions on the fringes of deserts are especially at risk. People who live there risk starvation, or moving to new homes elsewhere, which may cause conflict with local people.

Above: The area of the Antarctic atmosphere called the "ozone hole" opens up each year in mid-August and peaks in September. This image, created with data collected by the NASA Aura satellite, shows the hole at its peak in 2007. NASA scientists described the hole as average, peaking at 9.7 million square miles, roughly the size of North America. However, it is important to know that the hole did not exist at all in the 1970s.

Large illustration: The Sleipner Project off the coast of Norway was the world's first commercial CO2 capture and storage facility. Captured CO2 is stored in depleted gas reservoirs under the sea.

The Physical World

When viewed from space, the Earth is blue. This is because 70 percent of the surface of our planet is covered by oceans. The Earth is the only planet in the Solar System to have such large quantities of water, most of which is located in five large oceans. The Pacific Ocean is the biggest; it covers almost one-third of the surface of the planet and is larger than all the landmasses combined. We divide our world into two hemispheres—the Northern Hemisphere and the Southern Hemisphere—at an imaginary line called the Equator that runs around the planet half way between the North Pole and the South Pole.

Below: Satellite photograph of the "Blue Planet."

THE BLUE PLANET

The reflection of the Sun's light on the water that covers most of our planet gives Earth its unique blue color. Life on Earth began in the first oceans over three billion years ago. Single-celled forms of life developed from a mixture of chemicals and gradually formed DNA (deoxyribonucleic acid), which was able to reproduce itself. Every plant and animal that lives today began its evolutionary journey in these early oceans.

OCEAN RECORDS

In order of size, the oceans are: the Pacific Ocean, the Atlantic Ocean, the Indian Ocean, the Southern Ocean, and the Arctic Ocean. The Sea of Marmara, which lies between the Black and Mediterranean seas, is the smallest sea in the world.

Left: Fossil of Spriggina, one of the first multicelled organisms that lived in the oceans about 620 million years ago.

Right: The Cedar of Lebanon is a large conifer tree that grows mainly in the Middle East.

PLANTS AND TREES

Trees and other plants grow in most parts of the world, except in the deserts (where it is too dry), the tundra and polar regions (where it is too cold), and on the tallest mountains (where it is too cold and windy). A thick belt of conifer trees runs across the northern continents.

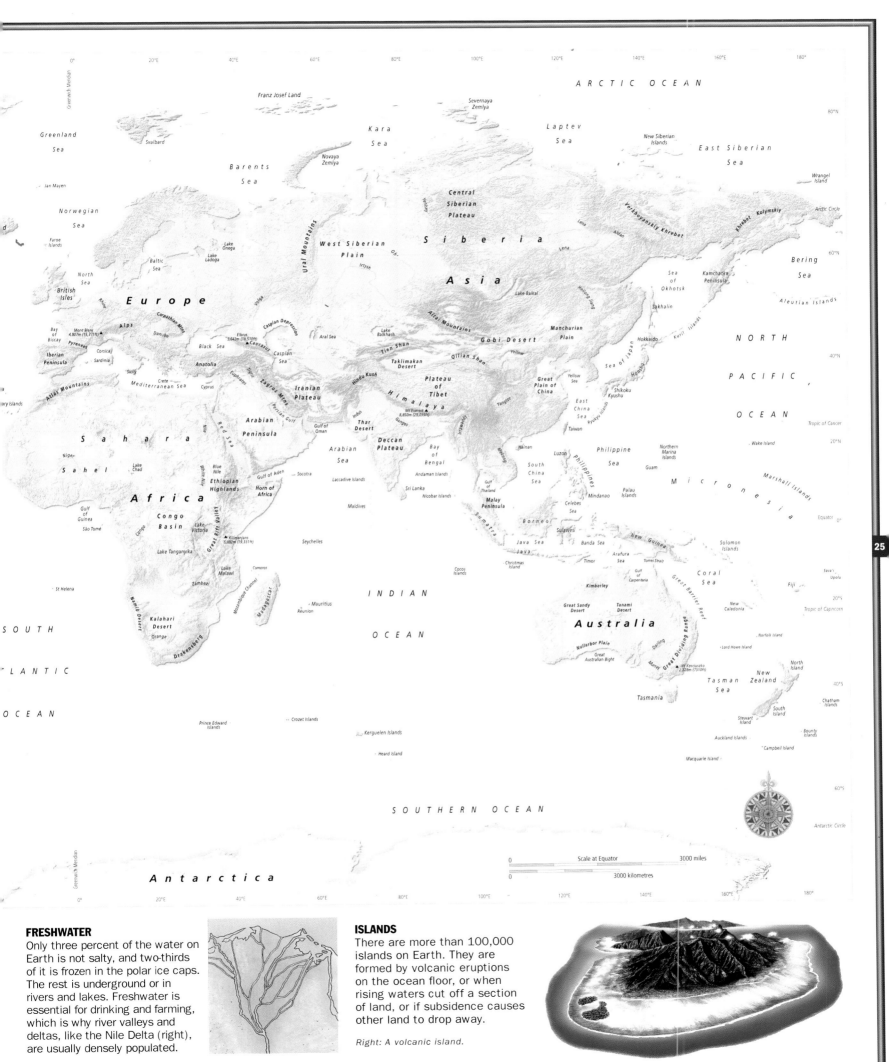

25

FRESHWATER
Only three percent of the water on Earth is not salty, and two-thirds of it is frozen in the polar ice caps. The rest is underground or in rivers and lakes. Freshwater is essential for drinking and farming, which is why river valleys and deltas, like the Nile Delta (right), are usually densely populated.

ISLANDS
There are more than 100,000 islands on Earth. They are formed by volcanic eruptions on the ocean floor, or when rising waters cut off a section of land, or if subsidence causes other land to drop away.

Right: A volcanic island.

The Political World

There are 194 independent countries in the world today, each with its own government and laws. Countries are divided by borders, which are shown in red on this map. However, not everyone agrees on these borders and many are disputed; we have shown disputed borders with a dotted red line. Many countries govern regions in other parts of the world. These areas are known as territories or dependencies (see page 120). The name of the governing country appears in parenthesis after the name of the territory on the maps in this atlas. Countries vary enormously in size—the Russian Federation is the largest country in the world today, while the Vatican City, in Italy, is the smallest.

Below: An Independence Day celebration in Gabon, Africa. In 1950, only four African nations were independent. Today they are all free and there are 53 independent states in Africa.

MORE AND MORE COUNTRIES
In 1950 there were only 82 independent countries in the world. Since then 112 more countries have appeared; many gained independence from their colonial European rulers (especially in Africa and Asia), while many others became independent when the Soviet Union broke up after 1990.

ANTARCTICA
Antarctica is the only continent with no permanent inhabitants. The region has no government and belongs to no country, although several countries have laid claim to areas within it. In summer more than 4,000 scientists carry out research there; only about 1,000 stay in winter.

Left: The Amundsen-Scott South Pole Station, in Antarctica. Astrophysicists study space from here where there is a clearer view than on most other places on Earth.

Right: Buying Fair Trade articles, like this chocolate and coffee, ensures that farmers get a fair price for their crops.

FAIR TRADE
Fair Trade is a movement that seeks to ensure that farmers and workers in poor countries are paid a fair price for their produce and work. Fair Trade values include sustainable farming methods, fair trading relationships, and self-sufficiency for producers.

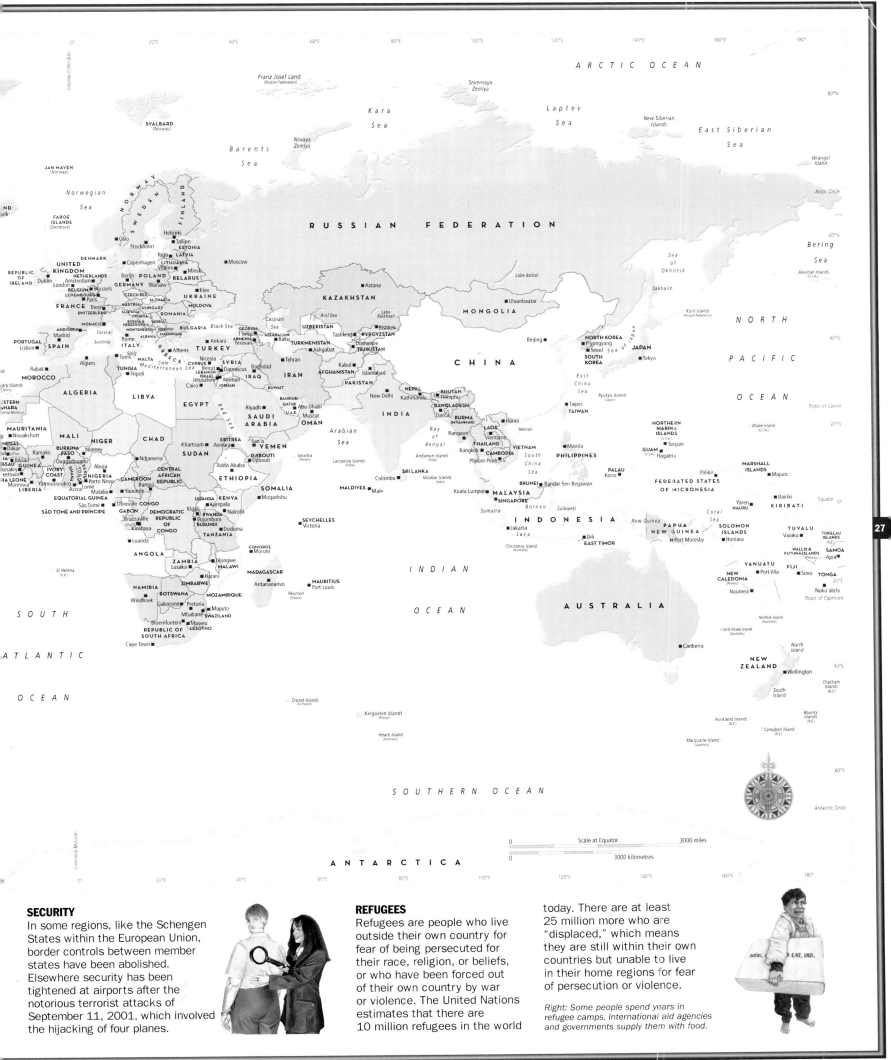

SECURITY

In some regions, like the Schengen States within the European Union, border controls between member states have been abolished. Elsewhere security has been tightened at airports after the notorious terrorist attacks of September 11, 2001, which involved the hijacking of four planes.

REFUGEES

Refugees are people who live outside their own country for fear of being persecuted for their race, religion, or beliefs, or who have been forced out of their own country by war or violence. The United Nations estimates that there are 10 million refugees in the world today. There are at least 25 million more who are "displaced," which means they are still within their own countries but unable to live in their home regions for fear of persecution or violence.

Right: Some people spend years in refugee camps. International aid agencies and governments supply them with food.

About Maps

There are many different kinds of maps, but they all visual representations (or pictures) of an area. Most maps focus on one or two key features or concepts, to make information clear or to highlight certain ideas or relationships. For example, the subway map of New York (far right) shows the subway lines and stations clearly marked but tells you very little else about the city. The political map of South America (right) clearly shows the countries but has little information about rivers, mountains, or other geographical features. Maps can show small areas, like a district in a city, or huge regions, including the whle world. There are even maps of the stars and the Universe. On most maps, real objects are shown as lines, colors, or symbols. In this atlas, for example, we have chosen to represent most cities with a round red dot and capital cities with a square dot. If you look carefully at the sample spread shown here you will learn how to read the maps in this atlas.

Left: Political maps show the countries in a given area clearly marked. They don't usually show many geographical features.

The regional and physical maps in this atlas all have locator globes to show you which area is being discussed.

Right: This ancient map shows the city of Constantinople (modern Istanbul) as it looked at the time of the Crusades.

All the place names on the regional and physical maps in this atlas have been indexed with the page number, a letter, and a number. To find a place, look up the name in the index, find the right page, and see where the letter and number co-ordinates meet on the map.

Above: An Islamic map of the Middle east from medieval times. Unlike modern maps, it shows south at the top (instead on north).

Left: A map of New York in 1660 when the city was still known as New Amsterdam.

France and Monaco

The second largest country in Europe, France stretches from the Mediterranean Sea in the south to the North Sea. In climate and culture, France straddles the continent, and is the only country to belong to both southern and northern Europe. France has played a central role in European civilization over the centuries and its long history is clearly visible in its towns and monuments, which range from prehistoric cave paintings and standing stones, to Roman temples and medieval castles and cathedrals, to 18th-century chateaux and modern skyscrapers. Travelers come from all over the world to admire these and to enjoy the country's superb food, wine, and entertainment; France is the world's number one tourist destination, with more than 79 million visitors each year. Much of France is covered in rich, fertile farmlands. French farmers use efficient technology and are the top producers of agricultural products in Europe. Services and industry, including the aerospace industry which produces Airbus airplanes, form the backbone of the French economy. France has welcomed immigrants from many parts of the world, especially from its former colonies in Africa and Asia. High unemployment has led to tension and rioting by some young immigrants in recent years.

Monaco
The Principality of Monaco is less than a mile square (1.95 sq km; only the Vatican City is smaller). It is mostly rocky outcrop crammed with luxury hotels and apartments and with million-dollar yachts in the harbor. Monaco has been ruled by the Grimaldi family since 1297. When Prince Rainier married Hollywood star Grace Kelly in 1956 this (along with the Mediterranean scenery and climate, generous tax laws, and annual Formula 1 "grand prix" motor race) attracted many wealthy visitors and celebrities to settle here.

Paris – City of Light
Founded over 2,000 years ago on a small island in the River Seine, Paris is called the city of light because it is a world center for commerce, education, and culture. Some of the world's most famous artists and writers have lived here. Its many famous art museums include the Louvre, which houses possibly the most famous painting in the world, the Mona Lisa by Leonardo Da Vinci. Other famous landmarks are the Arc de Triomphe, the Eiffel Tower (which was only meant to be there for 20 years), and the glorious palace and gardens of Versailles.

Left: France leads the world in high fashion, or "haute couture." Each season there are spectacular fashion shows in Paris with glamorous models striding the catwalks in the latest designer wear.

Fine food and wine
France is famous for its cooking and regional foods—from soft cheeses like Camembert and brie (delicious with French loaves called baguettes), to crêpes (thin rolled up pancakes), and cold meats. Other delicacies include escargots (the world's biggest consumers of snails) and cuisses de grenouilles (frogs' legs). Some frogs are eaten each year—protected in France they come from southeast Asia. France is the largest wine producer in the world. Famous wines include champagne, burgundy, and chardonnay.

Left: Some French specialities, clockwise from the top: red wine, a selection of cheeses, a baguette, a croissant, and crêpes.

Large rivers and lakes, tall mountains, and other important geographical features are all labeled and indexed.

Left: The Louise Weiss building in Strasbourg was opened in 1999. The wing-shaped building houses the debating chamber and the offices of the members of the European Parliament. Its 750-seat debating chamber is designed to host this institution's monthly sessions. The modern building has a 200-foot (60-m) high tower including 17 floors and 1,133 offices.

Strasbourg and the European Parliament
France was a founding member of the European Union (EU) in the 1950s and hosts the official seat of the Council of Europe in Strasbourg. Members meet there to decide a common European policy on a range of issues, from human rights to education and the environment. Currently there are 27 member states representing a combined population of some 800 million people. Along with New York and Geneva, Strasbourg is the only city in the world which is home to an international institution but is not a national capital.

Each regional map includes a scale in miles and kilometers to help you calculate distances on the map.

Sometimes, when an important island is too far away to be shown to scale on the map, we have placed it in a box and placed it beside the main country.

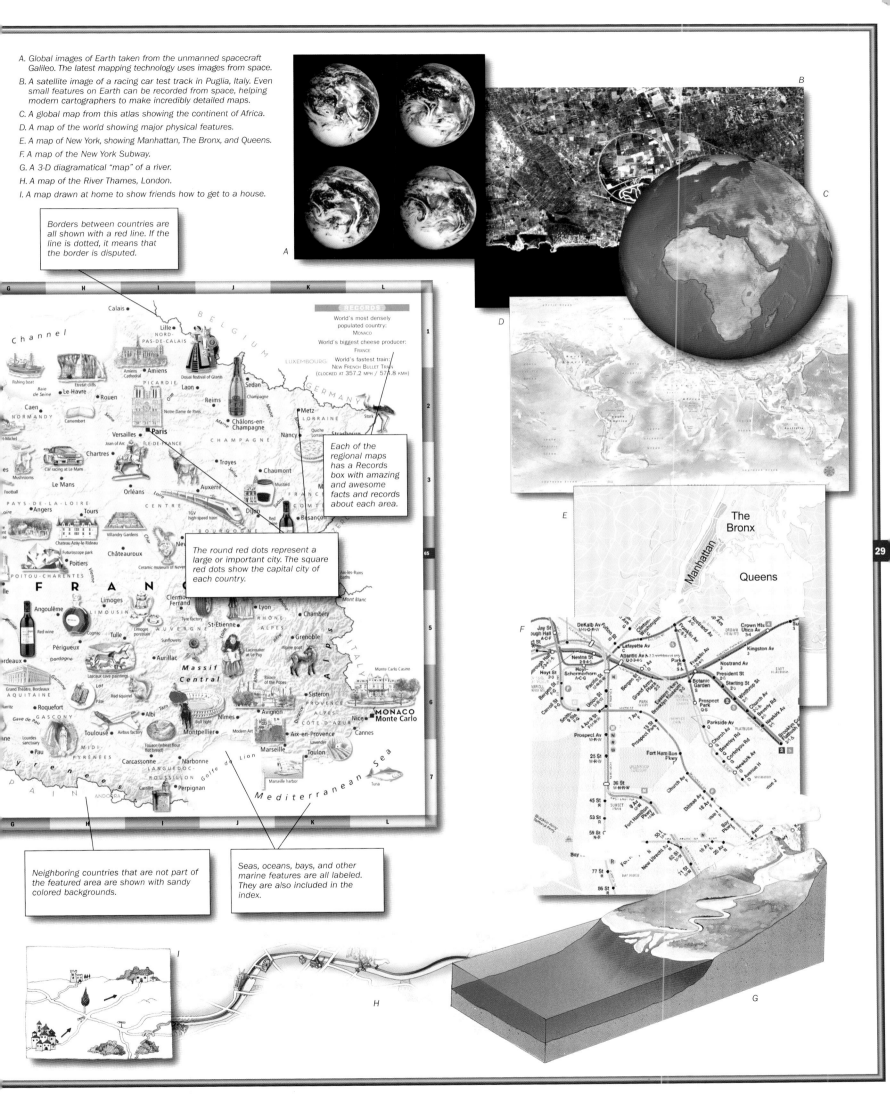

A. Global images of Earth taken from the unmanned spacecraft Galileo. The latest mapping technology uses images from space.

B. A satellite image of a racing car test track in Puglia, Italy. Even small features on Earth can be recorded from space, helping modern cartographers to make incredibly detailed maps.

C. A global map from this atlas showing the continent of Africa.

D. A map of the world showing major physical features.

E. A map of New York, showing Manhattan, The Bronx, and Queens.

F. A map of the New York Subway.

G. A 3-D diagramatical "map" of a river.

H. A map of the River Thames, London.

I. A map drawn at home to show friends how to get to a house.

Borders between countries are all shown with a red line. If the line is dotted, it means that the border is disputed.

Each of the regional maps has a Records box with amazing and awesome facts and records about each area.

The round red dots represent a large or important city. The square red dots show the capital city of each country.

Neighboring countries that are not part of the featured area are shown with sandy colored backgrounds.

Seas, oceans, bays, and other marine features are all labeled. They are also included in the index.

CLIMATE AND WEATHER

North America experiences every kind of climate, from the bitter cold of the far north to the humid heat of the tropics. Cold air from the frozen interiors of Greenland and the Arctic sweeps down on Canada bringing snow and icy conditions for much of the year. To the south, humid tropical air is carried northward by the Gulf of Mexico into the plains and the East Coast. The center section has a continental climate, which means that it is cold enough for snow in winter and hot or warm and rainy in the summer. Some regions here are frequently hit by "twisters" (tornadoes). The Southwest has a hot, dry, desert climate, while the south generally is tropical with a hurricane season. In 2005 the north-central Gulf Coast and New Orleans were devastated by Hurricane Katrina.

Queen Elizabeth Is

Brooks Range
Beaufort Sea
Banks Island
Victoria Island

Bering Strait
Bering Sea
Yukon
Mackenzie
Great Bear Lake

Mt McKinley ▲
Mackenzie Mountains
Great Slave Lake

Aleutian Range

Gulf of Alaska
Coast Mountains
Peace
Reindeer Lake

Aleutian Islands
Lake Athabasca

Rocky
Saskatchewan

Lake Man

Columbia

Snake

Mountains

Great Salt Lake

Sierra Nevada
Great Basin
Colorado

Grand Canyon
Colorado Plateau

Sonoran Desert

Rio Grand

PACIFIC OCEAN

Baja California
Gulf of California
Sierra Madre Occidental
Sierra Madre

NORTH AMERICA

There are just 500 miles between the icy North Pole and North America and only 500 miles from the south of the continent to the jungles of the equator. The two largest countries, Canada and the United

States, stretch across eight time zones between the Pacific and Atlantic Oceans, but the continent's southern tip shrinks to just 40 miles (60 km) and a single time zone from coast to coast. The spectacular chain of the jagged Rocky Mountains runs like a giant backbone down the west side.

The Rockies were forged 80 million years ago and level out eastward into the fertile farmlands of the Great Plains, or prairies. Further east are the five Great Lakes which you could still see if you were standing on the moon. They make up the largest fresh surface water system on Earth. Beyond them are the old, wooded Appalachian Mountains. To the North, the land is mostly snowbound with lots of lakes and forests. If you look at the globe (left) you can imagine how Alaska in the far northwest was once joined to Siberia on the Asian continent. This land bridge was crossed by the ancestors of the Native Americans about 30,000 years ago.

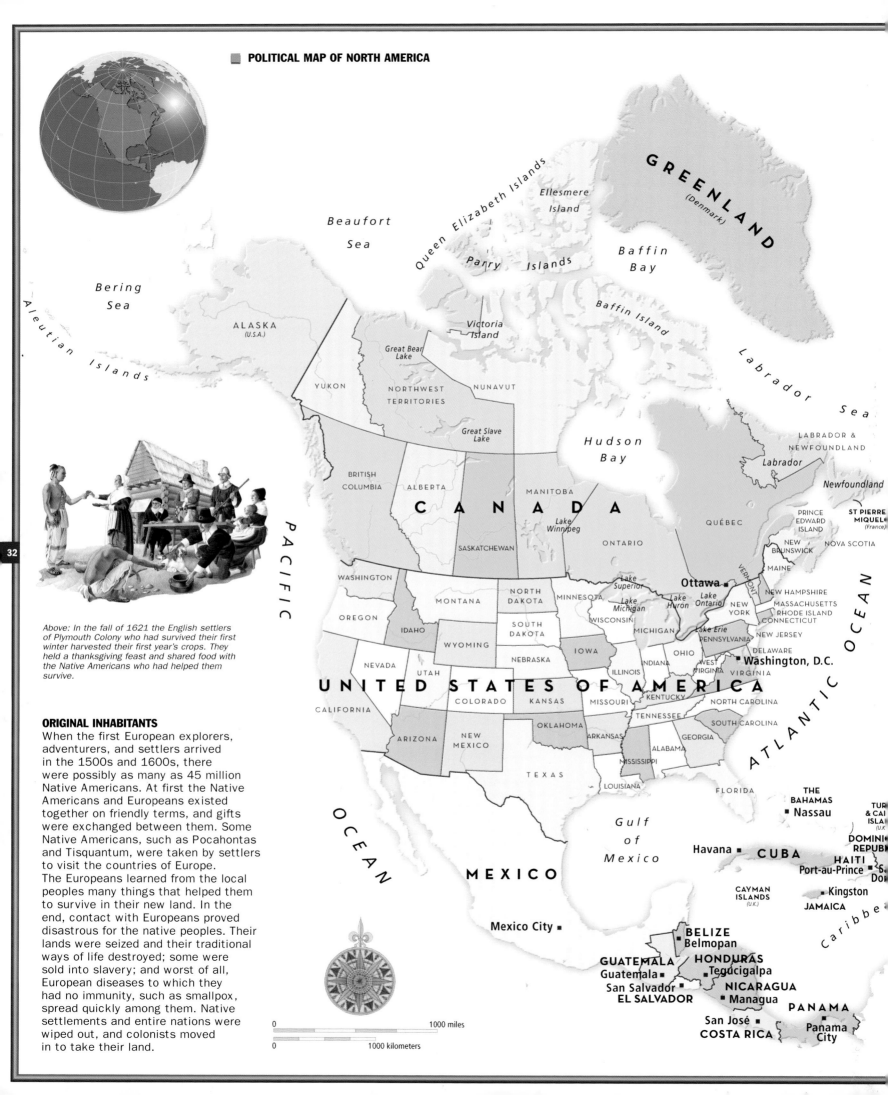

POLITICAL MAP OF NORTH AMERICA

GREENLAND
(Denmark)

Beaufort Sea

Queen Elizabeth Islands

Ellesmere Island

Parry Islands

Baffin Bay

Bering Sea

Aleutian Islands

ALASKA (U.S.A.)

Baffin Island

Labrador Sea

Victoria Island

Great Bear Lake

YUKON

NORTHWEST TERRITORIES

NUNAVUT

Hudson Bay

Great Slave Lake

LABRADOR & NEWFOUNDLAND

Labrador

Newfoundland

BRITISH COLUMBIA

ALBERTA

MANITOBA

C A N A D A

ONTARIO

QUÉBEC

PRINCE EDWARD ISLAND

ST PIERRE & MIQUELON (France)

SASKATCHEWAN

Lake Winnipeg

NEW BRUNSWICK

NOVA SCOTIA

MAINE

WASHINGTON

MONTANA

NORTH DAKOTA

MINNESOTA

Lake Superior

Ottawa

VERMONT

NEW HAMPSHIRE

OREGON

IDAHO

SOUTH DAKOTA

WISCONSIN

Lake Michigan

Lake Huron

Lake Ontario

NEW YORK

MASSACHUSETTS
RHODE ISLAND
CONNECTICUT

MICHIGAN

Lake Erie

NEW JERSEY

WYOMING

NEBRASKA

IOWA

OHIO

PENNSYLVANIA

DELAWARE

NEVADA

UTAH

ILLINOIS

INDIANA

WEST VIRGINIA

Washington, D.C.

U N I T E D   S T A T E S   O F   A M E R I C A

VIRGINIA

CALIFORNIA

COLORADO

KANSAS

MISSOURI

KENTUCKY

NORTH CAROLINA

TENNESSEE

ARIZONA

NEW MEXICO

OKLAHOMA

ARKANSAS

SOUTH CAROLINA

GEORGIA

ALABAMA

MISSISSIPPI

TEXAS

LOUISIANA

FLORIDA

PACIFIC OCEAN

Gulf of Mexico

M E X I C O

THE BAHAMAS
Nassau

TURKS & CAICOS ISLANDS (U.K.)

Havana

CUBA

DOMINICAN REPUBLIC

HAITI
Port-au-Prince

ATLANTIC OCEAN

CAYMAN ISLANDS (U.K.)

Kingston

JAMAICA

Caribbean

Mexico City

BELIZE
Belmopan

GUATEMALA
Guatemala

HONDURAS
Tegucigalpa

San Salvador
EL SALVADOR

NICARAGUA
Managua

San José
COSTA RICA

PANAMA
Panama City

Above: In the fall of 1621 the English settlers of Plymouth Colony who had survived their first winter harvested their first year's crops. They held a thanksgiving feast and shared food with the Native Americans who had helped them survive.

ORIGINAL INHABITANTS

When the first European explorers, adventurers, and settlers arrived in the 1500s and 1600s, there were possibly as many as 45 million Native Americans. At first the Native Americans and Europeans existed together on friendly terms, and gifts were exchanged between them. Some Native Americans, such as Pocahontas and Tisquantum, were taken by settlers to visit the countries of Europe. The Europeans learned from the local peoples many things that helped them to survive in their new land. In the end, contact with Europeans proved disastrous for the native peoples. Their lands were seized and their traditional ways of life destroyed; some were sold into slavery; and worst of all, European diseases to which they had no immunity, such as smallpox, spread quickly among them. Native settlements and entire nations were wiped out, and colonists moved in to take their land.

0   1000 miles

0   1000 kilometers

North America

North America includes the three large countries of Canada, the United States, and Mexico, as well as the 20 smaller nations that make up Central America and the Caribbean. The three main official languages in the region, all of European origin, are English, Spanish, and French. In the Caribbean a number of Creole languages are spoken, while in some isolated areas local indigenous languages still exist. Canada and the United States are both rich, industrialized nations with long-standing democratic governments. Mexico, which has the world's largest and fastest-growing Spanish-speaking population, has recovered well from a severe economic crisis in the mid-1990s. The countries of Central America and the Caribbean are poorer than their northern neighbors and have had varying degrees of success in establishing democratic governments. Tourism and agriculture form the basis of most economies here, with coffee, cotton, sugar, cocoa, spices, and fruit being grown for export.

SETTLING NORTH AMERICA

The native peoples of North America and the Amerindians of Central and South America are believed to have penetrated into America from Asia by way of the Bering Sea about 30,000 years ago when a land bridge existed between the two continents. They were nomadic hunter-gatherers moving where there was food and water. Some tribes settled into farming communities and in Central America the first Spanish settlers discovered highly organized civilizations, such as the Aztecs. The first Europeans to discover America were neither Christopher Columbus nor Amerigo Vespucci in the 1490s (and they didn't reach the North American mainland) but the Vikings from Scandinavia 500 years earlier. They were blown off course as they sailed to Iceland and Greenland in their wooden longships and landed in Newfoundland, leaving the only documented settlement at L'Anse aux Meadows.

VIRGIN ISLANDS (U.K.)
ANGUILLA (U.K.)
ANTIGUA & BARBUDA
GUADELOUPE (France)
DOMINICA
ST KITTS and NEVIS
MARTINIQUE (France)
BARBADOS
ST LUCIA
MONTSERRAT (U.K.)
ST VINCENT & THE GRENADINES
GRENADA
TRINIDAD & TOBAGO
NETHERLANDS ANTILLES (Netherlands)

Above: View of part of the Manhattan skyline looking across the Brooklyn Bridge.

Right: Statue of Abraham Lincoln, president of the United States during the Civil War. He was assassinated within a week of the end of the war.

HOW THEY BECAME THE UNITED STATES OF AMERICA

The name "America" first appeared on a map in 1507 drawn by the German mapmaker Waldseemueller. He wanted to honor the voyages of Amerigo Vespucci a few years earlier in search of a passage to the Orient. During the 17th century the British created 13 colonies on the East Coast around Massachusetts and Virginia. As settlers moved westwards across the Appalachians they met resistance from Native American tribes and French colonists and this led to the French and Indian Wars (1754–1763). The English colonists demanded freedom from their English rulers to govern themselves. This led to the Declaration of Independence in 1776 and the American Revolution which ended with British surrender in 1781. A full United States government was founded in 1788 and George Washington became the first US President in 1789. Other states were added to the original 13, though a bitter Civil War was fought from 1861–65 over slavery and the right of states to rule themselves. The last two states, Hawaii and Alaska, were added in 1959 and became the 49th and 50th states of the Union.

Above: An early version of the Stars and Stripes, when there were just 13 states in the Union.

CANADA

Country name Canada
Area 3,854,844 sq mi
(9,984,670 sq km)
Population 33,212,696
Government Parliamentary
democracy
Capital Ottawa
Currency Canadian dollar
Languages English, French
Main religions Roman Catholic 42%,
Protestant 24%
Literacy 99%
GDP per capita $38,400 (2007 est.)

UNITED STATES

Country name United States
of America
Area 3,793,840 sq mi
(9,826,630 sq km)
Population 303,824,646
Government Federal republic
Capital Washington, D.C.
Currency US dollar
Languages English, Spanish
Main religions Protestant 51%,
Roman Catholic 24%
Literacy 99%
GDP per capita $45,800 (2007 est.)

MEXICO

Country name United Mexican States
Area 761,606 sq mi
(1,972,550 sq km)
Population 109,955,400
Government Constitutional republic
Capital Mexico City
Currency Mexican peso
Languages Spanish, Nahuatl, Mayan,
Zaptec, Miztec, other indigenous
languages
Main religions Roman Catholic 76%,
Protestant 7%
Literacy 91%
GDP per capita $12,800 (2007 est.)

Above: Salsa, a favorite Mexican dish in its homeland and also north of the border.

NATIONS OF IMMIGRANTS

North America is truly a melting pot of different peoples. From the early prehistoric tribes to the first European colonists, who later brought Africans over as slaves, the continent has become home to people from every corner of the globe. Many immigrants, like the millions of Irish settlers who left Ireland during the potato famine of the 1850s, came to the New World to escape poverty at home. Others sought refuge from persecution, including the many Jews and other Europeans who came to escape extremist political regimes in Europe. In more recent times immigrants from Asia have sought a new life in North America. The Statue of Liberty, a gift to America from France, stands in New York harbor as a welcoming symbol to all new arrivals. The statue bears the words "*Give me your tired, your poor, Your huddled masses yearning to breathe free...*"

GUATEMALA

Country name Republic of Guatemala
Area 42,043 sq mi (108,890 sq km)
Population 13,002,206
Government Republic
Capital Guatemala City
Currency Quetzal, US dollar
Languages Spanish, Amerindian
languages
Main religions Roman Catholic,
Protestant, indigenous Mayan
beliefs
Literacy 70%
GDP per capita $4,700 (2007 est.)

BELIZE

Country name Belize
Area 8,867 sq mi (22,966 sq km)
Population 301,270
Government Parliamentary
democracy
Capital Belmopan
Currency Belize dollar
Languages Spanish, Creole
Main religions Roman Catholic 50%,
Protestant 27%
Literacy 77%
GDP per capita $7,900 (2007 est.)

HONDURAS

Country name Republic of Honduras
Area 43,278 sq mi (112,090 sq km)
Population 7,639,327
Government Republic
Capital Tegucigalpa
Currency Lempira
Languages Spanish, Indigenous
languages
Main religions Roman Catholic 97%,
Protestant 3%
Literacy 80%
GDP per capita $4,100 (2007 est.)

EL SALVADOR

Country name Republic
of El Salvador
Area 8,123 sq mi (21,040 sq km)
Population 7,066,403
Government Republic
Capital San Salvador
Currency US dollar
Languages Spanish, Nahua
Main religions Roman Catholic 83%,
other 17%
Literacy 80%
GDP per capita $5,800 (2007 est.)

NICARAGUA

Country name Republic of Nicaragua
Area 49,998 sq mi (129,494 sq km)
Population 5,785,846
Government Republic
Capital Managua
Currency Gold cordoba
Languages Spanish, Miskito,
Indigenous languages
Main religions Roman Catholic
72.9%, Evangelical 15.1%
Literacy 68%
GDP per capita $2,600 (2007 est.)

COSTA RICA

Country name Republic of Costa Rica
Area 19,730 sq mi (51,100 sq km)
Population 4,195,914
Government Republic
Capital San José
Currency Costa Rican colon
Languages Spanish, English
Main religions Roman Catholic
76.3%, Evangelical 13.7%
Literacy 95%
GDP per capita $10,300 (2007 est.)

PANAMA

Country name Republic of Panama
Area 30,193 sq mi (78,200 sq km)
Population 3,292,693
Government Republic
Capital Panamá
Currency Balboa, US dollar
Languages Spanish, English
Main religions Roman Catholic 85%,
Protestant 15%
Literacy 92%
GDP per capita $10,300 (2007 est.)

THE BAHAMAS

Country name Commonwealth
of The Bahamas
Area 5,382 sq mi (13,940 sq km)
Population 307,451
Government Parliamentary
democracy
Capital Nassau
Currency Bahamas dollar
Languages English, Creole
Main religions Baptist 35.4%,
Anglican 15.1%, Roman Catholic
13.5%
Literacy 96%
GDP per capita $25,000 (2007 est.)

CUBA

Country name Republic of Cuba
Area 42,803 sq mi (110,860 sq km)
Population 11,423,952
Government Communist state
Capital Havana
Currency Cuban peso
Languages Spanish
Main religions Roman Catholic,
Santeria
Literacy 99%
GDP per capita $4,500 (2007 est.)

JAMAICA

Country name Jamaica
Area 4,244 sq mi (10,991 sq km)
Population 2,804,332
Government Parliamentary
democracy
Capital Kingston
Currency Jamaican dollar
Languages English, English patois
Main religions Protestant 62.5%,
Roman Catholic 2.6%
Literacy 88%
GDP per capita $7,700 (2007 est.)

HAITI

Country name Republic of Haiti
Area 10,714 sq mi (27,750 sq km)
Population 8,924,553
Government Republic
Capital Port-au-Prince
Currency Gourde
Languages French, Creole
Main religions Roman Catholic 80%,
Protestant 16%
Literacy 53%
GDP per capita $1,300 (2007 est.)

DOMINICAN REPUBLIC

Country name Dominican Republic
Area 18,814 sq mi (48,730 sq km)
Population 9,507,133
Government Republic
Capital Santo Domingo
Currency Dominican peso
Languages Spanish
Main religions Roman Catholic 95%,
other 5%
Literacy 87%
GDP per capita $7,000 (2007 est.)

MEXICO CITY

With an estimated 23 million inhabitants, Mexico City is the biggest city in the Americas and the second largest in the world. The capital of the country, it is the center of government, the economy, industry, and culture in Mexico. The city is located in a large valley in the high plateaus of central Mexico. It was built over the Pre-Columbian Aztec city of Tenochtitlan. At 7,546 feet (2,300 m), it is the highest city in North America. Ringed by mountains, air pollution is a huge problem since the pollutants produced by cars and industry cannot escape. The government tries to control the pollution by planning "carless days," changing school hours, and closing factories. The historic center of the city has many beautiful buildings and the "floating gardens" of Xochimilco in a southern borough have been declared a UNESCO World Heritage Site.

ANTIGUA AND BARBUDA

Country name Antigua and Barbuda
Area 171 sq mi (442.6 sq km)
Population 69,842
Government Parliamentary democracy
Capital Saint John's
Currency East Caribbean dollar
Languages English, local dialects
Main religions Anglican 25.7%, Seventh Day Adventist 12.3%
Literacy 86%
GDP per capita $18,300 (2007 est.)

DOMINICA

Country name Commonwealth of Dominica
Area 291 sq mi (754 sq km)
Population 72,514
Government Parliamentary democracy
Capital Roseau
Currency East Caribbean dollar
Languages English, French patois
Main religions Roman Catholic 61.4%, Seventh Day Adventist 6%
Literacy 94%
GDP per capita $9,000 (2007 est.)

SAINT KITTS AND NEVIS

Country name Federation of Saint Kitts and Nevis
Area 101 sq mi (261 sq km)
Population 39,619
Government Parliamentary democracy
Capital Basseterre
Currency East Caribbean dollar
Languages English
Main religions Anglican, other Protestant, Roman Catholic
Literacy 98%
GDP per capita $13,900 (2007 est.)

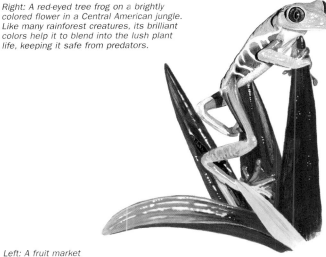

Right: A red-eyed tree frog on a brightly colored flower in a Central American jungle. Like many rainforest creatures, its brilliant colors help it to blend into the lush plant life, keeping it safe from predators.

Left: A fruit market in Dominica.

NATURAL RESOURCES

The United States has vast wheat, corn, and other agricultural and mining resources while Canada has huge oil, gas, and timber reserves. Mexico and Central America also have oil reserves and tourism is important throughout the region. The Caribbean produces bananas and other tropical fruits, as well as sugar, coffee, spices, seafood, and rum.

TOURISM

Many people are drawn to Hawaii, Mexico, Central America, and the Caribbean for their sandy beaches and crystal clear waters for swimming and scuba diving. Others visit the fabulous ruins of the ancient Mesoamerican civilizations found in Belize, Guatelmala, and Mexico. There are also tropical rain forests with rare and colorful wildlife for more adventurous travelers.

SAINT LUCIA

Country name Saint Lucia
Area 238 sq mi (616 sq km)
Population 172,884
Government Parliamentary democracy
Capital Castries
Currency East Caribbean dollar
Languages English, French patois
Main religions Roman Catholic 67.5%, Seventh Day Adventist 8.5%
Literacy 90%
GDP per capita $10,700 (2007 est.)

BARBADOS

Country name Barbados
Area 166 sq mi (431 sq km)
Population 281,968
Government Parliamentary democracy
Capital Bridgetown
Currency Barbados dollar
Languages English
Main religions Protestant 67%, Roman Catholic 4%
Literacy 99%
GDP per capita $19,300 (2007 est.)

SAINT VINCENT AND THE GRENADINES

Country name Saint Vincent and the Grenadines
Area 150 sq mi (389 sq km)
Population 118,432
Government Parliamentary democracy
Capital Kingstown
Currency East Caribbean dollar
Languages English, French patois
Main religions Anglican 47%, Methodist 28%, Roman Catholic 13%
Literacy 96%
GDP per capita $9,800 (2007 est.)

GRENADA

Country name Grenada
Area 133 sq mi (344 sq km)
Population 90,343
Government Parliamentary democracy
Capital Saint George's
Currency East Caribbean dollar
Languages English, French patois
Main religions Roman Catholic 53%, Anglican 13.8%
Literacy 96%
GDP per capita $10,500 (2007 est.)

TRINIDAD AND TOBAGO

Country name Republic of Trinidad and Tobago
Area 1,980 sq mi (5,128 sq km)
Population 1,047,366
Government Parliamentary democracy
Capital Port-of-Spain
Currency Trinidad and Tobago dollar
Languages English, Caribbean Hindustani
Main religions Roman Catholic 26%, Hindu 22.5%
Literacy 99%
GDP per capita $18,300 (2007 est.)

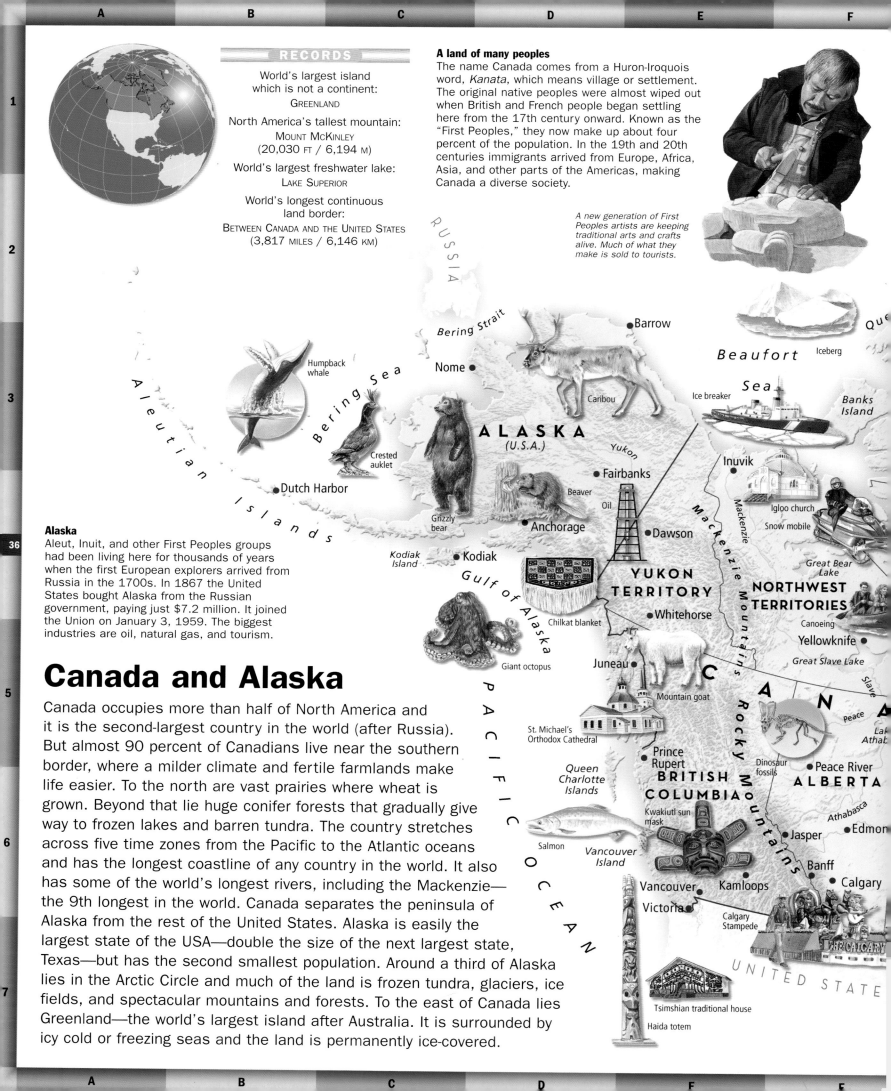

RECORDS

World's largest island
which is not a continent:
GREENLAND

North America's tallest mountain:
MOUNT McKINLEY
(20,030 FT / 6,194 M)

World's largest freshwater lake:
LAKE SUPERIOR

World's longest continuous
land border:
BETWEEN CANADA AND THE UNITED STATES
(3,817 MILES / 6,146 KM)

A land of many peoples

The name Canada comes from a Huron-Iroquois word, *Kanata*, which means village or settlement. The original native peoples were almost wiped out when British and French people began settling here from the 17th century onward. Known as the "First Peoples," they now make up about four percent of the population. In the 19th and 20th centuries immigrants arrived from Europe, Africa, Asia, and other parts of the Americas, making Canada a diverse society.

A new generation of First Peoples artists are keeping traditional arts and crafts alive. Much of what they make is sold to tourists.

Alaska

Aleut, Inuit, and other First Peoples groups had been living here for thousands of years when the first European explorers arrived from Russia in the 1700s. In 1867 the United States bought Alaska from the Russian government, paying just $7.2 million. It joined the Union on January 3, 1959. The biggest industries are oil, natural gas, and tourism.

Canada and Alaska

Canada occupies more than half of North America and it is the second-largest country in the world (after Russia). But almost 90 percent of Canadians live near the southern border, where a milder climate and fertile farmlands make life easier. To the north are vast prairies where wheat is grown. Beyond that lie huge conifer forests that gradually give way to frozen lakes and barren tundra. The country stretches across five time zones from the Pacific to the Atlantic oceans and has the longest coastline of any country in the world. It also has some of the world's longest rivers, including the Mackenzie—the 9th longest in the world. Canada separates the peninsula of Alaska from the rest of the United States. Alaska is easily the largest state of the USA—double the size of the next largest state, Texas—but has the second smallest population. Around a third of Alaska lies in the Arctic Circle and much of the land is frozen tundra, glaciers, ice fields, and spectacular mountains and forests. To the east of Canada lies Greenland—the world's largest island after Australia. It is surrounded by icy cold or freezing seas and the land is permanently ice-covered.

RUSSIA

Bering Strait

Barrow

Beaufort
Sea
Iceberg

Que

Humpback whale

Nome

Caribou

Ice breaker

Banks Island

Bering Sea

Crested auklet

ALASKA
(U.S.A.)

Yukon

Inuvik

Aleutian Islands

Dutch Harbor

Grizzly bear

Fairbanks

Beaver

Oil

Anchorage

Dawson

Mackenzie

Mackenzie Mountains

Igloo church

Snow mobile

Great Bear Lake

Kodiak Island

Kodiak

Gulf of Alaska

Chilkat blanket

YUKON
TERRITORY

Whitehorse

NORTHWEST
TERRITORIES

Canoeing

Yellowknife

Great Slave Lake

Giant octopus

Juneau

Mountain goat

CANADA

Slave

Peace

Lak
Athab

St. Michael's
Orthodox Cathedral

PACIFIC

Prince Rupert

Dinosaur fossils

Peace River

Queen
Charlotte
Islands

BRITISH
COLUMBIA

ALBERTA

Kwakiutl sun mask

Athabasca

Salmon

Vancouver
Island

Jasper

Edmon

OCEAN

Vancouver

Kamloops

Banff

Victoria

Calgary

Calgary
Stampede

THE CALGARY

UNITED STATE

Tsimshian traditional house

Haida totem

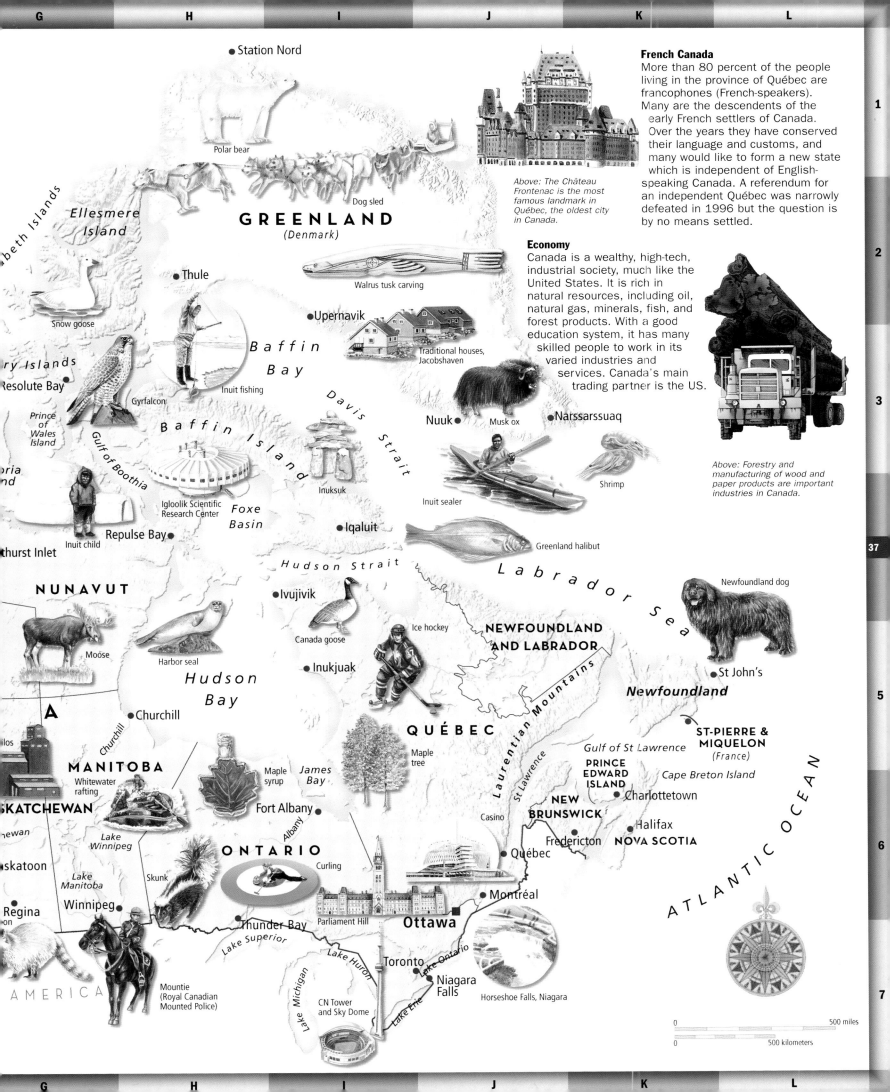

Station Nord

Polar bear

Dog sled

GREENLAND
(Denmark)

Thule

Walrus tusk carving

Upernavik

B a f f i n
Bay

Traditional houses,
Jacobshaven

Snow goose

Inuit fishing

Davis

Gyrfalcon

Nuuk

Musk ox

Narssarssuaq

Prince
of
Wales
Island

B a f f i n   *I s l a n d*

Strait

Inuksuk

Shrimp

Igloolik Scientific
Research Center

Foxe
Basin

Inuit sealer

Greenland halibut

Repulse Bay

Iqaluit

Hudson   Strait

L a b r a d o r   *S e a*

NUNAVUT

Newfoundland dog

Ivujivik

Moose

Canada goose

Ice hockey

NEWFOUNDLAND
AND LABRADOR

Harbor seal

Inukjuak

Newfoundland

Hudson
Bay

St John's

Churchill

QUÉBEC

Laurentian Mountains

ST-PIERRE &
MIQUELON
(France)

Gulf of St Lawrence

MANITOBA

Whitewater
rafting

Maple
syrup

James
Bay

Maple
tree

Cape Breton Island

PRINCE
EDWARD
ISLAND

Charlottetown

Lake
Winnipeg

Fort Albany

Casino

NEW
BRUNSWICK

KATCHEWAN

Halifax

Fredericton

NOVA SCOTIA

Lake
Manitoba

Skunk

ONTARIO

Curling

Québec

Skaton

Winnipeg

Montréal

Regina

Parliament Hill

Ottawa

Thunder Bay

Lake Superior

Lake Huron

Toronto

Niagara
Falls

AMERICA

Mountie
(Royal Canadian
Mounted Police)

CN Tower
and Sky Dome

Horseshoe Falls, Niagara

Lake Michigan

Lake Erie

Lake Ontario

French Canada

More than 80 percent of the people living in the province of Québec are francophones (French-speakers). Many are the descendents of the early French settlers of Canada. Over the years they have conserved their language and customs, and many would like to form a new state which is independent of English-speaking Canada. A referendum for an independent Québec was narrowly defeated in 1996 but the question is by no means settled.

Above: The Château Frontenac is the most famous landmark in Québec, the oldest city in Canada.

Economy

Canada is a wealthy, high-tech, industrial society, much like the United States. It is rich in natural resources, including oil, natural gas, minerals, fish, and forest products. With a good education system, it has many skilled people to work in its varied industries and services. Canada's main trading partner is the US.

Above: Forestry and manufacturing of wood and paper products are important industries in Canada.

ATLANTIC OCEAN

0 ——————— 500 miles

0 ——————— 500 kilometers

Eastern United States

With a population of just over 300 million people, the United States has the largest and most technologically advanced economy in the world. European settlement began in the East, and the Eastern states largely retain control over government and the economy. The capital city and seat of government is in Washington. The economy is driven from New York—the largest city in the US—and Chicago, both major hubs of finance and business. The Northeast is highly urbanized, with the major cities almost running together to form a single megacity, sometimes referred to as Bosnywash (Boston, New York, Washington). The more rural Southern states, settled by many French and Spanish immigrants and with a high proportion of African Americans, have distinctive customs, cuisines, and cultures of their own. Once known as the "breadbasket" of the US for its fertile soils and wheat, the Midwest is now industrialized and is home to the third-largest US city—Chicago.

Running the country

All three branches of the US government—legislative (Congress), executive (the President), and judiciary (Supreme Court)—are based in Washington D.C. The city is also home to more than 170 foreign embassies, the World Bank, and the International Monetary Fund (IMF). Many lobbying groups, trade unions, and professional associations are also located here, close to the seat of power.

Above: The central part of the Capitol Building in Washington, D.C. It houses the United States Congress, the legislative branch of the government. The cornerstone was laid by George Washington in 1793.

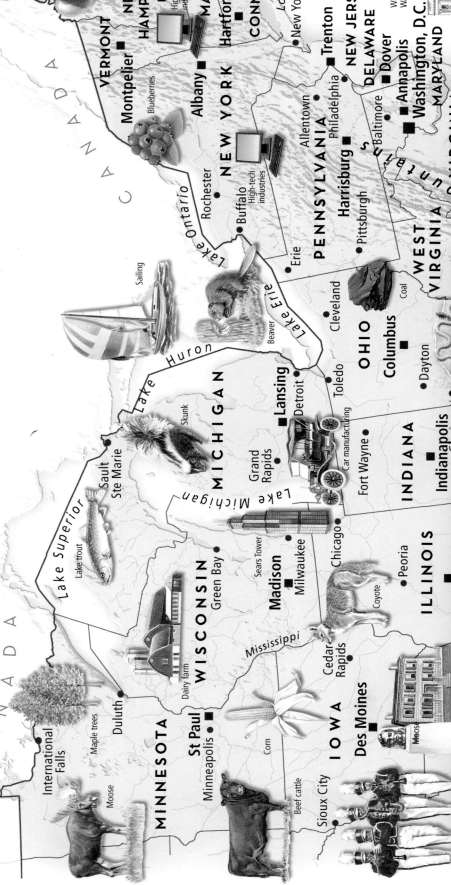

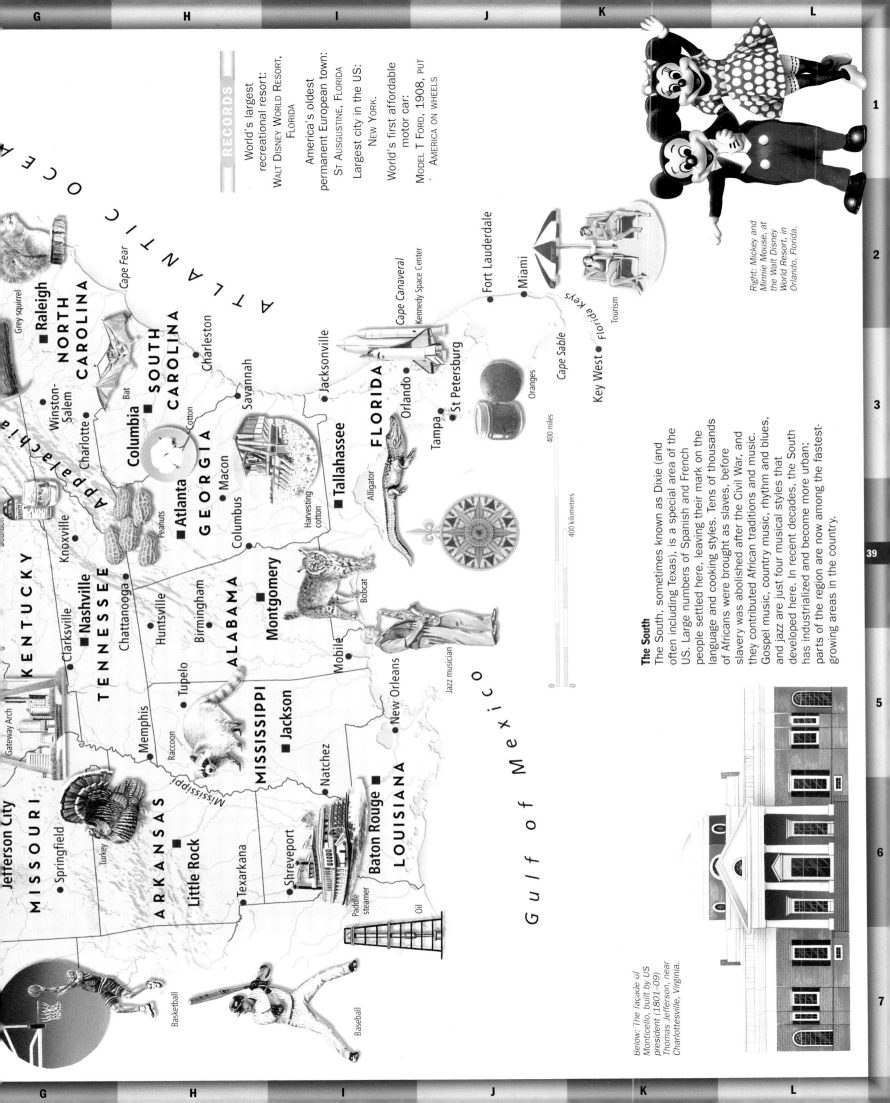

RECORDS

World's largest
recreational resort:
WALT DISNEY WORLD RESORT,
FLORIDA

America's oldest
permanent European town:
ST AUGUSTINE, FLORIDA

Largest city in the US:
NEW YORK.

World's first affordable
motor car:
MODEL T FORD, 1908, PUT
AMERICA ON WHEELS

ATLANTIC OCEAN

Grey squirrel

Cape Fear

NORTH CAROLINA

Raleigh

Winston-Salem
Charlotte
Bat

SOUTH CAROLINA

Columbia

Charleston

Cotton

Savannah

GEORGIA

Atlanta
Macon
Columbus

Peanuts

Harvesting cotton

Jacksonville

FLORIDA

Tallahassee

Orlando

Tampa
St Petersburg

Oranges

Cape Canaveral
Kennedy Space Center

Cape Sable

Florida Keys

Fort Lauderdale

Miami

Key West

Tourism

Alligator

KENTUCKY

Clarksville
Knoxville

TENNESSEE

Nashville
Chattanooga
Huntsville

Memphis

Tupelo

ALABAMA

Birmingham

Montgomery

Mobile

Bobcat

MISSISSIPPI

Jackson

New Orleans

Jazz musician

Appalachia

Tobacco

Gateway Arch

MISSOURI

Jefferson City
Springfield

Turkey

ARKANSAS

Little Rock

Texarkana

Raccoon

Mississippi

Natchez

Shreveport

LOUISIANA

Baton Rouge

Oil

Paddle steamer

Gulf of Mexico

400 miles

400 kilometers

0
0

Basketball

Baseball

Below: The façade of
Monticello, built by US
president (1801–09)
Thomas Jefferson, near
Charlottesville, Virginia.

Right: Mickey and
Minnie Mouse, at
the Walt Disney
World Resort, in
Orlando, Florida.

The South

The South, sometimes known as Dixie (and
often including Texas), is a special area of the
US. Large numbers of Spanish and French
people settled here, leaving their mark on the
language and cooking styles. Tens of thousands
of Africans were brought as slaves, before
slavery was abolished after the Civil War, and
they contributed African traditions and music.
Gospel music, country music, rhythm and blues,
and jazz are just four musical styles that
developed here. In recent decades, the South
has industrialized and become more urban;
parts of the region are now among the fastest-
growing areas in the country.

Western United States

This vast region, covering more than half the land area of the United States, is very diverse. It can be divided into several distinct, often overlapping areas. The Southwest, which includes the Grand Canyon, has some of the most stunning landscapes on the planet. Despite its overall low population density, it contains some large cities, such as Phoenix and Houston. The West Coast, or Pacific Seaboard, has several large cities, including Los Angeles (the second largest in the US), San Diego, San Francisco, and Seattle. Wealthy and quite densely populated, especially in the south, this region is known for its high-tech industries centered in the northern California region of Silicon Valley. California is the richest and most populous state in the US. According to some, if California were an independent state it would be ranked as the seventh or eighth largest economy in the world. To the east, straddling the Rockies, are the Mountain States. The spectacular mountain valleys and peaks are not suited to agriculture, although they are grazed by cattle and sheep. East of the mountains lie the Great Plains, with prairies stretching eastward as far as the eye can see.

Sports and entertainment

Sports are the most popular form of recreation in the US. Americans enjoy individual activities, such as jogging, golf, fishing, skiing, hiking, tennis, and hunting, as well as team sports, like baseball, basketball, and football. Spectator sports are also a major form of entertainment—the Super Bowl, the championship game of the National Football League, is watched on TV by almost a half of all American households. Americans take their leisure time seriously, and the variety of entertainment available is vast. Movies, concerts, theater, amusement parks, television, and bars are just some of the places people gather to have fun.

Right: Football, baseball, and basketball are the top three sports. Televised big games are watched by millions.

Right: This poster shows a detail from the poster for Casablanca, a Hollywood classic. California, and especially Los Angeles, remains the heart of the American film industry.

CANADA

WASHINGTON
Olympia • Seattle • Tacoma • Spokane • Walla Walla
Portland • Salem • Eugene

OREGON
Crescent City • Klamath Falls • Redding

NEVADA
Reno

MONTANA
Kalispell • Missoula • Helena • Bozeman • Billings • Great Falls

IDAHO
Lewiston • Boise • Idaho Falls

Salt Lake City • Ogden • Wells

WYOMING
Jackson • Casper • Laramie • Cheyenne

NORTH DAKOTA
Bismarck • Fargo

SOUTH DAKOTA
Pierre • Rapid City • Black Hills • Sioux Falls

NEBRASKA
North Platte • Omaha

MONTANA • Buffalo • Mount Rushmore

Missouri

ROCKY Mo

Cascade Range
Sierra
Great Salt Lake

Aircraft manufacturing
Sea lion
Giant sequoia tree
Victorian houses
Mountain lion
Crater lake
Grizzly bear
Black bear
Columbia
Snake
Bison
Bighorn sheep
Cataldo Mission
Beef cattle
Yellowstone National Park
Yellowstone Lake
Rock climbing
Missouri
Bald eagle
Whitewater rafting
Coyote
Salamander
Prairie dog
Sioux headdress
Missouri
Football
Halloween
Pumpkin pie
Roast turkey

Hamburger

Tornado

Rodeo

Galveston

Gulf of Mexico

• Tulsa

Topeka ■
• Wichita
KANSAS

• Oakley

Sunflowers

Red

Oklahoma City ■
OKLAHOMA

Dallas •
Fort Worth •
• Waco

Houston •

San Antonio •
Austin ■
TEXAS

Peanuts

Corpus Christi •
Laredo •

Brownsville •

Dodge City •

Boise City •

Skiing

Sheep farming

Amarillo •
• Lubbock
• Abilene

Odessa •

Oil

Oil pump

Del Rio •

Rio Grande

400 miles

Right: Isolated areas of the West are home to pumas (mountains lions), bears, coyotes, bighorn sheep, pronghorns, and many other wild animals.

RECORDS

World's largest active volcano:
MAUNO LOA, HAWAII

Hottest place in the US:
DEATH VALLEY, CALIFORNIA

Most popular sport:
FOOTBALL

World's largest economy:
UNITED STATES

Most internet users in the world:
UNITED STATES

Colorado Springs

Durango •

COLORADO

Yucca flower

Santa Fe ■
Albuquerque •
NEW MEXICO

Alamogordo •
El Paso •

Presidio •

Rio Grande

MEXICO

400 kilometers

Kachina doll

UTAH

Grand Canyon •
Flagstaff •

Grand Canyon
Grand Canyon

Lake Mead

Colorado

Nevada

Las Vegas •
San Bernardino •

Casino

Road runner

Phoenix ■
Scottsdale •
ARIZONA

Tucson •

Yuma •

Saguaro

Below: This Navajo man is preparing a small dry-painting in the traditional style. Sand, pollen, crushed flowers, and other objects are used.

Native American traditions
Native Americans now make up less than one percent of the population of the US. However, many are working to keep their languages and traditions alive, especially among the larger tribes such as the Cherokee and the Navajo. Pow wows, or meetings, are held so that people can share their experiences and reinforce a community feeling. Traditional styles of pottery, weaving, and other art forms are being taught to young people, and a thriving tourist trade is creating work for artists and craftspeople.

San Jose
Monterey •
Fresno •
Bakersfield •

High-tech industries

Film making
Los Angeles •
HOLLYWOOD

San Diego •

Garibaldi fish

CALIFORNIA

PACIFIC OCEAN

Hawaii
Hawaii—the most westerly of the 50 states—lies in the Pacific Ocean, about 1990 miles (3,200 km) off the coast of the North American mainland. It is made up of about 130 volcanic islands; some of the volcanos are still active, including Mauna Loa, the largest active volcano in the world. Hawaii was the last state to join the United States, in August 1959 (six months after Alaska). The first inhabitants of the islands were of Polynesian descent and many aspects of their culture are still maintained today.

Hawaiian Islands

Hawaiian Monk seal

Kauai •
Niihau •
Lihue •

Oahu
Honolulu •
Molokai
Lanai
Maui
Wailuku •
Kahoolawe

Hilo •
Hawaii

PACIFIC OCEAN

Hula dancer

HAWAII

100 miles
100 kilometers

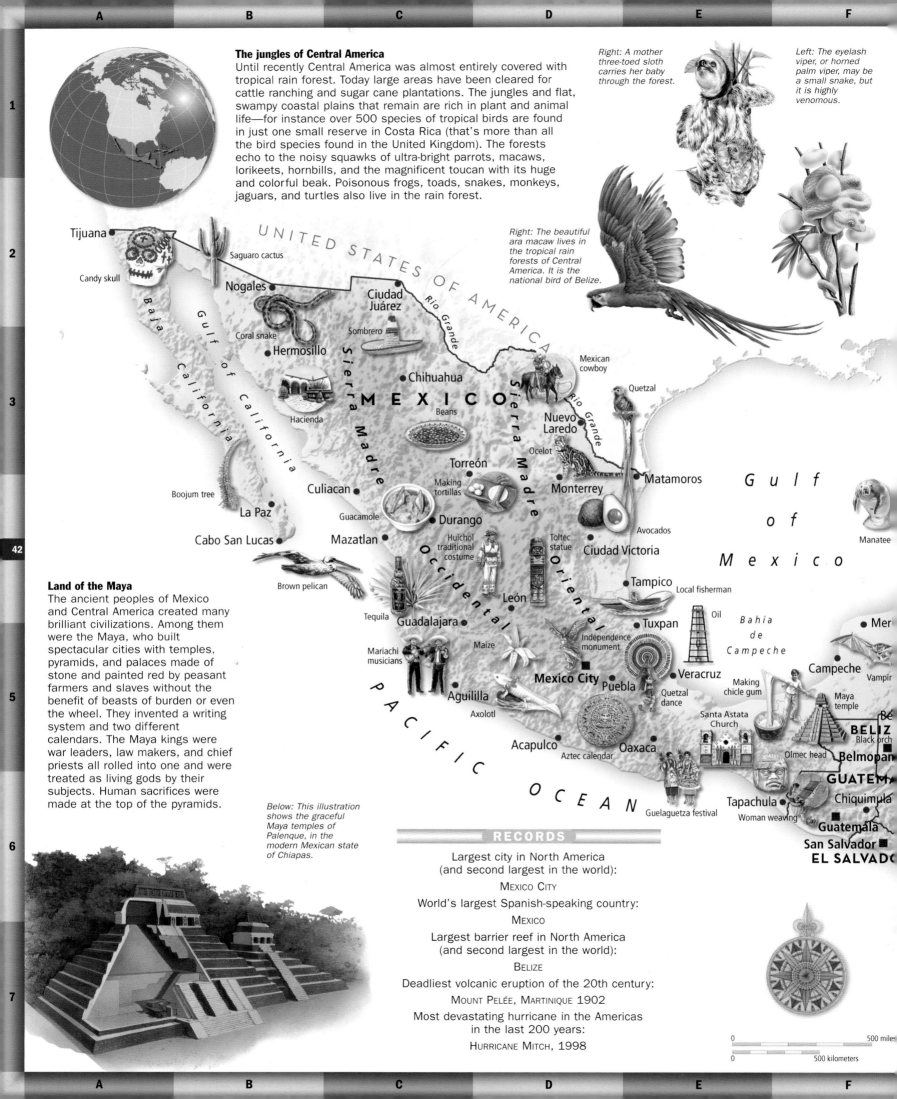

The jungles of Central America

Until recently Central America was almost entirely covered with tropical rain forest. Today large areas have been cleared for cattle ranching and sugar cane plantations. The jungles and flat, swampy coastal plains that remain are rich in plant and animal life—for instance over 500 species of tropical birds are found in just one small reserve in Costa Rica (that's more than all the bird species found in the United Kingdom). The forests echo to the noisy squawks of ultra-bright parrots, macaws, lorikeets, hornbills, and the magnificent toucan with its huge and colorful beak. Poisonous frogs, toads, snakes, monkeys, jaguars, and turtles also live in the rain forest.

Right: A mother three-toed sloth carries her baby through the forest.

Left: The eyelash viper, or horned palm viper, may be a small snake, but it is highly venomous.

Right: The beautiful ara macaw lives in the tropical rain forests of Central America. It is the national bird of Belize.

Land of the Maya

The ancient peoples of Mexico and Central America created many brilliant civilizations. Among them were the Maya, who built spectacular cities with temples, pyramids, and palaces made of stone and painted red by peasant farmers and slaves without the benefit of beasts of burden or even the wheel. They invented a writing system and two different calendars. The Maya kings were war leaders, law makers, and chief priests all rolled into one and were treated as living gods by their subjects. Human sacrifices were made at the top of the pyramids.

Below: This illustration shows the graceful Maya temples of Palenque, in the modern Mexican state of Chiapas.

Map labels

Tijuana
Candy skull
Saguaro cactus
UNITED STATES OF AMERICA
Nogales
Ciudad Juárez
Rio Grande
Coral snake
Sombrero
Hermosillo
Chihuahua
Mexican cowboy
Quetzal
Baja California
Gulf of California
Sierra Madre
MEXICO
Beans
Nuevo Laredo
Rio Grande
Hacienda
Sierra Madre
Ocelot
Torreón
Matamoros
Gulf of Mexico
Boojum tree
Culiacan
Making tortillas
Monterrey
La Paz
Guacamole
Durango
Avocados
Cabo San Lucas
Mazatlan
Huichol traditional costume
Toltec statue
Ciudad Victoria
Manatee
Brown pelican
Occidental
Oriental
Tampico
Local fisherman
Tequila
León
Oil
Bahía de Campeche
Guadalajara
Maize
Tuxpan
Mariachi musicians
Independence monument
Veracruz
Making chicle gum
Campeche
Vampir
Mexico City
Puebla
Maya temple
Aguililla
Quetzal dance
Santa Astata Church
Bé
Axolotl
BELIZ
Black orch
PACIFIC OCEAN
Acapulco
Aztec calendar
Oaxaca
Olmec head
Belmopan
GUATEM
Tapachula
Woman weaving
Chiquimula
Guelaguetza festival
Guatemala
San Salvador
EL SALVADO

RECORDS

Largest city in North America
(and second largest in the world):
MEXICO CITY

World's largest Spanish-speaking country:
MEXICO

Largest barrier reef in North America
(and second largest in the world):
BELIZE

Deadliest volcanic eruption of the 20th century:
MOUNT PELÉE, MARTINIQUE 1902

Most devastating hurricane in the Americas
in the last 200 years:
HURRICANE MITCH, 1998

0   500 miles
0   500 kilometers

The people
The first peoples in this region were the Amerindians whose ancestors came from the north. In the late 15th century Spanish and Portuguese explorers and soldiers started settling in the area and today most of the population is of mixed native and Spanish ancestry.

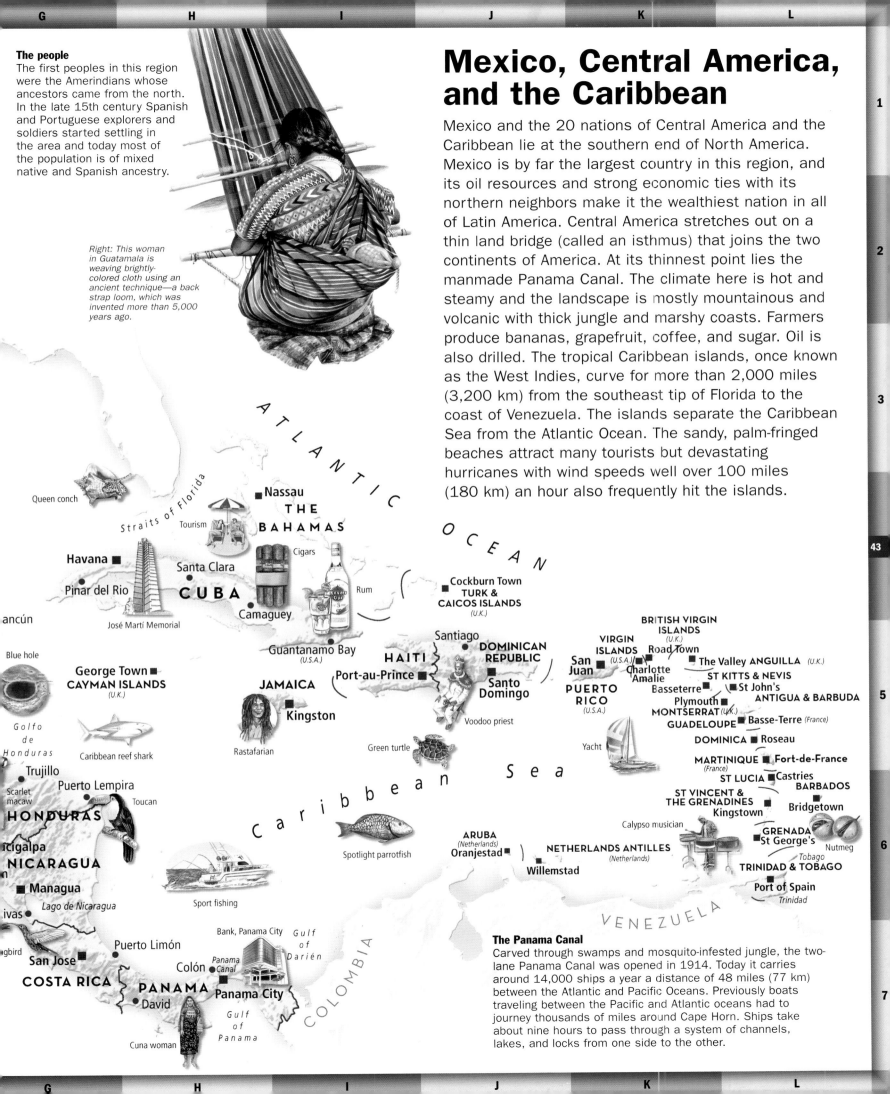

Right: This woman in Guatamala is weaving brightly-colored cloth using an ancient technique—a back strap loom, which was invented more than 5,000 years ago.

Mexico, Central America, and the Caribbean

Mexico and the 20 nations of Central America and the Caribbean lie at the southern end of North America. Mexico is by far the largest country in this region, and its oil resources and strong economic ties with its northern neighbors make it the wealthiest nation in all of Latin America. Central America stretches out on a thin land bridge (called an isthmus) that joins the two continents of America. At its thinnest point lies the manmade Panama Canal. The climate here is hot and steamy and the landscape is mostly mountainous and volcanic with thick jungle and marshy coasts. Farmers produce bananas, grapefruit, coffee, and sugar. Oil is also drilled. The tropical Caribbean islands, once known as the West Indies, curve for more than 2,000 miles (3,200 km) from the southeast tip of Florida to the coast of Venezuela. The islands separate the Caribbean Sea from the Atlantic Ocean. The sandy, palm-fringed beaches attract many tourists but devastating hurricanes with wind speeds well over 100 miles (180 km) an hour also frequently hit the islands.

ATLANTIC OCEAN

Queen conch

Straits of Florida

Nassau
Tourism
THE BAHAMAS

Cigars

Havana ■
Santa Clara
CUBA
Pinar del Rio
Rum
Camaguey
José Martí Memorial

ancún

Cockburn Town ■
TURK & CAICOS ISLANDS
(U.K.)

Blue hole

Guantanamo Bay
(U.S.A.)

Santiago ●
DOMINICAN REPUBLIC
HAITI
Port-au-Prince ■

BRITISH VIRGIN ISLANDS
(U.K.)
VIRGIN ISLANDS
(U.S.A.)
San Juan ■ Road Town ■
The Valley ■ **ANGUILLA** *(U.K.)*
Charlotte Amalie
ST KITTS & NEVIS
Basseterre ■ ■ St John's

George Town ■■
CAYMAN ISLANDS
(U.K.)

JAMAICA

Rastafarian

Santo Domingo

Voodoo priest

Kingston

Green turtle

Golfo de Honduras

Caribbean reef shark

PUERTO RICO
(U.S.A.)
Plymouth ■
MONTSERRAT *(U.K.)*
GUADELOUPE ■ Basse-Terre *(France)*
ANTIGUA & BARBUDA
DOMINICA ■ Roseau
Yacht
MARTINIQUE ■ **Fort-de-France**
(France)
ST LUCIA ■ Castries
BARBADOS

Trujillo
Scarlet macaw
Puerto Lempira
Toucan
HONDURAS
cigalpa
NICARAGUA
Managua ■
Lago de Nicaragua
ivas ●

Caribbean Sea

Spotlight parrotfish

Sport fishing

ARUBA
(Netherlands)
Oranjestad ■
NETHERLANDS ANTILLES
(Netherlands)
Willemstad ■

Calypso musician

ST VINCENT & THE GRENADINES ■
Kingstown
GRENADA
■ St George's
Nutmeg
Bridgetown
Tobago
TRINIDAD & TOBAGO
Port of Spain
Trinidad

gbird
San Jose ●
COSTA RICA

Bank, Panama City
Puerto Limón
Colón ● *Panama Canal*
PANAMA
Panama City
David ●
Gulf of Darién
COLOMBIA

Gulf of Panama

Cuna woman

VENEZUELA

The Panama Canal
Carved through swamps and mosquito-infested jungle, the two-lane Panama Canal was opened in 1914. Today it carries around 14,000 ships a year a distance of 48 miles (77 km) between the Atlantic and Pacific Oceans. Previously boats traveling between the Pacific and Atlantic oceans had to journey thousands of miles around Cape Horn. Ships take about nine hours to pass through a system of channels, lakes, and locks from one side to the other.

CLIMATE AND WEATHER

Three-quarters of South America lies within the tropics but the continent has a wide variety of climates. Most of South America receives plenty of rain, although the deserts of northern Chile are among the driest places on Earth. Colombia has the highest rainfall, closely followed by the coastal regions of the northeast, the Amazon Basin, and southern Chile. The hottest temperatures occur in the Gran Chaco in Argentina. Weather in the Andes is driven by altitude with Ecuador's capital, Quito, at 9,000 feet (2,800 m) enjoying cool spring nights and pleasant warm days, even though it lies on the equator. To the north, a perpetual snowline climate is found above 14,500 feet (4,300 m) in Columbia and yet at sea level, a few miles away, bananas are grown.

Caribbean Sea

Gulf of
Panama

Llanos

Orinoco

Guiana
Highlands

Negro

Putumayo

Marañón

Ucayali

Amazon

Amazon Basin

Madeira

A n d e s

Lake
Titicaca

Altiplano

PACIFIC

Atacama Desert

Gran
Chaco

OCEAN

▲ Mt Aconcagua

Pampas

Pa

A
n
d
e
s

Negro

P
a
t
a
g
o
n
i
a

Chico

Golfo de San Jorge

Bahía Grande

Tierra del
Fuego

Cape Horn

SOUTH AMERICA

The world's fourth largest continent, South America takes up 12 percent of the planet's total land area (its northern neighbor North America occupies 16 percent). It extends further south than any other continent as it narrows to Cape Horn, which lies only 650 miles (1,050 km) off the Antarctic continent. South America has a backbone of mountains hugging its Pacific Ocean coast known as the Andes. They stretch from the tiny isthmus (land bridge) of Panama in the north to the barren uplands of Tierra del Fuego ("land of fire") in the south. With many peaks rising above 20,000 feet (6100 m), the Andes, unlike the Rocky Mountains of North America, have no low passes for highway or rail crossings. This continuous mountain chain is the longest on the planet. The lowlands to the east of the Andes are drained by two large river systems—the vast Amazon Basin to the north and the basin of the Gran Chaco to the south. Huge grasslands known as the Pampas and the Llanos are separated by the Amazon rainforest, one of the last great wilderness areas left on Earth.

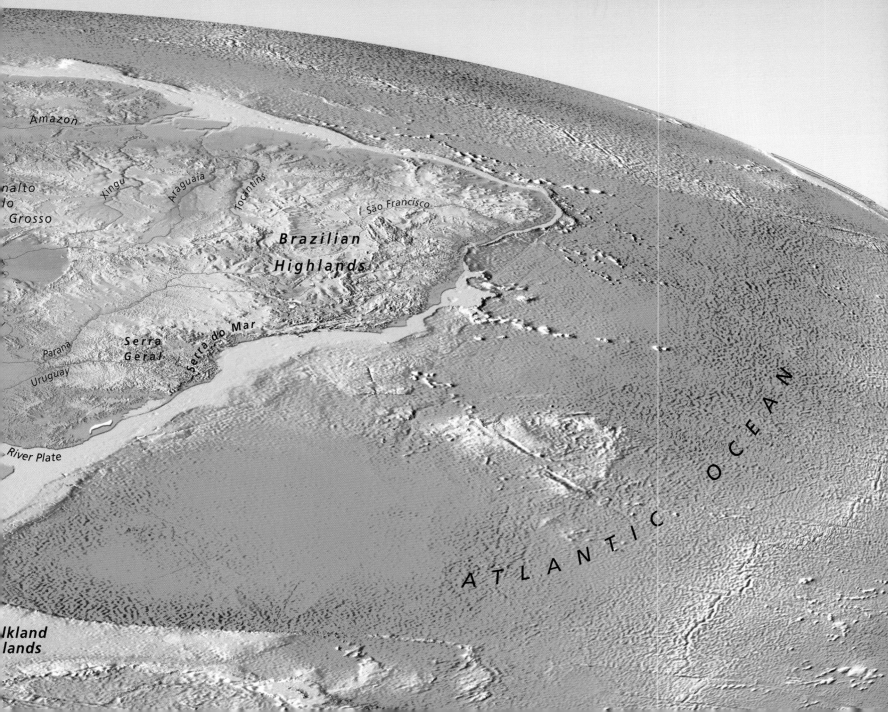

POLITICAL MAP OF SOUTH AMERICA

RESOURCES AND TRADE
South America is rich in mineral and food resources. Gold and silver have been mined there for centuries and today precious stones such as diamonds and emeralds are exported all over the world. Colombia produces more emeralds than any other country. Sugar, coffee, rice, fruit, fish, coal, iron, oil, natural gas, and copper (of which Chile is the world's biggest producer) are also important to the economy. At the moment there are two free-trade groups—Mercosaur and the Andean Community—but plans are being made to join all the countries on the continent in a single free-trade organization to be known as the Union of South American Nations.

LIFE IN THE BARRIOS
Despite South America's economic progress, there is still much poverty, with millions living in sprawling shantytowns called barrios and favelas. With little affordable housing available, people build shacks for themselves out of scrap metal, wood, and found objects, crammed next to each other on overcrowded hillsides on the edges of the cities. Clean, running water and sanitation is scarce. One of the shantytowns of Caracas, in Venezuela, called José Félix Ribas barrio, is said to be among the largest in Latin America with 120,000 dwellers.

In many large cities of South America, including Rio de Janeiro in Brazil and Santiago in Chile, children who have lost their families or been abandoned by them, live in groups on the streets.

Caribbean Sea

ATLANTIC OCEAN

PACIFIC OCEAN

ATLANTIC OCEAN

Galápagos Islands
(Ecuador)

■ Caracas
Lake Maracaibo
VENEZUELA

Orinoco

■ Georgetown
GUYANA ■ Paramaribo
■ Bogotá   SURINAME   ■ Cayenne
COLOMBIA   FRENCH GUIANA
                              (France)

Negro

Quito ■
ECUADOR   *Amazon*   *Amazon*

Madeira

Ucayali

B R A Z I L

PERU   *São Francisco*

Lima ■

                    BOLIVIA
Lake Titicaca   ■ La Paz   ■ Brasília

              ■ Sucre
                        Paraguay
                              PARAGUAY   *Paraná*
                                    ■ Asunción
                              Paraná

                    Uruguay

                    Paraná

            URUGUAY
Santiago ■   ■ Montevideo
        Buenos Aires ■ *River Plate*
C H I L E
      ARGENTINA

FALKLAND ISLANDS
(U.K.)
Stanley

Cape Horn

0		1000 miles

0		1000 kilometers

46

The Christ the Redeemer statue overlooks Rio de Janeiro. With about 12 million inhabitants, Rio is the second largest city in Brazil.

GROWING CITIES

In the 20th century huge numbers of South Americans began leaving the countryside and moving to the cities. Now nearly 80 percent of the population lives in urban areas. The new arrivals are often poor and many settle in shantytowns on the edges of cities. The big cities have gleaming high-rise buildings and often beautiful historic areas in their centers with shopping, transportation, and cultural life similar to that of cities in North America or Europe. The largest cities include Sao Paulo and Rio de Janeiro (Brazil), Santiago (Chile), Buenos Aires (Argentina), and Bogotá (Colombia).

South America

There are 12 independent nations in South America, including the world's fifth biggest country, Brazil. The main languages are Portuguese (in Brazil) and Spanish, but some 350 indigenous languages are spoken too. In many cases attempts are being made to preserve these languages and to prevent them from dying out. Many countries in the region, especially Brazil, have experienced strong economic growth in the first decade of the 21st century. By some calculations Brazil is already the seventh largest economy in the world and the second biggest economy in the Americas (after the United States). Most South Americans live in large cities where many wealthy and middle class people live comfortable lifestyles. Even so, millions of people still live in dire poverty; an estimated 60 percent of Bolivians live below the poverty line along with 31 percent of Brazilians. The political turmoil with revolutions and military dictatorships of the 20th century has largely ended and since the 1980s most countries have had democratically elected governments.

FOOD FOR THOUGHT

South America exports a wide range of foods, from soybeans and peanuts to beef, wheat, and fruit. Sugar and coffee are valuable crops as are all sorts of nuts, including Brazil nuts (named after the country). What many people don't realize is that a lot of common foods, such as potatoes, peanuts, chili peppers, tomatoes, cocoa, and pineapples, originally came from Central or South America and were unknown in Europe until the early settlers brought them back. Since then they have spread around the world.

Potatoes

Pineapples

Peanuts

COLOMBIA

Country name Republic of Colombia
Area 439,736 sq mi
(1,138,910 sq km)
Population 45,013,674
Government Republic
Capital Bogotá
Currency Colombian peso
Languages Spanish
Main religions Roman Catholic 90%,
Literacy 93%
GDP per capita $6,700 (2007 est.)

VENEZUELA

Country name Bolivarian Republic
of Venezuela
Area 352,144 sq mi
(912,050 sq km)
Population 26,414,815
Government Federal republic
Capital Caracas
Currency Bolivar
Languages Spanish, Indigenous
languages
Main religions Roman Catholic 96%,
Protestant 2%
Literacy 93%
GDP per capita $12,200 (2007 est.)

GUYANA

Country name Cooperative Republic
of Guyana
Area 83,000 sq mi
(214,970 sq km)
Population 770,794
Government Republic
Capital Georgetown
Currency Guyana dollar
Languages English, Indigenous
languages, Creole, Caribbean
Hindustani, Urdu
Main religions Christian 50%,
Hindu 35%, Muslim 10%
Literacy 99%
GDP per capita $3,800 (2007 est.)

SURINAME

Country name Republic of Suriname
Area 63,038 sq mi
(163,270 sq km)
Population 475,996
Government Republic
Capital Paramaribo
Currency Surinam dollar
Languages Dutch, English, Sranang
Tongo, Caribbean Hindustani,
Javanese
Main religions Hindu 27.4%,
Protestant 25.2%, Roman Catholic
22.8%, Muslim 19.6%
Literacy 90%
GDP per capita $7,800 (2007 est.)

ECUADOR

Country name Republic of Ecuador
Area 109,483 sq mi
(283,560 sq km)
Population 13,927,650
Government Republic
Capital Quito
Currency US dollar
Languages Spanish, Indigenous
languages
Main religions Roman Catholic 95%,
other 5%
Literacy 91%
GDP per capita $7,200 (2007 est.)

PERU

Country name Republic of Peru
Area 496,141 sq mi
(1,285,220 sq km)
Population 29,180,899
Government Republic
Capital Lima
Currency Nuevo sol
Languages Spanish, Quechua,
Aymara, Indigenous languages
Main religions Roman Catholic 81%,
Seventh Day Adventist 1.4%
Literacy 88%
GDP per capita $7,800 (2007 est.)

BRAZIL

Country name Federative Republic
of Brazil
Area 3,286,488 sq mi
(8,511,965 sq km)
Population 191,908,598
Government Federal republic
Capital Brasília
Currency Real
Languages Portuguese, Spanish,
German, Italian, Japanese, English,
Indigenous languages
Main religions Roman Catholic
73.6%, Protestant 15.4%
Literacy 89%
GDP per capita $9,700 (2007 est.)

BOLIVIA

Country name Republic of Bolivia
Area 423,940 sq mi
(1,098,580 sq km)
Population 9,247,816
Government Republic
Capital La Paz (administrative),
Sucre (judicial)
Currency Boliviano
Languages Spanish, Quechua, Aymara
Main religions Roman Catholic 95%,
Protestant 5%
Literacy 87%
GDP per capita $4,000 (2007 est.)

CHILE

Country name Republic of Chile
Area 292,260 sq mi
(756,950 sq km)
Population 16,454,143
Government Republic
Capital Santiago
Currency Chilean peso
Languages Spanish, Mapudungun,
German
Main religions Roman Catholic 70%,
Evangelical 15.1%
Literacy 96%
GDP per capita $13,900 (2007 est.)

PARAGUAY

Country name Republic of Paraguay
Area 157,047 sq mi
(406,750 sq km)
Population 6,831,306
Government Republic
Capital Asunción
Currency Guaraní
Languages Spanish, Guaraní
Main religions Roman Catholic
89.6%, Protestant 6.2%
Literacy 94%
GDP per capita $4,500 (2007 est.)

ARGENTINA

Country name Argentine Republic
Area 1,067,958 sq mi
(2,766,890 sq km)
Population 40,677,348
Government Republic
Capital Buenos Aires
Currency Argentine peso
Languages Spanish, Italian, English,
German, French
Main religions Roman Catholic 92%,
Protestant 2%, Jewish 2%
Literacy 97%
GDP per capita $13,300 (2007 est.)

URUGUAY

Country name Oriental Republic
of Uruguay
Area 68,039 sq mi
(176,220 sq km)
Population 3,477,778
Government Republic
Capital Montevideo
Currency Uruguayan peso
Languages Spanish, Portunol
Main religions Roman Catholic 66%,
Protestant 2%, Jewish 1%
Literacy 98%
GDP per capita $11,600 (2007 est.)

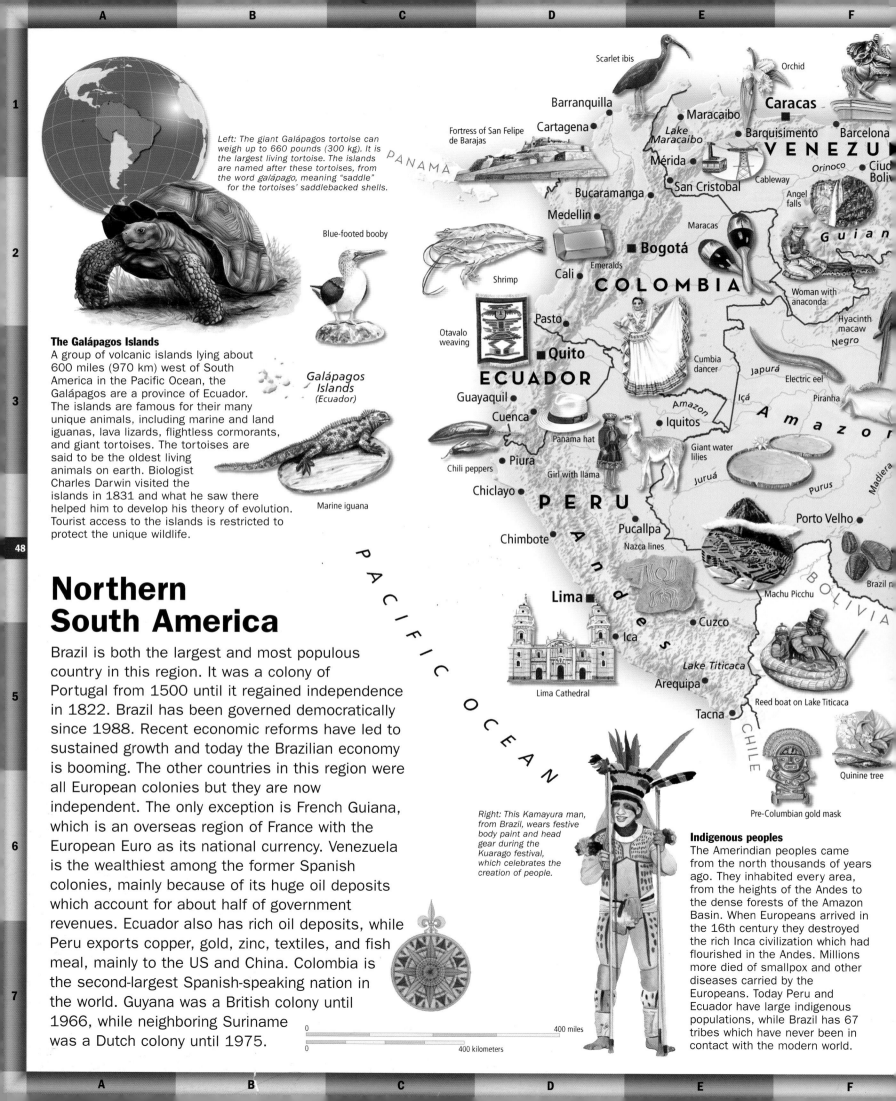

The Galápagos tortoise can weigh up to 660 pounds (300 kg). It is the largest living tortoise. The islands are named after these tortoises, from the word *galápago*, meaning "saddle" for the tortoises' saddlebacked shells.

Blue-footed booby

The Galápagos Islands

A group of volcanic islands lying about 600 miles (970 km) west of South America in the Pacific Ocean, the Galápagos are a province of Ecuador. The islands are famous for their many unique animals, including marine and land iguanas, lava lizards, flightless cormorants, and giant tortoises. The tortoises are said to be the oldest living animals on earth. Biologist Charles Darwin visited the islands in 1831 and what he saw there helped him to develop his theory of evolution. Tourist access to the islands is restricted to protect the unique wildlife.

Galápagos Islands (Ecuador)

Marine iguana

Northern South America

Brazil is both the largest and most populous country in this region. It was a colony of Portugal from 1500 until it regained independence in 1822. Brazil has been governed democratically since 1988. Recent economic reforms have led to sustained growth and today the Brazilian economy is booming. The other countries in this region were all European colonies but they are now independent. The only exception is French Guiana, which is an overseas region of France with the European Euro as its national currency. Venezuela is the wealthiest among the former Spanish colonies, mainly because of its huge oil deposits which account for about half of government revenues. Ecuador also has rich oil deposits, while Peru exports copper, gold, zinc, textiles, and fish meal, mainly to the US and China. Colombia is the second-largest Spanish-speaking nation in the world. Guyana was a British colony until 1966, while neighboring Suriname was a Dutch colony until 1975.

Scarlet ibis

Orchid

Fortress of San Felipe de Barajas

Barranquilla
Maracaibo
Caracas
Cartagena
Lake Maracaibo
Barquisimento
Barcelona
Mérida
VENEZU
Orinoco
Ciud
Boliv
Cableway
Bucaramanga
San Cristobal
Angel falls
Medellin
Maracas
G u i a n
Bogotá
Woman with anaconda
Emeralds
Cali
COLOMBIA
Shrimp
Hyacinth macaw
Negro
Pasto
Otavalo weaving
Quito
Cumbia dancer
Japurá
Electric eel
ECUADOR
Içá
Piranha
Guayaquil
Amazon
A m a z o r
Cuenca
Iquitos
Chili peppers
Panama hat
Giant water lilies
Piura
Juruá
Girl with llama
Chiclayo
Purus
Madiera
P E R U
Porto Velho
Pucallpa
Chimbote
Nazca lines
Brazil n
Machu Picchu
B O L I V I A
Lima
Cuzco
Ica
Lake Titicaca
Lima Cathedral
Arequipa
Reed boat on Lake Titicaca
Tacna
CHILE
Quinine tree
Pre-Columbian gold mask

PANAMA

PACIFIC OCEAN

Right: This Kamayura man, from Brazil, wears festive body paint and head gear during the Kuarago festival, which celebrates the creation of people.

Indigenous peoples

The Amerindian peoples came from the north thousands of years ago. They inhabited every area, from the heights of the Andes to the dense forests of the Amazon Basin. When Europeans arrived in the 16th century they destroyed the rich Inca civilization which had flourished in the Andes. Millions more died of smallpox and other diseases carried by the Europeans. Today Peru and Ecuador have large indigenous populations, while Brazil has 67 tribes which have never been in contact with the modern world.

0   400 miles

0   400 kilometers

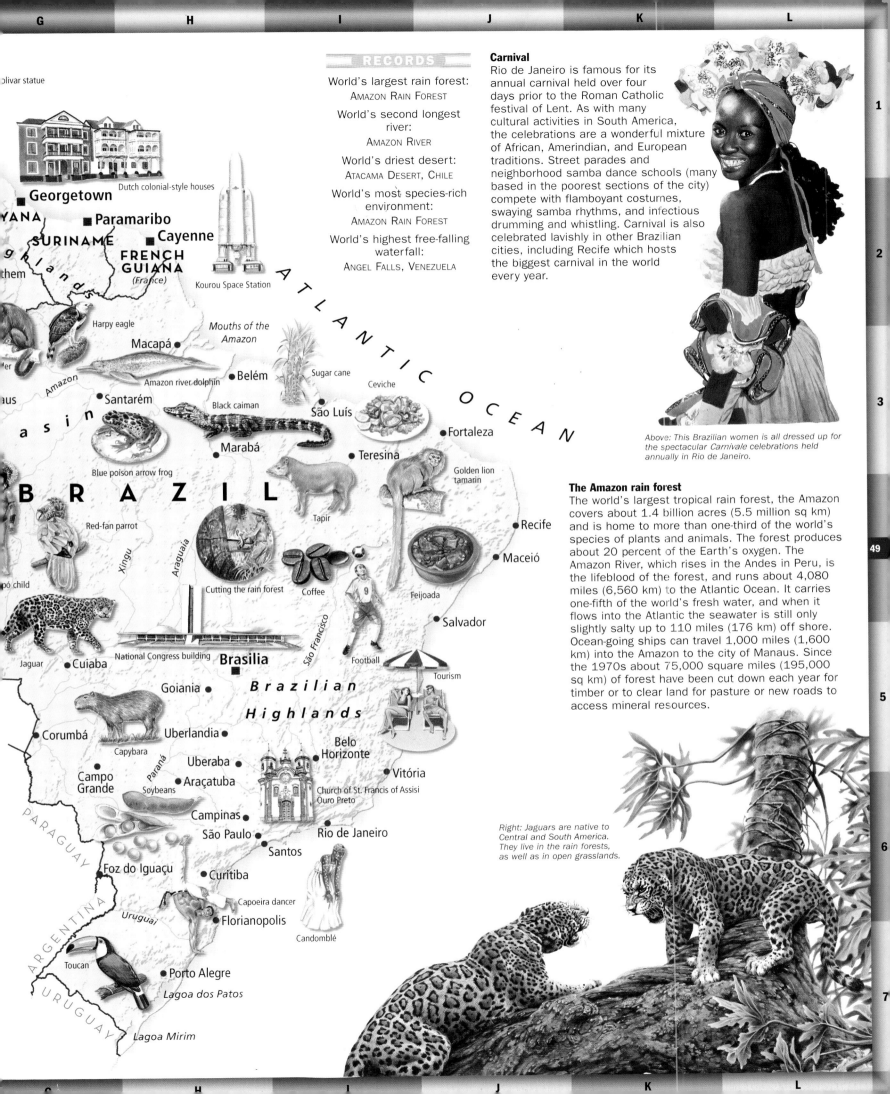

Bolivar statue

Dutch colonial-style houses

Georgetown

Paramaribo

Cayenne

GUYANA

SURINAME

FRENCH GUIANA
(France)

Kourou Space Station

Highlands

them

RECORDS

World's largest rain forest:
AMAZON RAIN FOREST

World's second longest river:
AMAZON RIVER

World's driest desert:
ATACAMA DESERT, CHILE

World's most species-rich environment:
AMAZON RAIN FOREST

World's highest free-falling waterfall:
ANGEL FALLS, VENEZUELA

Carnival

Rio de Janeiro is famous for its annual carnival held over four days prior to the Roman Catholic festival of Lent. As with many cultural activities in South America, the celebrations are a wonderful mixture of African, Amerindian, and European traditions. Street parades and neighborhood samba dance schools (many based in the poorest sections of the city) compete with flamboyant costumes, swaying samba rhythms, and infectious drumming and whistling. Carnival is also celebrated lavishly in other Brazilian cities, including Recife which hosts the biggest carnival in the world every year.

Above: This Brazilian women is all dressed up for the spectacular Carnivale celebrations held annually in Rio de Janeiro.

ATLANTIC OCEAN

Amazon

Harpy eagle

Mouths of the Amazon

Macapá

Amazon river dolphin

Belém

Sugar cane

Ceviche

Santarém

Black caiman

São Luís

Marajá

aus

Fortaleza

asin

Blue poison arrow frog

Teresina

Golden lion tamarin

B R A Z I L

Tapir

Red-fan parrot

Recife

pó child

Xingu

Araguaia

Cutting the rain forest

Coffee

Feijoada

Maceió

Jaguar

National Congress building

Brasilia

São Francisco

9

Football

Salvador

Cuiabá

Brazilian Highlands

Tourism

Goiania

Capybara

Corumbá

Uberlandia

Paraná

Paraná

Belo Horizonte

Campo Grande

Uberaba

Araçatuba

Soybeans

Church of St. Francis of Assisi
Ouro Preto

Vitória

PARAGUAY

Campinas

São Paulo

Rio de Janeiro

Santos

Foz do Iguaçu

Curitiba

Uruguai

Capoeira dancer

ARGENTINA

Uruguai

Florianopolis

Candomblé

Toucan

Porto Alegre

URUGUAY

Lagoa dos Patos

Lagoa Mirim

The Amazon rain forest

The world's largest tropical rain forest, the Amazon covers about 1.4 billion acres (5.5 million sq km) and is home to more than one-third of the world's species of plants and animals. The forest produces about 20 percent of the Earth's oxygen. The Amazon River, which rises in the Andes in Peru, is the lifeblood of the forest, and runs about 4,080 miles (6,560 km) to the Atlantic Ocean. It carries one-fifth of the world's fresh water, and when it flows into the Atlantic the seawater is still only slightly salty up to 110 miles (176 km) off shore. Ocean-going ships can travel 1,000 miles (1,600 km) into the Amazon to the city of Manaus. Since the 1970s about 75,000 square miles (195,000 sq km) of forest have been cut down each year for timber or to clear land for pasture or new roads to access mineral resources.

Right: Jaguars are native to Central and South America. They live in the rain forests, as well as in open grasslands.

49

Southern South America

All of the countries in this region were once colonies of Spain and a strong Spanish influence remains. A large majority of the inhabitants are Roman Catholics and Spanish is the main language. Argentina is the largest and richest country in this region and it is recovering well from an economic meltdown in 2001. Bolivia is the poorest country in southern South America. Despite rich natural resources, economic growth has been slow and many people live in extreme poverty. Over half the population of Bolivia are Amerindians, mainly Aymaras and Quechuas. Long, narrow Chile is one of South America's most stable and prosperous regions. Copper is a major export item and Chile is also the world's fifth-largest exporter of wine. Both Chile and Argentina have women as presidents. Uruguay and Paraguay are major exporters of agricultural products.

50

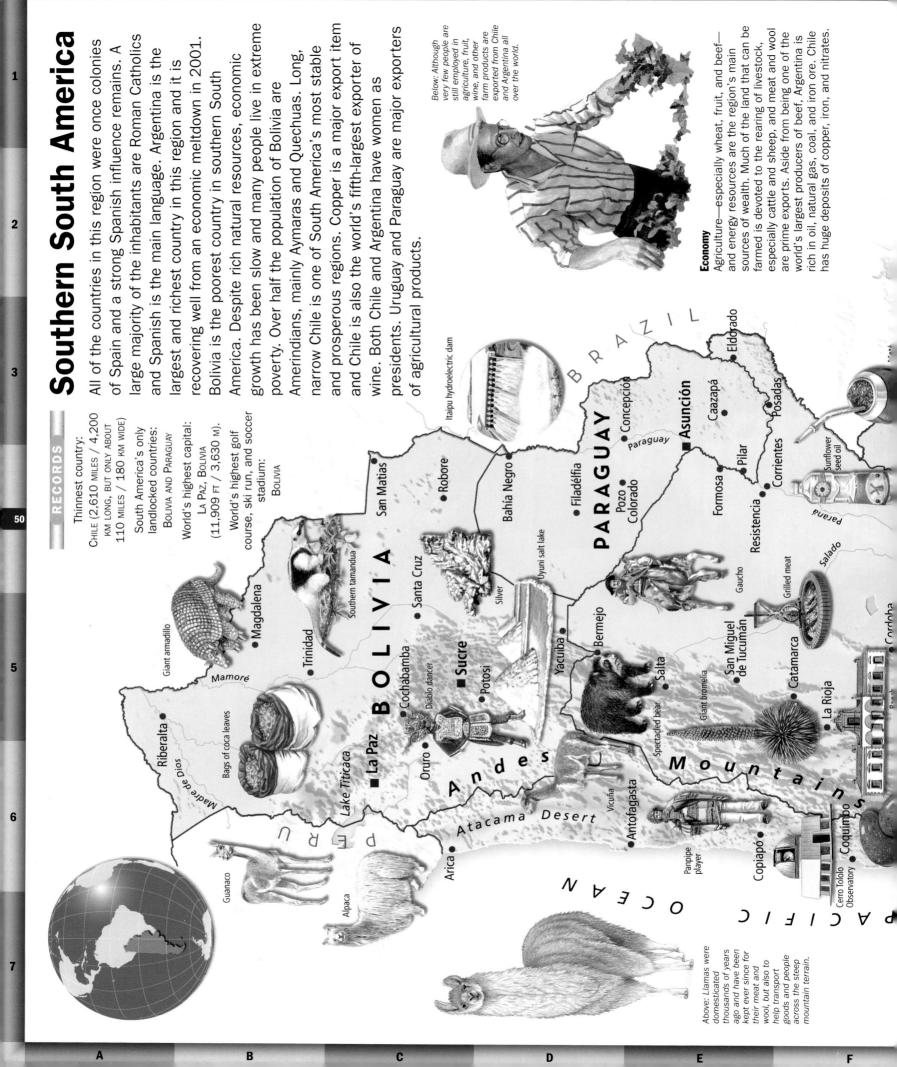

Below: Although very few people are still employed in agriculture, fruit, wine, and other farm products are exported from Chile and Argentina all over the world.

Economy

Agriculture—especially wheat, fruit, and beef—and energy resources are the region's main sources of wealth. Much of the land that can be farmed is devoted to the rearing of livestock, especially cattle and sheep, and meat and wool are prime exports. Aside from being one of the world's largest producers of beef, Argentina is rich in oil, natural gas, coal, and iron ore. Chile has huge deposits of copper, iron, and nitrates.

Above: Llamas were domesticated thousands of years ago and have been kept ever since for their meat and wool, but also to help transport goods and people across the steep mountain terrain.

Itaipu hydroelectric dam

BRAZIL

Eldorado

PARAGUAY

Concepción
Caazapá
Posadas
Asunción
Paraguay
Pilar
Corrientes
Filadélfia
Resistencia
Pozo Colorado
Formosa
Bahia Negro
Sunflower seed oil
Parana

San Matias
Robore

Silver
Uyuni salt lake
Salado
Gaucho
Grilled meat

BOLIVIA

Santa Cruz
Southern tamandua
Magdalena
Trinidad
Cochabamba
Diablo dancer
Sucre
Potosi
Yacuiba
Bermejo
Salta
San Miguel de Tucumán
Giant bromelia
Catamarca
La Rioja
Córdoba
Spectacled bear

Giant armadillo

Mamoré

Oruro
La Paz
Lake Titicaca
Bags of coca leaves
Riberalta
Madre de Dios

Andes
Mountains

PERU

Vicuña
Atacama Desert
Antofagasta
Arica
Panpipe player
Copiapó
Coquimbo
Cerro Tololo Observatory

Guanaco
Alpaca

PACIFIC OCEAN

Right: This tiny Inca statue was found in a boy's grave. It probably represents a god.

Below: These young people are dressed in traditional costume for market day in the Andes.

Ancient civilizations of the Andes

The Andes region has been home to many important civilizations, including the Moche, Chavín, and Nazca. But the greatest of them all was the Inca Empire with its huge network of roads, complex religion, developed farming methods, large cities, and great wealth. Inca artisans crafted beautiful jewelry and images in gold, silver, and copper by hammering them and stretching them into wire or melting them and casting them in molds. All this was destroyed by the Spanish Conquistadores in the early 1500s. However the Spanish invaders never found the incredible (now ruined) city of Machu Picchu, "the Lost City of the Incas," which was only rediscovered in 1911 by an American archeologist named Hiram Bingham (who apparently inspired the figure of Indiana Jones).

The people

The *pollera* clothing of highland Amerindians in Bolivia and Peru is very distinctive. They often wear a th-century European "bowler hat" combined with a silky shawl known as a *manta*. The colorful skirts and brightly colored hats are a tourist attraction today. The custom goes back to colonial times, when the Spanish rulers, after a series of uprisings, required the local peoples to abandon their traditional dress and wear the garments then popular in Spain. In Argentina, another distinct group are the cowboys, called *gauchos*, who once worked on cattle ranches on the Pampas in large numbers working on the cattle ranches. They were armed with *boleadoras*—three hardrock leather balls tied to a rope—that they used to stop the cattle escaping. They remain important as a cultural attraction.

PACIFIC OCEAN

ATLANTIC OCEAN

Trinidad
Montevideo
Rocha
Mercado del Puerto, restaurant
River Plate
Buenos Aires
Mar del Plata
Tango

CHILE
Santiago
Talca
Concepción
Presidential Palace
Monkey puzzle tree
Valdivia
Puerto Montt
Isla de Chiloé
Pisco container
Chilean firebush
Cerro Fitz Roy
Condor

ARGENTINA
Pampas
Polo
Salado
Chinchilla
Beef cattle
Neuquen
Colorado
Negro
Bahía Blanca
Viedma
Puerto Madryn
Chubut
Mara
Chico
Deseado
Comodoro Rivadavia
Perito Moreno
Puerto San Julián
Patagonia
Bahía Grande
Moreno glacier
Sheep
Calafate
Río Gallegos
Puerto Natales
Strait of Magellan
Punta Arenas
Lenga tree
Tierra del Fuego
Ushuaia
Cape Horn
Traditional religion

FALKLAND ISLANDS (U.K.)
Stanley
East Falkland
Magellan penguin
West Falkland
Sea lion
Southern right whale
Albatross

400 miles
400 kilometers

CLIMATE AND WEATHER

Southern Europe has hot, dry summers and relatively warm, wet winters. In northwestern Europe, north of the Pyrenees and the Alps, the weather is cooler and wetter, while to the east the winters can be extremely cold. As might be expected, the far north experiences long, bitterly cold winters and short, fairly cool summers. Iceland, the Faroe Islands, the Shetlands, and other islands in the North Atlantic, are generally warmer than other places in the world of similar latitude because of the warm North Atlantic Current which carries warm water north and prevents the seas from freezing over.

Norwegian Sea

Iceland

Faroe Islands

Shetland Islands

Outer Hebrides

Orkney Islands

Vänern

OCEAN

ATLANTIC

Skagerrak

Kattegat

Jylland

North Sea

Fyn

Sjaelland

Ireland British Isles

Pennines

Elbe

Thames

Hartz Mountains

Ore Moun

English Channel

Rhine

Bohemian Forest

Mosel

Seine

Danube

Loire

Black Forest

Bay of Biscay

Massif Central

Lake Geneva

ALPS

Dolomites

Mt Blanc

Po

Garonne

Rhône

Apenni

Pyrenees

Ligurian Sea

Adri

Douro

Corsica

Iberian Peninsula

Ebro

Balearic Islands

Minorca

Sardinia

Tyrrhenian Sea

Sierra Morena

Majorca

Guadalquivir

Ibiza

SistemasBeticos

Mt Etn

Mediterranean

Sicily

Sea

EUROPE

Europe, the second smallest continent (after Australia), is physically joined to the continent of Asia. The Eurasian landmass is traditionally divided into Europe and Asia at the Ural Mountains in Russia. Europe's main mountain ranges, including the Pyrenees, the Alps, and the Carpathians, run west to east across the continent. These mountains block the cold winds from the north, making the southern regions of Europe much warmer and drier. The south is also more mountainous, with less fertile farmland. To the north of the mountain chains lies the huge Northern European Plain, which stretches from southern England to the Ural Mountains. A large part of this plain has fertile soils and has been turned into farmland. To the north and east of the plain there are vast areas of grasslands, known as the steppes, as well as forests and tundra. The peninsula of Scandinavia in the far north juts out into the chilly Arctic seas. Europe is drained by many large rivers, including the Volga, the Dneiper, the Danube, the Rhine, the Rhône, the Loire, and the Tagus. Apart from the fresh water they provide, these rivers have been used for transportation since ancient times.

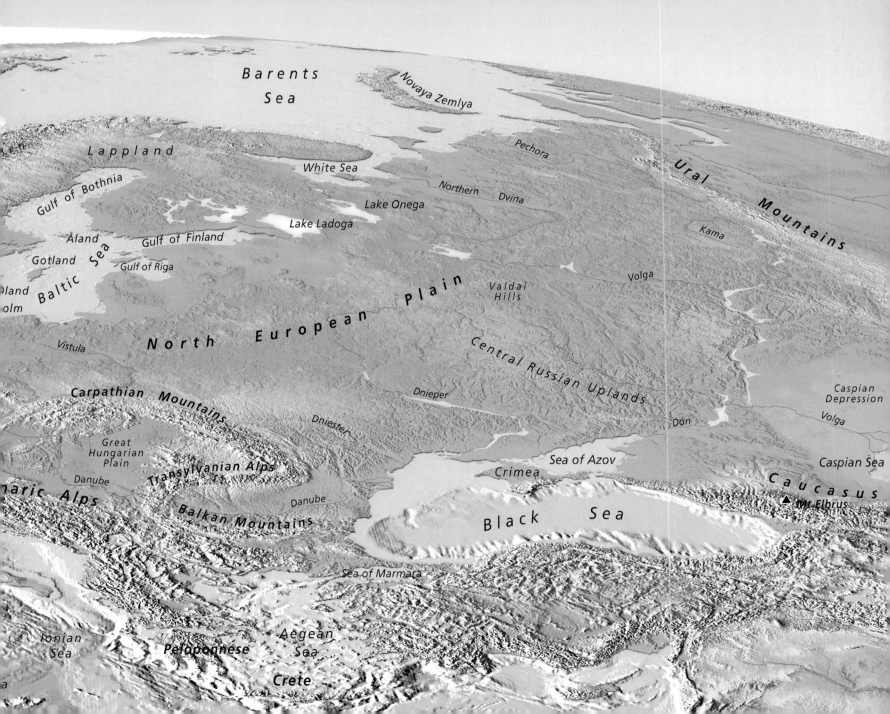

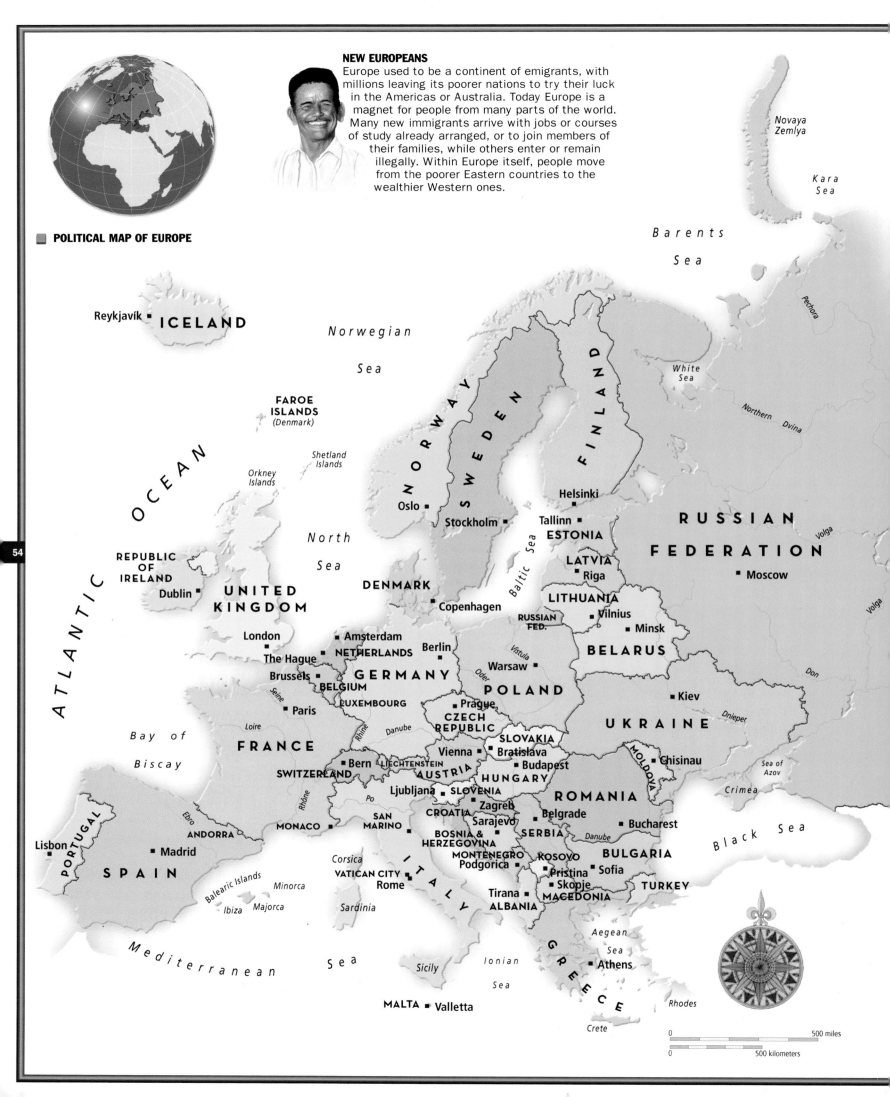

NEW EUROPEANS

Europe used to be a continent of emigrants, with millions leaving its poorer nations to try their luck in the Americas or Australia. Today Europe is a magnet for people from many parts of the world. Many new immigrants arrive with jobs or courses of study already arranged, or to join members of their families, while others enter or remain illegally. Within Europe itself, people move from the poorer Eastern countries to the wealthier Western ones.

■ POLITICAL MAP OF EUROPE

54

Novaya Zemlya

Kara Sea

Barents Sea

Pechora

Reykjavík ■ **ICELAND**

Norwegian Sea

FAROE ISLANDS (Denmark)

Shetland Islands

Orkney Islands

White Sea

Northern Dvina

N O R W A Y

S W E D E N

F I N L A N D

Oslo ■

Helsinki ■

Stockholm ■

Tallinn ■

ESTONIA

RUSSIAN FEDERATION

A T L A N T I C   O C E A N

North Sea

LATVIA

■ Riga

Volga

■ Moscow

REPUBLIC OF IRELAND

DENMARK

LITHUANIA

Dublin ■

UNITED KINGDOM

■ Copenhagen

Baltic Sea

■ Vilnius

■ Minsk

Volga

RUSSIAN FED.

London ■

■ Amsterdam

Berlin ■

BELARUS

NETHERLANDS

The Hague ■

Vistula

Warsaw ■

Brussels ■

GERMANY

BELGIUM

■ **LUXEMBOURG**

Oder

■ Prague

POLAND

■ Kiev

Dnieper

Seine

■ Paris

CZECH REPUBLIC

UKRAINE

Loire

Rhine

Danube

SLOVAKIA

Bay of Biscay

FRANCE

■ Bern

Vienna ■

■ Bratislava

MOLDOVA

■ Chisinau

LIECHTENSTEIN

AUSTRIA

■ Budapest

SWITZERLAND

HUNGARY

Rhône

Po

Ljubljana ■

SLOVENIA

ROMANIA

Sea of Azov

Crimea

Ebro

MONACO

SAN MARINO

CROATIA

■ Zagreb

■ Belgrade

■ Bucharest

Black Sea

ANDORRA

Sarajevo ■

Lisbon ■

■ Madrid

Corsica

VATICAN CITY

BOSNIA & HERZEGOVINA

SERBIA

Danube

PORTUGAL

SPAIN

I T A L Y

Rome ■

MONTENEGRO

Podgorica ■

KOSOVO

Pristina ■

■ Sofia

BULGARIA

Balearic Islands

Minorca

MACEDONIA

■ Skopje

TURKEY

Ibiza

Majorca

Sardinia

Tirana ■

ALBANIA

M e d i t e r r a n e a n   S e a

Sicily

Ionian Sea

Aegean Sea

G R E E C E

■ Athens

Rhodes

MALTA ■ Valletta

Crete

0   500 miles

0   500 kilometers

Europe

With over 40 countries, Europe is a crowded continent where empires have risen and fallen, and countries have come and gone (and come back again!). You may have heard of the Ancient Greek and Ancient Roman Empires, but Europe also had a Byzantine Empire, Ottoman Empire, Holy Roman Empire, Austro-Hungarian Empire, and British Empire. Inside and outside these empires, countries battled for freedom and independence and sometimes supremacy. In the 20th century alone there were two World Wars—earth-shattering global conflicts started by European squabbles. After World War II in 1945, Europe was divided by an "Iron Curtain" between West and East. The West, including France, West Germany, and Great Britain, was free and democratic. It enjoyed close relations with the USA. The East had East Germany, Czechoslovakia, and Yugoslavia (countries which no longer exist) and Bulgaria, Hungary, and others (which do). They were under Soviet Russian domination. In the 1990s Communism collapsed and Europe began the long haul back to being reunited.

A VIBRANT HISTORY

Right: Statue of Charles the Great, who built a great empire in the 8–9th centuries.

Europe was the birthplace of "Western Civilization" in which tremendous leaps were made in our understanding of the arts, sciences, medicine, technology, warfare, politics, and philosophy. The first great leap was made by the Ancient Greeks (c.450 BCE) and a later flowering of ideas took place during the Renaissance (1450–1620). Europe was also the first to have large-scale mechanized farming (from the 1700s) and industrial factories with iron and steam-driven machinery (from the 1730s). This is not to say that Arab, American, Indian, or Chinese cultures were not exploring and inventing similar things: it's just the Europeans were the first to "capitalize" and exploit them across the world.

EUROPEAN UNION

Member States Austria, Belgium, Bulgaria, Cyprus, Czech Republic, Denmark, Estonia, Finland, France, Germany, Greece, Hungary, Ireland, Italy, Latvia, Lithuania, Luxembourg, Malta, Netherlands, Poland, Portugal, Romania, Slovakia, Slovenia, Spain, Sweden, UK. CANDIDATE COUNTRIES: Croatia, Macedonia, Turkey

Area 4,324,782 sq km

Population 490,426,060 (July 2007 est.)

Government Intergovernmental and supranational organization

Capital Brussels (Belgium), Strasbourg (France), Luxembourg

Currency Euro, British pound, Bulgarian lev, Czech koruna, Danish krone, Estonian kroon, Hungarian forint, Latvian lat, Lithuanian litas, Polish zloty, Romanian leu, Slovak koruna, Swedish krona

Languages Bulgarian, Czech, Danish, Dutch, English, Estonian, Finnish, French, Gaelic, German, Greek, Hungarian, Italian, Latvian, Lithuanian, Maltese, Polish, Portuguese, Romanian, Slovak, Slovene, Spanish, Swedish

Religions Roman Catholic, Protestant, Orthodox, Muslim, Jewish

Literacy 98%

GDP per capita $32,900 (2007 est.)

UNITED EUROPE

The European Union began in the 1950s when Belgium, West Germany, France, Italy, Luxembourg, and the Netherlands formed the European Economic Community (EEC). These doubled to 12 countries in 1986. Today the European Union (EU) is a rich and powerful group of 27 democratic European countries with several more "candidate countries" wanting to join. It has made laws removing frontiers so people can travel, study, work, and trade freely, creating the Euro (the single European currency), ensuring safer food and a greener environment, creating better living standards in poorer regions, allowing for cheaper phone calls and air travel, and fighting crime and terror.

Below: 15 countries in the EU have adopted the Euro as their currency.

55

ICELAND
Country name Republic of Iceland
Area 39,768 sq mi (103,000 sq km)
Population 304,367
Government Parliamentary republic
Capital Reykjavik
Currency Icelandic krona
Languages Icelandic, English, Nordic languages, German
Main religions Evangelical Lutheran 90%, other Christian 8%, Roman Catholic 2%
Literacy 99,9%
GDP per capita $38,800 (2007 est.)

FINLAND
Country name Republic of Finland
Area 130,558 sq mi (338,145 sq km)
Population 5,244,749
Government Parliamentary republic
Capital Helsinki
Currency Euro
Languages Finnish, Swedish, Sami, Russian
Main religions Evangelical Lutheran 82.5%, Orthodox 1.1%
Literacy 100%
GDP per capita $35,300 (2007 est.)

NORWAY
Country name Kingdom of Norway
Area 125,020 sq mi (323,802 sq km)
Population 4,644,457
Government Constitutional monarchy and parliamentary democracy
Capital Oslo
Currency Norwegian krone
Languages Norwegian, Sami, Finnish
Main religions Evangelical Lutheran 85.7%, Pentecostal 1%, Roman Catholic 1%
Literacy 100%
GDP per capita $53,000 (2007 est.)

SWEDEN
Country name Kingdom of Sweden
Area 173,732 sq mi (449,964 sq km)
Population 9,045,389
Government Constitutional monarchy and parliamentary democracy
Capital Stockholm
Currency Swedish krona
Languages Swedish, Sami, Finnish
Main religions Evangelical Lutheran 87%, other 13%
Literacy 99%
GDP per capita $36,500 (2007 est.)

DENMARK
Country name Kingdom of Denmark
Area 16,638 sq mi (43,094 sq km)
Population 5,484,723
Government Constitutional monarchy and parliamentary democracy
Capital Copenhagen
Currency Danish krone
Languages Danish, Faroese, Greenlandic, German
Main religions Evangelical Lutheran 90%, other Christian 3%, Muslim 2%
Literacy 99%
GDP per capita $37,400 (2007 est.)

IRELAND
Country name Republic of Ireland
Area 27,135 sq mi (70,280 sq km)
Population 4,156,119
Government Parliamentary republic
Capital Dublin
Currency Euro
Languages English, Irish Gaelic
Main religions Roman Catholic 88.4%, Church of Ireland 3%, other Christian 1.6%
Literacy 99%
GDP per capita $43,100 (2007 est.)

UNITED KINGDOM
Country name United Kingdom of Great Britain and Northern Ireland
Area 94,525 sq mi (244,820 sq km)
Population 60,943,912
Government Constitutional monarchy and parliamentary democracy
Capital London
Currency pound
Languages English, Welsh, Scottish Gaelic
Main religions Christian 71.6%, Muslim 2.7%, Hindu 1%
Literacy 99%
GDP per capita $35,100 (2007 est.)

NETHERLANDS
Country name Kingdom of the Netherlands
Area 16,033 sq mi (41,526 sq km)
Population 16,645,313
Government Constitutional monarchy and parliamentary democracy
Capital Amsterdam
Currency Euro
Languages Dutch, Frisian
Main religions Roman Catholic 31%, Dutch Reformed 13%, Calvinist 7%, Muslim 5.5%
Literacy 99%
GDP per capita $38,500 (2007 est.)

BELGIUM
Country name Kingdom of Belgium
Area 11,786 sq mi (30,528 sq km)
Population 10,403,951
Government Constitutional monarchy and parliamentary democracy
Capital Brussels
Currency Euro
Languages Dutch, French, German
Main religions Roman Catholic 75%, other (includes Protestant) 25%
Literacy 99%
GDP per capita $35,300 (2007 est.)

LUXEMBOURG
Country name Grand Duchy of Luxembourg
Area 998,46 sq mi (2,586 sq km)
Population 486,006
Government Constitutional monarchy and parliamentary democracy
Capital Luxembourg
Currency Euro
Languages Luxembourgish, German, French
Main religions Roman Catholic 87% (2000 est.)
Literacy 100%
GDP per capita $80,500 (2007 est.)

ART

For many centuries Europe was the center of art in the Western world. Great paintings, such as the *Mona Lisa* (right), painted by Leonardo da Vinci in 1503–06, hang in European art galleries and people flock to see them. Many European cities and towns are themselves like outdoor art galleries, with architecture and sculpture permanently on display in their buildings, fountains, and cityscapes. Some very old cities, like Rome or Athens, have buildings and art that date from over 2,000 years ago. Since they also have architecture from many periods in between they are fascinating places to visit.

FRANCE
Country name French Republic
Area 248,428 sq mi (643,427 sq km)
Population 64,057,790
Government Parliamentary republic
Capital Paris
Currency Euro
Languages French, Breton, Provencal, Alsatian, Corsican, Catalan, Basque, Flemish, Gascon
Main religions Roman Catholic 83%-88%, Protestant 2%, Jewish 1%, Muslim 5%-10%
Literacy 99%
GDP per capita $33,200 (2007 est.)

MONACO
Country name Principality of Monaco
Area 0,75 sq mi (1,95 km)
Population 32,796
Government Constitutional monarchy and parliamentary democracy
Capital Monaco
Currency Euro
Languages French, English, Italian, Monegasque
Main religions Roman Catholic 90%, other 10%
Literacy 99%
GDP per capita $30,000 (2007 est.)

GERMANY
Country name Federal Republic of Germany
Area 137,846 sq mi (357,021 sq km)
Population 82,369,548
Government Parliamentary federal republic
Capital Berlin
Currency Euro
Languages German, Turkish
Main religions Protestant 34%, Roman Catholic 34%, Muslim 3.7%
Literacy 99%
GDP per capita $34,200 (2007 est.)

SWITZERLAND
Country name Swiss Confederation
Area 15,942 sq mi (41,290 sq km)
Population 7,581,520
Government Parliamentary federal republic
Capital Bern
Currency Swiss franc
Languages German, French, Italian, Romansch
Main religions Roman Catholic 41.8%, Protestant 35.3%, Muslim 4.3%, Orthodox 1.8%
Literacy 99%
GDP per capita $39,400 (2007 est.)

LIECHTENSTEIN
Country name Principality of Liechtenstein
Area 62 sq mi (160 sq km)
Population 34,498
Government Constitutional monarchy and parliamentary democracy
Capital Vaduz
Currency Swiss franc
Languages German, Alemannic dialect
Main religions Roman Catholic 76.2%, Protestant 7%
Literacy 100%
GDP per capita $25,000 (2007 est.)

AUSTRIA
Country name Republic of Austria
Area 32,382 sq mi (83,870 sq km)
Population 8,205,533
Government Parliamentary republic
Capital Vienna
Currency Euro
Languages German, Turkish, Serbian, Croatian, Slovenian, Hungarian
Main religions Roman Catholic 73.6%, Protestant 4.7%, Muslim 4.2% Catholic 2%
Literacy 98%
GDP per capita $38,400 (2007 est.)

SPAIN
Country name Kingdom of Spain
Area 194,897 sq mi (504,782 sq km)
Population 40,491,051
Government Constitutional monarchy and parliamentary democracy
Capital Madrid
Currency Euro
Languages Castilian Spanish, Catalan, Galician, Basque
Main religions Roman Catholic 94%
Literacy 97,9%
GDP per capita $30,100 (2007 est.)

PORTUGAL
Country name Portuguese Republic
Area 35,672 sq mi (92,391 sq km)
Population 10,676,910
Government Parliamentary republic
Capital Lisbon
Currency Euro
Languages Portuguese, Mirandese
Main religions Roman Catholic 84.5%, other Christian 2.2%
Literacy 93,3%
GDP per capita $21,700 (2007 est.)

ITALY
Country name Italian Republic
Area 116,305 sq mi (301,230 sq km)
Population 58,145,321
Government Parliamentary republic
Capital Rome
Currency Euro
Languages Italian, German, French, Slovene, Albanian
Main religions Roman Catholic 90%
Literacy 98,4%
GDP per capita $30,400 (2007 est.)

VATICAN CITY
Country name The Holy See (State of the Vatican City)
Area 0,17 sq mi (0,44 sq km)
Population 824
Government Ecclesiastical
Capital Vatican City
Currency Euro
Languages Italian, Latin, French, various other languages
Main religions Roman Catholic
Literacy 100%

SAN MARINO
Country name Republic of San Marino
Area 24 sq mi (61 sq km)
Population 29,251
Government Parliamentary republic
Capital San Marino
Currency Euro
Languages Italian
Main religions Roman Catholic
Literacy 96%
GDP per capita $34,600

MALTA
Country name Republic of Malta
Area 122 sq mi (316 sq km)
Population 403,532
Government Parliamentary republic
Capital Valletta
Currency Euro
Languages Maltese, English
Main religions Roman Catholic 98%
Literacy 92,8%
GDP per capita $53,400 (2007 est.)

AN AGING POPULATION

European women are having fewer and fewer children and many choose to have none at all. This means that the median age of people across Europe is increasing and that population growth is slowing sharply. Soon the population of many countries will begin to decrease. See pages 16–17 for more detailed information on demographics and aging populations.

HUNGARY
Country name Republic of Hungary
Area 35,919 sq mi (93,030 sq km)
Population 9,930,915
Government Parliamentary republic
Capital Budapest
Currency Forint
Languages Hungarian, Roma, German, Slavic languages, Romanian
Main religions Roman Catholic 51.9%, Calvinist 15.9%, Lutheran 3%, Greek Catholic 2.6%
Literacy 99,4%
GDP per capita $19,000 (2007 est.)

CZECH REPUBLIC
Country name Czech Republic
Area 30,450 sq mi (78,866 sq km)
Population 10,220,911
Government Parliamentary republic
Capital Prague
Currency Czech koruna
Languages Czech, Slovak, German, Polish, Roma
Main religions Unaffiliated 59%, Roman Catholic 26.8%, Protestant 2.1%
Literacy 99%
GDP per capita $24,200 (2007 est.)

SLOVAKIA
Country name Slovak Republic
Area 18,859 sq mi (48,845 sq km)
Population 5,455,407
Government Parliamentary republic
Capital Bratislava
Currency Slovak koruna
Languages Slovak, Hungarian, Roma, Czech
Main religions Roman Catholic 68.9%, Protestant 10.8%, Greek Catholic 4.1%
Literacy 99,6%
GDP per capita $20,300 (2007 est.)

POLAND
Country name Republic of Poland
Area 120,728 sq mi (312,685 sq km)
Population 38,500,696
Government Parliamentary republic
Capital Warsaw
Currency Zloty
Languages Polish, Ukrainian, German
Main religions Roman Catholic 89.8%, Eastern Orthodox 1.3%, Protestant 0.3%
Literacy 99,8%
GDP per capita $16,300 (2007 est.)

BULGARIA
Country name Republic of Bulgaria
Area 42,822 sq mi (110,910 sq km)
Population 7,262,675
Government Parliamentary republic
Capital Sofia
Currency Lev
Languages Bulgarian, Turkish, Roma
Main religions Bulgarian Orthodox 82.6%, Muslim 12.2%
Literacy 98,2%
GDP per capita $11,300 (2007 est.)

ROMANIA

Country name Romania
Area 91,699 sq mi
(237,500 sq km)
Population 22,246,862
Government Parliamentary republic
Capital Bucharest
Currency Lei
Languages Romanian, Hungarian,
Roma, German
Main religions Eastern Orthodox
86.8%, Protestant 7.5%, Roman
Catholic 4.7%
Literacy 97,3%
GDP per capita $11,400 (2007 est.)

SLOVENIA

Country name Republic of Slovenia
Area 7,827 sq mi (20,273 sq km)
Population 2,007,711
Government Parliamentary republic
Capital Ljubljana
Currency Euro
Languages Slovenian, Serbo-
Croatian
Main religions Catholic 57.8%,
Muslim 2.4%, Orthodox 2.3%
Literacy 99,7%
GDP per capita $27,200 (2007 est.)

CROATIA

Country name Republic of Croatia
Area 21,830 sq mi (56,542 sq km)
Population 4,491,543
Government Parliamentary republic
Capital Zagreb
Currency Kuna
Languages Croatian, Serbian
Main religions Roman Catholic
87.8%, Orthodox 4.4%
Literacy 98,1%
GDP per capita $15,500 (2007 est.)

BOSNIA AND HERZEGOVINA

Country name Bosnia and
Herzegovina
Area 19,741 sq mi (51,129 sq km)
Population 4,590,310
Government Parliamentary republic
Capital Sarajevo
Currency Converted mark
Languages Bosnian, Croatian, Serbian
Main religions Muslim 40%, Orthodox
31%, Roman Catholic 15%
Literacy 96,7%
GDP per capita $7,000 (2007 est.)

SERBIA

Country name Republic of Serbia
Area 29,912 sq mi (77,474 sq km)
Population 10,159,046
Government Parliamentary republic
Capital Belgrade
Currency Serbian dinar
Languages Serbian, Hungarian,
Bosnian, Roma
Main religions Serbian Orthodox
85%, Roman Catholic 5.5%,
Muslim 3.2%, Protestant 1.1%,
Literacy 98,9%
GDP per capita $10,400 (2007 est.)

MONTENEGRO

Country name Montenegro
Area 5,415 sq mi (14,026 sq km)
Population 678,177
Government Parliamentary republic
Capital Podgorica
Currency Euro
Languages Montenegrin, Serbian,
Bosnian, Albanian, Croatian
Main religions Orthodox 74%,
Muslim 18%, Roman Catholic 2%
Literacy 93%
GDP per capita $3,800 (2007 est.)

KOSOVO

Country name Republic of Kosovo
Area 4,203 sq mi (10,887 sq km)
Population 2,126,708
Government Parliamentary republic
Capital Pristina
Currency Euro, Serbian Dinar
Languages Albanian, Serbian,
Bosnian, Turkish, Roma
Main religions Muslim, Serbian
Orthodox, Roman Catholic
Literacy -
GDP per capita $1,800 (2007 est.)

ALBANIA

Country name Republic of Albania
Area 11,100 sq mi (28,748 sq km)
Population 3,619,778
Government Parliamentary republic
Capital Tirana
Currency Lek
Languages Albanian, Greek, Vlach,
Roma
Main religions Muslim 70%,
Albanian Orthodox 20%, Roman
Catholic 10%
Literacy 98,7%
GDP per capita $6,300 (2007 est.)

MACEDONIA

Country name Republic of
Macedonia
Area 9,781 sq mi (25,333 sq km)
Population 2,061,315
Government Parliamentary republic
Capital Skopje
Currency Macedonian denar
Languages Macedonian, Albanian,
Turkish, Roma, Serbian
Main religions Macedonian
Orthodox 64.7%, Muslim 33.3%
Literacy 98,2%
GDP per capita $8,500 (2007 est.)

GREECE

Country name Hellenic Republic
Area 50,942 sq mi
(131,940 sq km)
Population 10,722,816
Government Parliamentary republic
Capital Athens
Currency Euro
Languages Greek, English, French
Main religions Greek Orthodox 98%,
Muslim 1.3%,
Literacy 97,8%
GDP per capita $29,200 (2007 est.)

CYPRUS

Country name Republic of Cyprus
Area 3,571 sq mi (9,250 sq km)
Population 792,604
Government Parliamentary republic
Capital Nicosia
Currency Euro
Languages Greek, Turkish, English
Main religions Greek Orthodox 78%,
Muslim 18%
Literacy 97,6%
GDP per capita $46,900 (2007 est.)

ECONOMY

There are large variations
in living standards across
Europe, with an obvious
divide between East and
West. Many Eastern
European countries are still
recovering after the
collapse of the Soviet
Union and Yugoslavia at
the end of the 20th
century while Western
European countries all have
high GDPs and high
standards of living.

ESTONIA

Country name Republic of Estonia
Area 17,461 sq mi (45,226 sq km)
Population 1,307,605
Government Parliamentary republic
Capital Tallinn
Currency Estonian kroon
Languages Estonian, Russian
Main religions Evangelical Lutheran
13.6%, Orthodox 12.8%
Literacy 99,8%
GDP per capita $21,100 (2007 est.)

LATVIA

Country name Republic of Latvia
Area 24,937 sq mi (64,589 sq km)
Population 2,245,423
Government Parliamentary republic
Capital Riga
Currency Lat
Languages Latvian, Russian,
Lithuanian
Main religions Lutheran, Roman
Catholic, Russian Orthodox
Literacy 99,7%
GDP per capita $17,400 (2007 est.)

LITHUANIA

Country name Republic of Lithuania
Area 25,173 sq mi (65,200 sq km)
Population 3,565,205
Government Parliamentary republic
Capital Vilnius
Currency Litas
Languages Lithuanian, Belarusian,
Russian, Polish
Main religions Roman Catholic 79%,
Russian Orthodox 4.1%, Protestant
1.9%
Literacy 99,6%
GDP per capita $17,700 (2007 est.)

UKRAINE

Country name Ukraine
Area 233,089 sq mi
(603,700 sq km)
Population 45,994,287
Government Parliamentary republic
Capital Kiev
Currency Hryvnia
Languages Ukrainian, Russian,
Romanian, Polish, Hungarian
Main religions Ukrainian Orthodox (Kyiv
Patriarchate 50.4%, Moscow Patriarchate
26.1%), Ukrainian Greek Catholic 8%,
Ukrainian Autocephalous Orthodox 7.2%
Literacy 99.4%
GDP per capita $6,900 (2007 est.)

MOLDOVA

Country name Republic of Moldova
Area 13,066 sq mi (33,843 sq km)
Population 4,324,450
Government Parliamentary republic
Capital Chisinau
Currency Moldovan leu
Languages Moldovan (almost
identical to the Romanian
language), Russian, Gagauz
(a Turkish dialect)
Main religions Eastern Orthodox
98%, Jewish 1.5%
Literacy 99,1%
GDP per capita $2,900 (2007 est.)

BELARUS

Country name Republic of Belarus
Area 80,154 sq mi
(207,600 sq km)
Population 9,685,768
Government Parliamentary republic
Capital Minsk
Currency Belarusian ruble
Languages Belarusian, Russian
Main religions Eastern Orthodox
80%, other (including Roman
Catholic, Protestant, Jewish, and
Muslim) 20%
Literacy 99.6%
GDP per capita $10,900 (2007 est.)

RUSSIA

Country name Russian Federation
Area 6,592,771 sq mi
(17,075,200 sq km)
Population 140,702,094
Government Parliamentary republic
Capital Moscow
Currency Russian ruble
Languages Russian, Tartar, Ukrainian,
Chuvash, Bashkir, Belarusian,
Moldovan
Main religions Russian Orthodox
15-20%, Muslim 10-15%
Literacy 99.4%
GDP per capita $14,700 (2007 est.)

RELIGION IN EUROPE

Most Europeans are
Christians. The
Vatican City, in
Rome, is the center
of the Roman
Catholic Church.
Most Roman Catholics
live in Southern Europe.
Further east, the Orthodox
Christian Church is more
popular, while in northern
Europe, many people follow
Protestant faiths. Islam is
a fast-growing religion in
countries like France
where many immigrants
come from Islamic
countries.

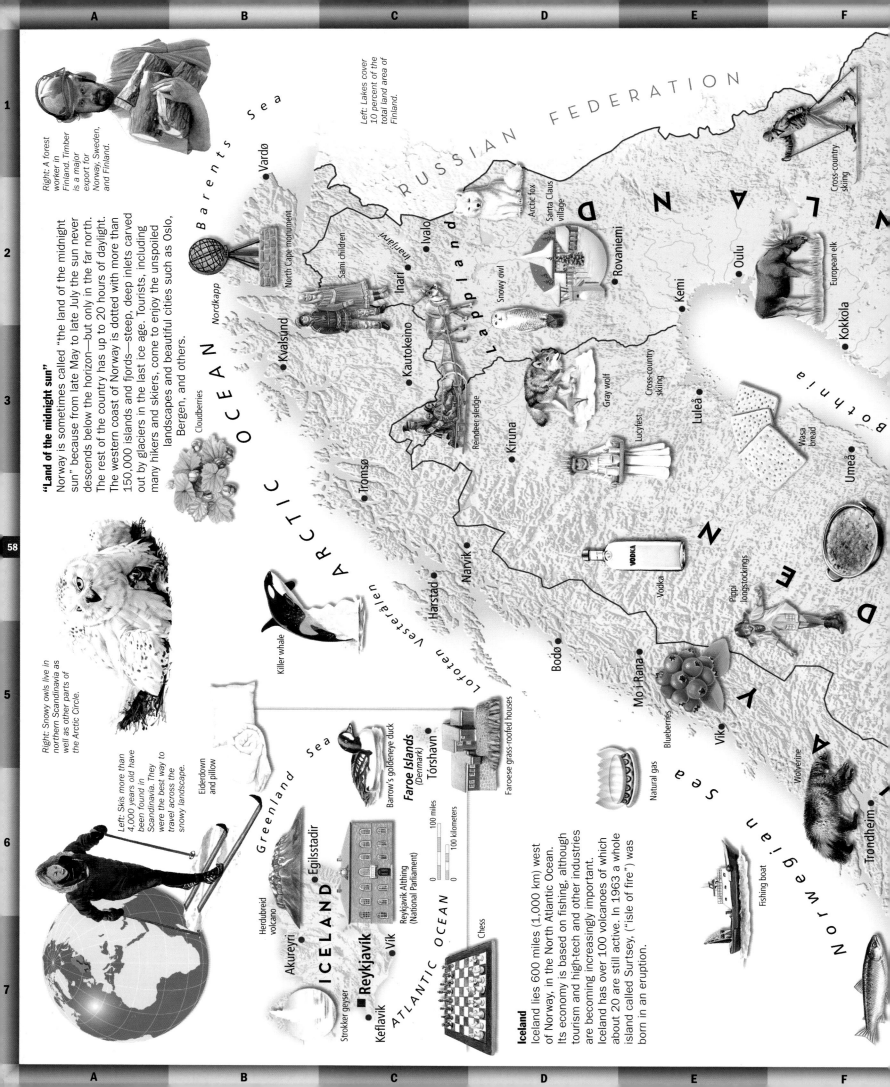

A   B   C   D   E   F

Right: A forest worker in Finland. Timber is a major export for Norway, Sweden, and Finland.

Barents Sea

RUSSIAN FEDERATION

Left: Lakes cover 10 percent of the total land area of Finland.

"Land of the midnight sun"

Norway is sometimes called "the land of the midnight sun" because from late May to late July the sun never descends below the horizon—but only in the far north. The rest of the country has up to 20 hours of daylight. The western coast of Norway is dotted with more than 150,000 islands and fjords—steep, deep inlets carved out by glaciers in the last ice age. Tourists, including many hikers and skiers, come to enjoy the unspoiled landscapes and beautiful cities such as Oslo, Bergen, and others.

Cloudberries

Vardø

North Cape monument

Nordkapp

Kvalsund

Sami children

Inari

Ivalo

Inari

Kautokeino

Arctic fox

Santa Claus village

Snowy owl

Rovaniemi

LAPLAND

Lappland

Kemi

Oulu

European elk

Cross-country skiing

Kokkola

ARCTIC OCEAN

Tromsø

Reindeer sledge

Kiruna

Gray wolf

Luleå

Cross-country skiing

Wasa bread

Umeå

Bothnia

Right: Snowy owls live in northern Scandinavia as well as other parts of the Arctic Circle.

Narvik

Harstad

VODKA

Vodka

Pippi longstockings

SWEDEN

Lofoten Vesterålen

Killer whale

Bodø

Mo i Rana

Blueberries

Vik

Wolverine

Greenland Sea

Barrow's goldeneye duck

Faroe Islands (Denmark)
Tórshavn

Faroese grass-roofed houses

Natural gas

Norwegian Sea

Trondheim

Left: Skis more than 4,000 years old have been found in Scandinavia. They were the best way to travel across the snowy landscape.

Eiderdown and pillow

Herdubreid volcano

Egilsstadir

Reykjavik Althing (National Parliament)

100 miles

100 kilometers

ICELAND

Akureyri

Strokker geyser

Reykjavik

Keflavik

Vik

ATLANTIC OCEAN

Chess

Fishing boat

Iceland

Iceland lies 600 miles (1,000 km) west of Norway, in the North Atlantic Ocean. Its economy is based on fishing, although tourism and high-tech and other industries are becoming increasingly important. Iceland has over 100 volcanoes of which about 20 are still active. In 1963 a whole island called Surtsey, ("isle of fire") was born in an eruption.

A   B   C   D   E   F

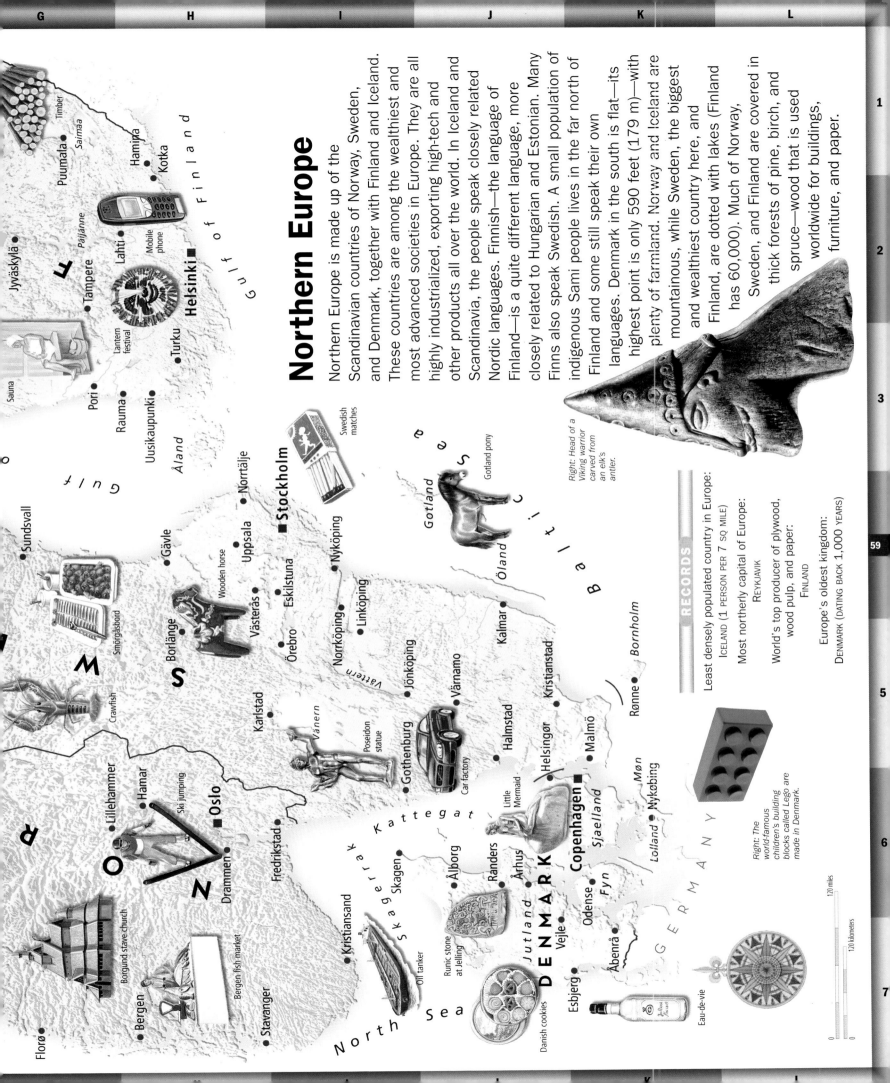

Northern Europe

Northern Europe is made up of the Scandinavian countries of Norway, Sweden, and Denmark, together with Finland and Iceland. These countries are among the wealthiest and most advanced societies in Europe. They are all highly industrialized, exporting high-tech and other products all over the world. In Iceland and Scandinavia, the people speak closely related Nordic languages. Finnish—the language of Finland—is a quite different language, more closely related to Hungarian and Estonian. Many Finns also speak Swedish. A small population of indigenous Sami people lives in the far north of Finland and some still speak their own languages. Denmark in the south is flat—its highest point is only 590 feet (179 m)—with plenty of farmland. Norway and Iceland are mountainous, while Sweden, the biggest and wealthiest country here, and Finland, are dotted with lakes (Finland has 60,000). Much of Norway, Sweden, and Finland are covered in thick forests of pine, birch, and spruce—wood that is used worldwide for buildings, furniture, and paper.

Right: Head of a Viking warrior carved from an elk's antler.

RECORDS

Least densely populated country in Europe:
ICELAND (1 PERSON PER 7 SQ MILE)

Most northerly capital of Europe:
REYKJAVIK

World's top producer of plywood, wood pulp, and paper:
FINLAND

Europe's oldest kingdom:
DENMARK (DATING BACK 1,000 YEARS)

Right: The world-famous children's building blocks called Lego are made in Denmark.

Timber

Saimaa

Puumala

Hämina

Kotka

Mobile phone

Jyväskylä

Päijänne

Tampere

Lahti

Lantern festival

Helsinki

Gulf of Finland

Sauna

Pori

Rauma

Uusikaupunki

Turku

Åland

Gulf

Swedish matches

Sundsvall

Gotland pony

Norrtälje

Gävle

Stockholm

Uppsala

Gotland

Eskilstuna

Nyköping

Wooden horse

Smörgåsbord

Borlänge

Västerås

Örebro

Linköping

Öland

Baltic Sea

Norrköping

Crawfish

Jönköping

Värnamo

Kalmar

Karlstad

Vänern

Poseidon statue

Gothenburg

Car factory

Halmstad

Kristianstad

Rønne

Bornholm

Lillehammer

Hamar

Ski jumping

Oslo

Fredrikstad

Drammen

Karlstad

Vättern

Helsingør

Malmö

Little Mermaid

Copenhagen

Sjælland

Møn

Nyköbing

Lolland

Borgund stave church

Bergen fish market

Bergen

Stavanger

Florø

Kristiansand

Skagen

Skagerrak

Kattegat

Ålborg

Randers

Århus

Odense

Fyn

Åbenrå

Esbjerg

Vejle

DENMARK

Jutland

Runic stone at Jelling

Oil tanker

Danish cookies

Eau-de-vie

GERMANY

North Sea

120 miles

120 kilometers

The British Isles

Lying in northwestern Europe and separated from it by the English Channel (though there is a rail tunnel underneath) and North Sea, the United Kingdom (UK) takes up most of the British Isles. It is a bit smaller than Wyoming. The largest of the islands is Great Britain, which is divided into the countries of England, Scotland, and Wales. The next largest island is Ireland, made up of Northern Ireland (which is part of the UK), and the Irish Republic (with the UK's only land border) which takes up about 85 percent of the island. Ireland is mainly lush, gently rolling farmland with lakes and peat bogs. The UK is just under 600 miles (1,000 km) long, from the far southwest of Cornwall to the northern tip of the Scottish mainland. Beyond that are the Orkney and Shetland Islands. Scotland has mountains and highlands—the highest mountain, Ben Nevis, at 4,406 feet (1,343 m) is here. Wales is both mountainous and hilly, while England has moors and dales but mostly farmland, fields, heaths, and woodland.

Celebrating cultural identities

The peoples of Scotland, Ireland, and Wales are proud of their local traditions and languages. Ancient Celtic languages are still spoken by some in these areas and attempts have been made to preserve and revive their use, especially in Wales. Many tourists come to these areas to visit ancient castles and often to trace their family roots, as well as to buy traditional local products, such as tartan and whisky. Since the 1960s, the UK has also become home to many immigrants, especially from former colonies in Africa, the Caribbean, and Asia. These people have enriched British culture with their religions, languages, and traditions.

Left: Performers of street theater during the Edinburgh Fringe Festival

Largest city in Europe:
LONDON

Longest river:
THE SEVERN
(200 MILES /
322 KM LONG)

Largest lake:
LOUGH NEAGH
(153 SQUARE MILES /
396 SQ KM)

Second longest undersea tunnel in the world (after Japan's Seikan Tunnel):
THE CHANNEL TUNNEL
(30 MILES /
48 KM LONG)

Weatherwatch

The weather appears to be a great topic of conversation in the UK: it is generally mild and temperate—which means it rains a lot with damp grey clouds carried in from the Atlantic. Despite the endless drizzle and occasional floods, the UK also has severe droughts and water shortages.

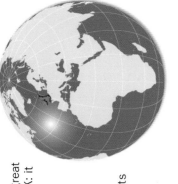

Shetland pony

Lerwick

Shetland Islands

Farming, fishing, and industry

Rich oil fields were found under the North Sea in the 1960s, and along with natural gas, they boosted the Scottish economy by creating work on oil rigs and refineries. Oil reserves are now running dry so other industries such as chemicals and electronics are taking over. Once a rich source of fish, the seas surrounding the UK have been overfished and have to be carefully monitored. Farming on the mainland remains highly productive and mechanized with only two percent of the population working on farms.

Norway pout

Cod

Haddock

Peterhead

Pictish stone

Aberdeen

Kirkwall

John o'Groats

Orkney Islands

Highland cattle

Golf

Dundee orange marmalade

Dundee

Grampian Mountains

Edinburgh
Edinburgh Fringe Festival

Tweed

Berwick-upon-Tweed

Inverness

Loch Ness

Braemar

Traditional dress and bagpipes

Durness

▲ Ben Nevis

Whisky

Glasgow

Tweed coat

Eilean Donan Castle

Fort Augustus

Fort William

S C O T L A N D

Stornoway

Isle of Lewis

Portree

Skye

Rum

Mull

Oban

Scotch thistle

Jura

Outer Hebrides

Inner Hebrides

Islay

North Uist

South Uist

O C E A N

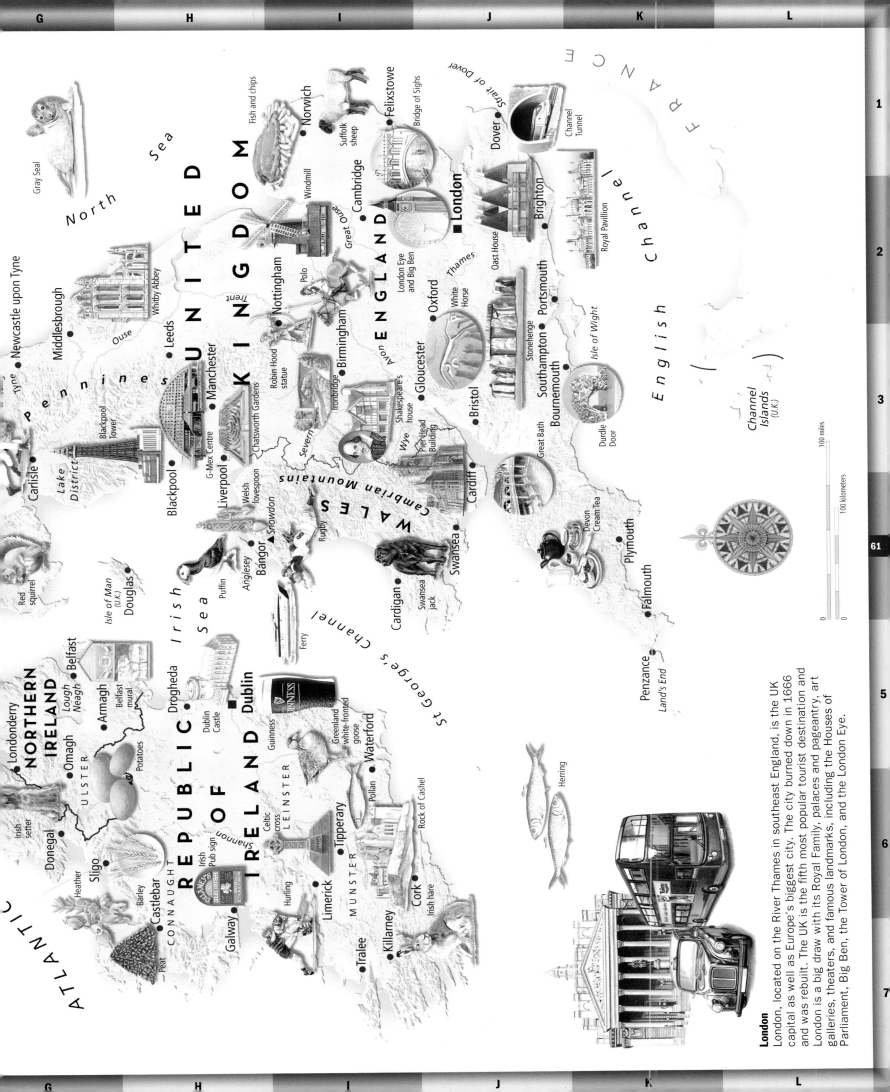

Gray Seal

North Sea

Fish and chips

• Norwich

Suffolk sheep

• Felixstowe

Bridge of Sighs

Strait of Dover

F R A N C E

• Dover

Channel Tunnel

U N I T E D

Windmill

Cambridge

• London

Great Ouse

Brighton

Royal Pavilion

K I N G D O M

London Eye and Big Ben

Newcastle upon Tyne

Whitby Abbey

Middlesbrough

Ouse

Leeds

Nottingham

Polo

Oxford

Thames

White Horse

Oast House

Portsmouth

Southampton

Stonehenge

Isle of Wight

English Channel

Tyne

Pennines

Manchester

Birmingham

E N G L A N D

Gloucester

Bournemouth

Great Bath

Durdle Door

Carlisle

Blackpool Tower

Lake District

G-Mex Centre

Chatsworth Gardens

Robin Hood statue

Ironbridge

Shakespeare's house

Avon

Bristol

Channel Islands (U.K.)

Red squirrel

Liverpool

Snowdon

Welsh lovespoon

Severn

Wye

Pier Head Building

Cardiff

W A L E S

Cambrian Mountains

Devon Cream Tea

Plymouth

Falmouth

Blackpool

Bangor

Anglesey

Rugby

Swansea

Swansea Jack

100 miles

100 kilometers

61

Isle of Man (U.K.)

Douglas

Puffin

Cardigan

Irish Sea

St George's Channel

Penzance

Land's End

Londonderry

NORTHERN IRELAND

Belfast

Lough Neagh

Armagh

Belfast mural

Drogheda

Dublin Castle

Dublin

Ferry

ULSTER

Omagh

Donegal

Potatoes

Guinness

Greenland white-fronted goose

Waterford

Herring

Irish setter

Heather

Sligo

Barley

Castlebar

Peat

CONNAUGHT

R E P U B L I C   O F   I R E L A N D

Irish Pub sign

Shannon

LEINSTER

Celtic cross

Rock of Cashel

Pollan

Galway

Tralee

Killarney

Hurling

Limerick

MUNSTER

Tipperary

Cork

Irish hare

A T L A N T I C

London

London, located on the River Thames in southeast England, is the UK capital as well as Europe's biggest city. The city burned down in 1666 and was rebuilt. The UK is the fifth most popular tourist destination and London is a big draw with its Royal Family, palaces and pageantry, art galleries, theaters, and famous landmarks, including the Houses of Parliament, Big Ben, the Tower of London, and the London Eye.

Spain, Portugal, and Andorra

Spain and Portugal are neighbors on the prominent southwest bulge of Europe called the Iberian Peninsula. It is separated from the rest of Europe by the Pyrenees Mountains. The peninsula is dominated by the vast Meseta plateau in the center which is rimmed and divided by mountains. The capital city of Madrid is located here. Both Spain and Portugal are hot and dry countries. The province of Almeria in Spain has Europe's only desert. Portugal is much smaller than Spain—it is about the size of Maine. The River Tagus divides the more mountainous north from the lower-lying south and Lisbon, the capital city, lies on the estuary where the river meets the Atlantic Ocean. For much of the 20th century both Spain and Portugal were ruled by right-wing dictators. In the 1970s they both became modern democracies and have experienced steady economic growth ever since. Both countries joined the European Union in 1986 and adopted the Euro as their currency on January 1, 2002. The majority of people are now employed in industry and services, with fewer than ever earning a living as farmers. The tiny independent country of Andorra nestles in the western Pyrenees. Its economy relies on tourism, with more than nine million visitors every year.

Islands in the Atlantic Ocean
The Canaries are made up of seven islands that lie off the coast of Africa. They were conquered by the Spanish in the 15th century and are still governed from Spain. Together with Madeira and the Azores, which are governed by Portugal, they are favorite tourist destinations.

Art, tradition, and culture
Spain and Portugal have rich and varied cultural traditions and both countries are major tourist destinations. People come to admire the old towns and buildings and to enjoy traditional events such as bullfighting and Flamenco music and dance, as well as the museums, food, wine, and beaches. Works by modern artists such as Picasso, Gaudí, Miró, and Dalí are also admired.

Left: Pablo Picasso's *Guernica* is a famous anti-war painting provoked by the first aerial bombing of civilians in 1937 during the Spanish Civil War. The enormous work is in the Prado Museum in Madrid.

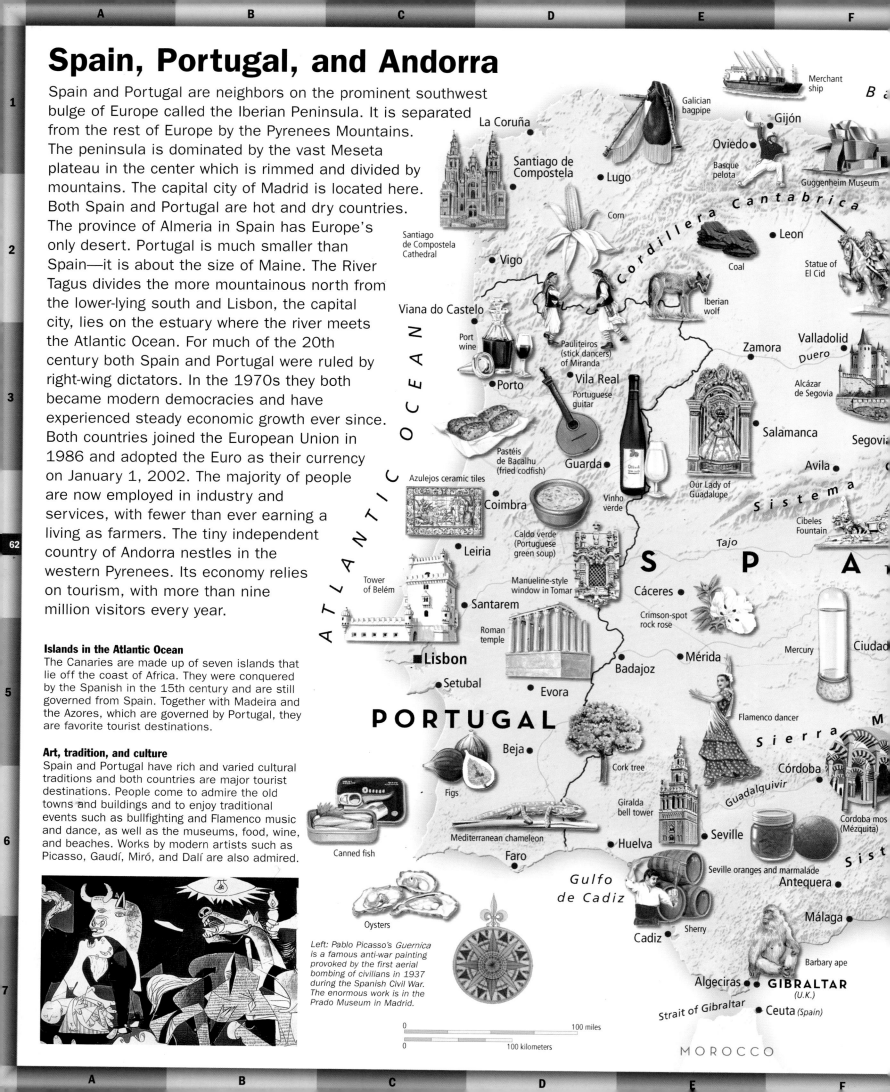

Merchant ship
Galician bagpipe
La Coruña
Santiago de Compostela
Lugo
Gijón
Oviedo
Basque pelota
Guggenheim Museum
Santiago de Compostela Cathedral
Cordillera Cantabrica
Corn
Leon
Coal
Statue of El Cid
Vigo
Iberian wolf
Zamora
Valladolid
Duero
Viana do Castelo
Port wine
Pauliteiros (stick dancers) of Miranda
Alcázar de Segovia
Porto
Vila Real
Portuguese guitar
Salamanca
Segovia
Pastéis de Bacalhu (fried codfish)
Guarda
Avila
Our Lady of Guadalupe
Sistema
Azulejos ceramic tiles
Coimbra
Vinho verde
Cibeles Fountain
Caldo verde (Portuguese green soup)
Tajo
Leiria
Manueline-style window in Tomar
Cáceres
S P A
Tower of Belém
Santarem
Crimson-spot rock rose
Mercury
Ciudad
Roman temple
Mérida
Lisbon
Badajoz
Setubal
Evora
PORTUGAL
Flamenco dancer
Sierra
M
Beja
Córdoba
Cork tree
Figs
Giralda bell tower
Cordoba mos (Mézquita)
Mediterranean chameleon
Seville
Sist
Canned fish
Huelva
Seville oranges and marmalade
Faro
Antequera
Gulfo de Cadiz
Málaga
Oysters
Sherry
Cadiz
Barbary ape
Algeciras
GIBRALTAR (U.K.)
Strait of Gibraltar
Ceuta (Spain)
MOROCCO

0 100 miles
0 100 kilometers

Languages and religion

Castilian is the official language of Spain, but there are four other official regional languages too. These are: Aranese, Basque, Catalan, and Galician. Several other regional languages are also in use. In the two Spanish cities in North Africa—Ceuta and Mellila—Arabic and Berber are spoken. Portuguese is the main language in Portugal but Mirandese, spoken in the northwest of the country, is now also an official regional language. Most people in the Iberian Peninsula are Roman Catholics, although only a small minority attend church on a regular basis.

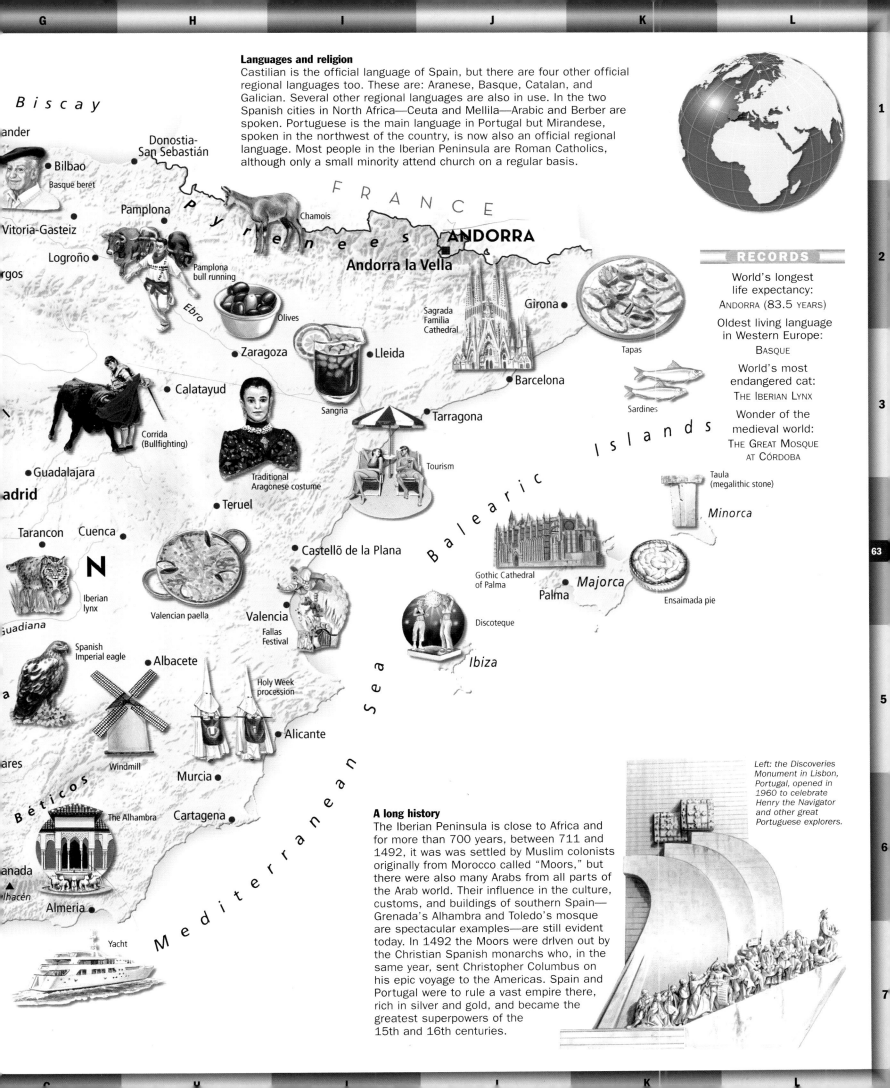

Biscay

ander

Bilbao

Basque beret

Vitoria-Gasteiz

rgos

Logroño

Donostia-San Sebastián

Pamplona

Pyrenees

Chamois

FRANCE

ANDORRA

Andorra la Vella

Pamplona bull running

Ebro

Olives

Zaragoza

Lleida

Sagrada Familia Cathedral

Girona

Calatayud

Sangria

Barcelona

Corrida (Bullfighting)

Traditional Aragonese costume

Tarragona

Tourism

Balearic Islands

Tapas

Sardines

Guadalajara

adrid

Teruel

Tarancon

Cuenca

N

Castellō de la Plana

Gothic Cathedral of Palma

Minorca

Taula (megalithic stone)

Iberian lynx

uadiana

Valencian paella

Valencia

Fallas Festival

Majorca

Palma

Ensaimada pie

Spanish Imperial eagle

Albacete

Holy Week procession

Discoteque

Ibiza

Mediterranean Sea

Windmill

Alicante

ares

Béticos

Murcia

The Alhambra

Cartagena

anada

lhacén

Almeria

Yacht

RECORDS

World's longest life expectancy:
ANDORRA (83.5 YEARS)

Oldest living language in Western Europe:
BASQUE

World's most endangered cat:
THE IBERIAN LYNX

Wonder of the medieval world:
THE GREAT MOSQUE AT CÓRDOBA

63

A long history

The Iberian Peninsula is close to Africa and for more than 700 years, between 711 and 1492, it was was settled by Muslim colonists originally from Morocco called "Moors," but there were also many Arabs from all parts of the Arab world. Their influence in the culture, customs, and buildings of southern Spain—Grenada's Alhambra and Toledo's mosque are spectacular examples—are still evident today. In 1492 the Moors were driven out by the Christian Spanish monarchs who, in the same year, sent Christopher Columbus on his epic voyage to the Americas. Spain and Portugal were to rule a vast empire there, rich in silver and gold, and became the greatest superpowers of the 15th and 16th centuries.

Left: the Discoveries Monument in Lisbon, Portugal, opened in 1960 to celebrate Henry the Navigator and other great Portuguese explorers.

France and Monaco

The second largest country in Europe, France stretches from the Mediterranean Sea in the south to the North Sea. In climate and culture, France straddles the continent, and is the only country to belong to both southern and northern Europe. France has played a central role in European civilization over the centuries and its long history is clearly visible in its towns and monuments, which range from prehistoric cave paintings and standing stones, to Roman temples and medieval castles and cathedrals, to 18th-century chateaux and modern skyscrapers. Travelers come from all over the world to admire these and to enjoy the country's superb food, wine, and entertainment; France is the world's number one tourist destination, with more than 79 million vistors each year. Much of France is covered in rich, fertile farmlands. French farmers use efficient technology and are the top producers of agricultural products in Europe. Services and industry, including the aerospace industry which produces Airbus airplanes, form the backbone of the French economy. France has welcomed immigrants from many parts of the world, especially from its former colonies in Africa and Asia. High unemployment has led to tension and rioting by some young immigrants in recent years.

Paris – City of Light

Founded over 2,000 years ago on a small island in the River Seine, Paris is called the city of light because it is a world center for commerce, education, and culture. Some of the world's most famous artists and writers have lived here. Its many famous art museums include the Louvre, which houses possibly the most famous painting in the world, the *Mona Lisa* by Leonardo Da Vinci. Other famous landmarks are the Arc de Triomphe, the Eiffel Tower (which was only meant to be there for 20 years), and the glorious palace and gardens of Versailles.

Left: France leads the world in high fashion, or "haute couture." Each season there are spectacular fashion shows in Paris with glamorous models striding the catwalks in the latest designer wear.

Strasbourg and the European Parliament

France was a founding member of the European Union (EU) in the 1950s and hosts the official seat of the Council of Europe in Strasbourg. Members meet there to decide a common European policy on a range of issues, from human rights to education and the environment. Currently there are 27 member states representing a combined population of some 800 million people. Along with New York and Geneva, Strasbourg is the only city in the world which is home to an international institution but is not a national capital.

Monaco

The Principality of Monaco is less than a mile square (1.95 sq km; only the Vatican City is smaller). It is mostly rocky outcrop crammed with luxury hotels and apartments and with million-dollar yachts in the harbor. Monaco has been ruled by the Grimaldi family since 1297. When Prince Rainier married Hollywood star Grace Kelly in 1956 this (along with the Mediterranean scenery and climate, generous tax laws, and annual Formula 1 "grand prix" motor race) attracted many wealthy visitors and celebrities to settle here.

Left: Some French specialities, clockwise from the top: red wine, a selection of cheeses, a baguette, a croissant, and crêpes.

Fine food and wine

France is famous for its cooking and regional foods—from soft cheeses like Camembert and brie (delicious with French loaves called baguettes), to *crêpes* (thin rolled up pancakes), and cold meats. Other delicacies include *escargots* (snails—France is the world's biggest consumer of snails with 40,000 tons consumed per year) and *cuisses de grenouilles* (frogs' legs; about 70 million frogs are eaten each year). Frogs are protected in France so most are imported from southeast Asia. Together with Italy, France is the largest producer of wine in the world. Famous French wines include champagne, burgundy, and chardonnay.

Left: The Louise Weiss building in Strasbourg was opened in 1999. The wing-shaped building houses the debating chamber and the offices of the members of the European Parliament. Its 750-seat debating chamber is designed to host this institution's monthly sessions. The modern building has a 200-foot (60-m) high tower including 17 floors and 1,133 offices.

En

Cha
Isla
(to

Herrings

Golfe de

Tall ship festival

Traditional Breton costume

● Brest

B R I T T A N Y

Quimpe
escargo

Megalithic stones at Carnac

Egret

St-Nazair

Heron

A T L A N T I C   O C E A N

B a y

La Ro

Sardines

Corsica

0 _____ 50 miles

0 _____ 50 kilometers

Figatelli and brocciu

Bastia

Bastia harbour

CORSICA

Ajaccio

Napoleon

Cormorant

● Bonifacio

0 _____ 100 miles

0 _____ 100 kilometers

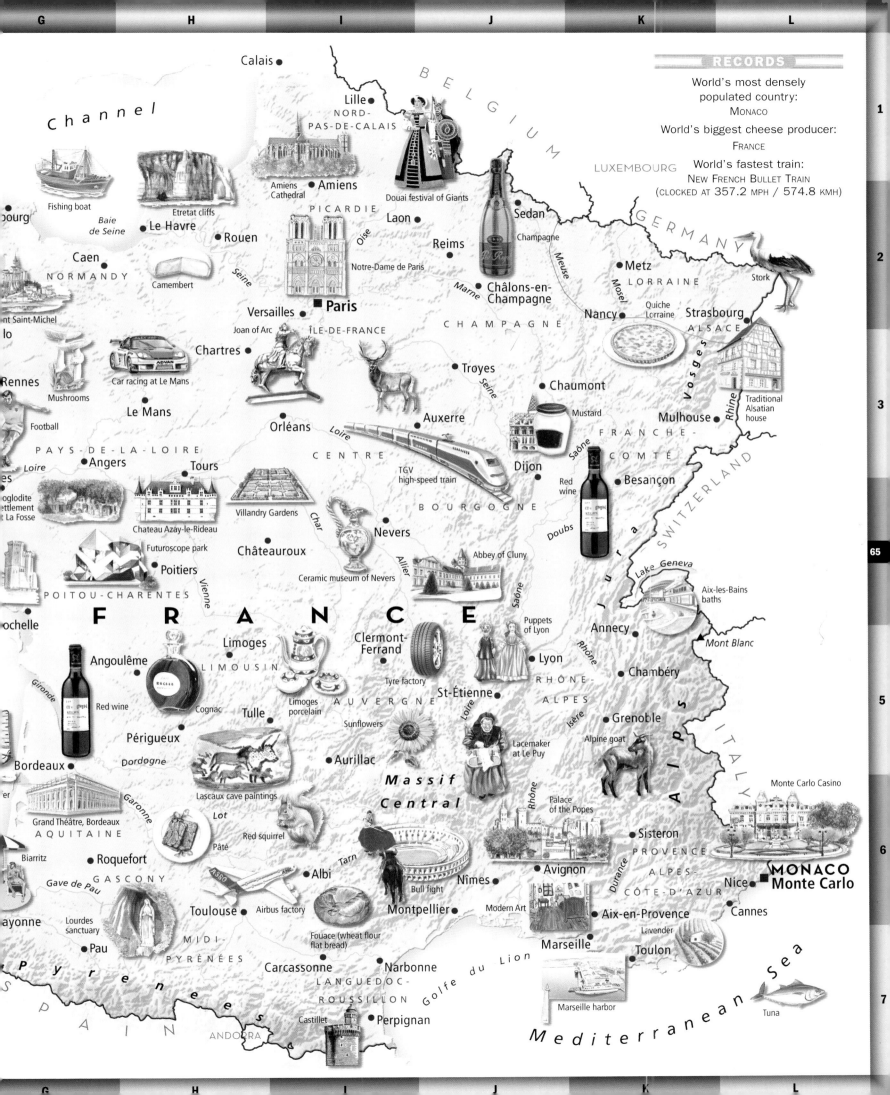

Calais

Channel

Lille
NORD-
PAS-DE-CALAIS

Fishing boat

Baie
de Seine

Etretat cliffs

Amiens
Cathedral

Amiens

Douai festival of Giants

PICARDIE

Le Havre

Rouen

Caen

NORMANDY

Camembert

ont Saint-Michel

lo

Versailles

Paris

Notre-Dame de Paris

Laon

Reims

Sedan

Champagne

RECORDS

World's most densely
populated country:
MONACO

World's biggest cheese producer:
FRANCE

World's fastest train:
NEW FRENCH BULLET TRAIN
(CLOCKED AT 357.2 MPH / 574.8 KMH)

LUXEMBOURG

GERMANY

Châlons-en-
Champagne

Metz

LORRAINE

Stork

Nancy

Quiche
Lorraine

Strasbourg

ALSACE

CHAMPAGNE

Joan of Arc

Chartres

ÎLE-DE-FRANCE

Troyes

Chaumont

Vosges

Mulhouse

Rhine

Traditional
Alsatian
house

Car racing at Le Mans

Rennes

Mushrooms

Le Mans

Football

Orléans

Loire

CENTRE

Auxerre

TGV
high-speed train

FRANCHE-
COMTÉ

Mustard

Dijon

Red
wine

Besançon

PAYS-DE-LA-LOIRE

Loire

es

Angers

Tours

Jura

SWITZERLAND

oglodite
ttlement
La Fosse

Chateau Azay-le-Rideau

Villandry Gardens

Char

BOURGOGNE

Doubs

Futuroscope park

Poitiers

Ceramic museum of Nevers

Nevers

Châteauroux

Abbey of Cluny

Allier

Saône

Lake Geneva

Aix-les-Bains
baths

POITOU-CHARENTES

Vienne

F R A N C E

Puppets
of Lyon

Annecy

Mont Blanc

ochelle

Limoges

Clermont-
Ferrand

Rhône

Lyon

Chambéry

Angoulême

LIMOUSIN

Gironde

Red wine

Cognac

Tulle

Limoges
porcelain

AUVERGNE

Tyre factory

Sunflowers

St-Étienne

Loire

RHÔNE-
ALPES

Isère

Grenoble

Alpine goat

Périgueux

Dordogne

Aurillac

Lacemaker
at Le Puy

Bordeaux

Lascaux cave paintings

Massif

Rhône

Monte Carlo Casino

Grand Théâtre, Bordeaux

AQUITAINE

Lot

Red squirrel

Central

Palace
of the Popes

Sisteron

PROVENCE

Biarritz

Roquefort

GASCONY

Pâté

Tarn

Albi

Bull fight

Nîmes

Avignon

ALPES-
CÔTE-D'AZUR

MONACO
Monte Carlo

ayonne

Gave de Pau

Lourdes
sanctuary

Pau

MIDI-
PYRÉNÉES

Toulouse

Airbus factory

Montpellier

Modern Art

Marseille

Aix-en-Provence

Lavender

Nice

Cannes

Fouace (wheat flour
flat bread)

Toulon

Carcassonne

Narbonne

LANGUEDOC-
ROUSSILLON

Golfe du Lion

Marseille harbor

Tuna

SPAIN

Castillet

Perpignan

ANDORRA

Mediterranean Sea

Garonne

65

Benelux

Belgium, the Netherlands, and Luxembourg (known as Benelux, from the first letters of the country names), lie together on a very low and flat delta where four rivers—the Rhine, Scheldt, Meuse, and Yser—empty into the North Sea. Almost one-third of the Netherlands is below sea level, and the region's highest point is only 2,303 feet (700 m)—which explains why the area is also known as the "Low Countries!" In fact often the highest thing you see are the windmills—there were once 10,000 of them channeling flood water away from Amsterdam. Engineers have reclaimed much of the soggy, marshy shoreline using canals, earth defenses (called dykes), and natural sand dunes. Because the land is so low-lying, people use the canals—they ice skate on them in winter—and cycle paths to travel. The drained soil is very fertile and vast fields of tulips and other flowers are grown. Luxembourg is the 20th smallest country in the world and was a large steel producer. Now it is a banking center. Belgium lies at the heart of Europe with a short coastline of just 42 miles (67 km). Belgium has many canals on which large barges transport goods. The whole region is densely populated and all three countries are economically well developed with high living standards.

RECORDS

Europe's largest and busiest port:
ROTTERDAM (NUMBER 3 IN THE WORLD, AFTER SINGAPORE AND SHANGHAI)

World's largest producer and exporter of tulips:
THE NETHERLANDS

World's first printed newspaper:
ANTWERP'S "NIEUWE TIJDINGEN" (1605)

Europe's highest GDP per capita:
LUXEMBOURG ($80,500)

Left: The cultivation of tulips is highly lucrative and farmers use technologically advanced methods to produce the strongest plants and the most beautiful blooms.

Tulipmania

The tulip is a flower originally from Central Asia. It was first cultivated by the Turks in about 1000 CE (our word "tulip" derives from *tulbent*, the Turkish word for turban), and was introduced to Western Europe and the Netherlands in the 17th century, first as a medical product, then as a bright garden flower. Sales rose quickly: in the early 17th century some varieties could cost more than an Amsterdam house.

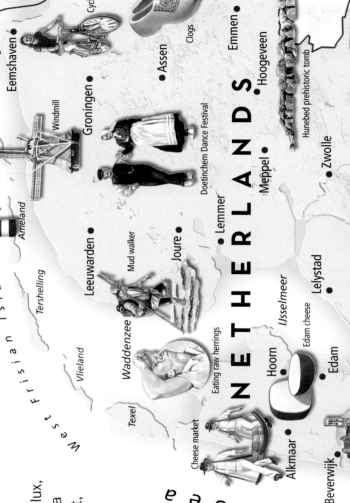

GERMANY

NETHERLANDS

North Sea

West Frisian Islands

Ice skating
Cyclist
Clogs
Eemshaven
Emmen
Schiermonnikoog
Assen
Hoogeveen
Windmill
Groningen
Hunebed prehistoric tomb
Pofferjes
Enschede
Ameland Lighthouse
Ameland
Doetinchem Dance Festival
Meppel
Zwolle
IJssel
Deventer
Zutphen
Brewery
Doetinchem
Terschelling
Leeuwarden
Mud walker
Joure
Lemmer
Het Loo Palace and gardens
Apeldoorn
Café
Arnhem
Vlieland
IJsselmeer
Lelystad
Schröder House
Rhine
Nijmegen
Oss
Texel
Waddenzee
Edam cheese
Amsterdam
St. Jan Cathedral
's-Hertogenbosch
Eating raw herrings
Hoorn
Edam
Naarden
Utrecht
Traditional Volendam
Cheese market
Alkmaar
Tulips
Gouda
Maa
Beverwijk
Singel waterway
Leiden
Peace Palace
Rotterdam
Delft porcelain
Dordrecht
Blue mussels
Haarlem
The Hague
Hoek van Holland
Container ship
Dam
Oosters
Mackerel

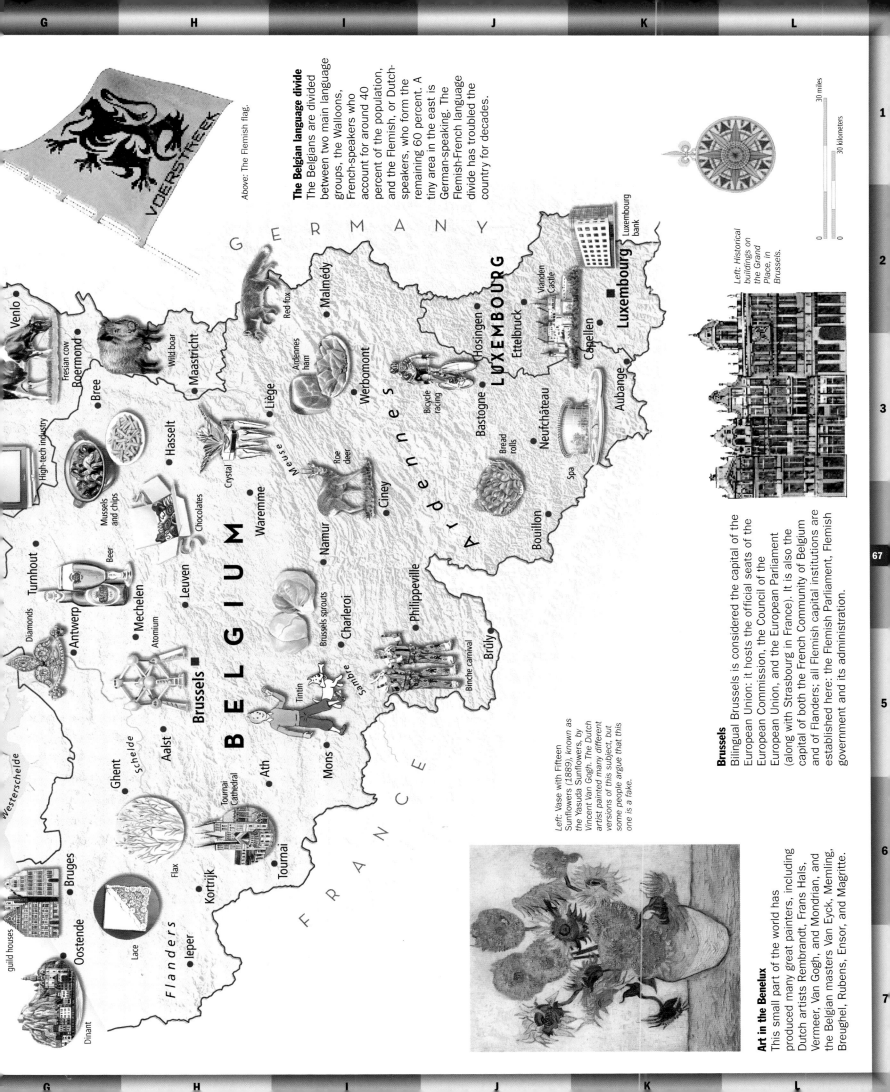

Above: The Flemish flag.

The Belgian language divide

The Belgians are divided between two main language groups, the Walloons, French-speakers who account for around 40 percent of the population, and the Flemish, or Dutch-speakers, who form the remaining 60 percent. A tiny area in the east is German-speaking. The Flemish-French language divide has troubled the country for decades.

Left: Historical buildings on the Grand Place, in Brussels.

30 miles
30 kilometers

GERMANY

Red fox

Malmédy

Ardennes ham

Werbomont

Bicycle racing

Hosingen

Vianden Castle

Ettelbruck

Capellen

Luxembourg bank

LUXEMBOURG

Luxembourg

Venlo

Fresian cow

Roermond

Wild boar

Bree

Maastricht

Liège

Hasselt

High-tech industry

Crystal

Waremme

Roe deer

Ciney

Namur

Bastogne

Neufchâteau

Bread rolls

Aubange

Meuse

Mussels and chips

Chocolates

Beer

Turnhout

Leuven

Brussels sprouts

Charleroi

Philippeville

Spa

Bouillon

Ardennes

Diamonds

Antwerp

Mechelen

Atomium

Sambre

Binche carnival

Brûly

67

Left: Vase with Fifteen Sunflowers (1889), known as the Yasuda Sunflowers, by Vincent Van Gogh. The Dutch artist painted many different versions of this subject, but some people argue that this one is a fake.

Tintin

Ghent

Aalst

Ath

Mons

Schelde

Westerschelde

Tournai Cathedral

Tournai

Flax

Bruges

Kortrijk

Oostende

Ieper

Lace

Flanders

guild houses

Dinant

FRANCE

BELGIUM

Brussels

Bilingual Brussels is considered the capital of the European Union: it hosts the official seats of the European Commission, the Council of the European Union, and the European Parliament (along with Strasbourg in France). It is also the capital of both the French Community of Belgium and of Flanders; all Flemish capital institutions are established here: the Flemish Parliament, Flemish government and its administration.

Art in the Benelux

This small part of the world has produced many great painters, including Dutch artists Rembrandt, Frans Hals, Vermeer, Van Gogh, and Mondrian, and the Belgian masters Van Eyck, Memling, Breughel, Rubens, Ensor, and Magritte.

Germany, Austria, Switzerland, and Liechtenstein

Germany is the industrial and economic "engine room" of Europe. It has the largest economy on the continent. From the North and Baltic Seas to the snowy Alps in the south, Germany's vast elevated plains and wide, open lowlands are criss-crossed by superfast *autobahn*, carrying goods on the oldest motorway network in the world and the only one in Europe without a speed limit (on some routes). Huge barges ply Germany's canals and major rivers, including the Rhine, Danube, and Elbe, carrying farm and factory produce. The country is roughly the size of Montana and situated even farther north. Westerley winds from the Atlantic Ocean provide plenty of rainfall and long periods of overcast weather. The Germany we know today was only reunified as a single nation on October 3, 1990 after it had been split into two opposing states—East Germany and West Germany. The mountainous countries of Austria and Switzerland lie south of Germany, tucked under the hilly, wooded, snow-capped Alps. The Swiss are famous for watchmaking—the Swiss company Patek Philippe invented the wristwatch in 1868. Liechtenstein is tiny—only 15 miles (24 km) long and 7 miles (12 km) wide. It is a banking center and, bizarrely, the world's largest exporter of false teeth.

Right: This half-timbered house in Germany has been standing since the Middle Ages.

An industrial powerhouse

Germany is the world's third largest economy. After World War II (1939–45) it rebuilt its shattered economy to become the world's third producer of motor vehicles, including the famous Mercedes Benz, BMW, and Volkswagen, and the second largest producer of hops (for beer). Germany is one of the largest exporters of goods around the world, including cars, computer equipment, machinery, and chemical products.

POLAND

Oder

Baltic Sea

Berlin
Brandenburg Gate

Wild cat

Cottbus

Semper Opera House

Soccer

Pig

Beets

Elbe

Leipzig

Rostock

Potatoes

Volkswagen

Saale

Stork

Magdeburg

Harz

Wolfsburg

Elbe

Wartburg Castle

Kiel

Lubeck

Hamburg

Hannover

Hamburg Old Town

High-tech industry

Bremen

Bielefeld

European hare

Kassel

DENMARK

Bremerhaven

Osnabruck

Weser

Nordfriesische Inseln

Bremen statue of Roland

Cattle

Ems

Koln Cathedral

Ostfriesische Inseln

Wilhelmshaven

North Sea

Tugboat

Essen

Rhine barge

Dusseldorf

NETHERLANDS

Right: A coal miner in Germany. Heavy industry and high technology go hand in hand in Germany today.

SLOVAKIA

HUNGARY

CZECH REPUBLIC

SLOVENIA

ITALY

AUSTRIA

GERMANY

SWITZERLAND

LIECHTENSTEIN

FRANCE

BELGIUM

LUXEMBOURG

Schönbrunn Palace

Danube

Vienna ■
Sachertorte

Lipizzaner, at the Spanish Riding School

Chamois

Graz

Graz Clock Tower

St Michael

Melk Abbey

Mur

Waltz

Klagenfurt

Linz

Alpine marmot

Spittal

Drau

The Alps

Mozart candy

Salzburg

Bruck

Alpine star

Edelweiss

Grossglockner ▲

Passau

Bavarian costume

Gray wolf

Regensberg

Danube

Trombone player at Oktoberfest

Beer mug

Munich ●

Golden dachl

Bearded vulture

Innsbruck

Landeck

Inn

Zugspitze ▲

Bamberg Old Town Hall

Bamberg ●

Nuremberg ●

Main

Augsburg ●

Neuschwanstein Castle

Vaduz Castle

St Moritz

Würzburg ●

Brezel

Ulm ●

Bodensee

Bregenz

St Gallen

LIECHTENSTEIN
Vaduz ■

Chur

Chalet

European Central Bank

erra

Mannheim ●

Neckar

Stuttgart ●

Mercedes

Swabian Jura

Karlsruhe ●

Chapel bridge, Lucerne

Zurich ●

Emmental cheese

Luzern ●

Rhine

Banking

St Moritz

Alphorn player

Lugano ●

Chemical industry

Frankfurt am Main ●

Rhine

Mainz ●

Black Forest

Freiburg ●

Cuckoo clock

Bern ■

Biel

Basel ●

Rhine

Watch

Brig ●

Rhône

Matterhorn ▲

Walser woman in traditional costume

Bonn ●

Mosel

Saarbrucken ●

Lausanne ●

Lake Geneva

Martigny ●

Geneva ●

Chateau de Chillon

Trier Porta Nigra

Franz Anton Ketterer made the first cuckoo clock in Schönwald in Germany's Black Forest region in the mid-17th century. He imitated the cuckoo's call by using bellows and whistles to produce two different sounds. The world's biggest cuckoo clocks are both located in Schonach im Schwarzwald, Baden-Württemberg. One cuckoo measures nearly 15 feet (5 m) across.

Classical music

Austria is famous for its classical music and was the birthplace of the amazing child prodigy Wolfgang Amadeus Mozart: when he was five he wrote a concert for harpsichord that only the most accomplished musicians could perform. Another Austrian composer, Johann Strauss, wrote *The Blue Danube* and many other world-famous waltzes. The European Union anthem is *Ode To Joy*—the melody for which was composed by the German composer Ludwig van Beethoven for his 9th Symphony. JS Bach is another German classical composer famous for, among other things, his *Brandenburg Concertos.*

100 miles

100 kilometers

0

St. Bernard dogs were bred by monks in the Alps to rescue people. One famous dog, called Bray, is said to have saved at least 40 lives.

69

The Alps

The Alps have most of the highest mountains in Europe. Well over 30 peaks are above 13,000 feet (4,000 m) and they stretch from southeastern France though Italy, Germany, Austria, and Switzerland. The snowy slopes attract millions of skiers paying billions of Euros every winter to the world's most famous ski resorts—St. Moritz, St. Anton, Davos, Gstaad, and Kitzbuehel—and home of the first Downhill World Championships and first Winter Olympics.

Italy and Malta

Italy is made up of a long, boot-shaped peninsula stretching down into the Mediterranean Sea, the two large islands of Sicily and Sardinia, and about 70 smaller isles. Two tiny independent states—the Vatican City and San Marino—lie within Italian borders. In the north, Italy is separated from the rest of Europe by the Alps, the tallest mountain range in Europe. The peninsula is divided in half down the middle by the Apennine Mountains. The climate is mild Mediterranean, with the south much hotter and drier than the north. Italy is a prosperous, industrialized country with a well-developed economy. There is still, however, quite a large difference between the wealthy north and the poorer southern regions and the islands. The south is also still plagued by the Mafia and other organized crime groups. Throughout Italy most people are employed in office jobs; factory work has declined steeply in the last few decades, and very few people are now employed in agriculture. Malta is located to the south of Italy and is made up of three major islands. Situated at the crossroads of some of the world's busiest shipping routes, Malta is heavily involved in shipbuilding and boat repairs. Tourism also makes a large contribution to the local economy.

Above: Plastic "butterfly" sunglasses decorated with sparkling crystals like these were worn by Italian filmstars and socialites in the 1950s.

Design, fashion, and *La dolce vita*
In the 20th century Italy became famous for its chic but affordable fashion, ultra modern design, and glamorous lifestyles. *La Dolce Vita*, which means "the sweet life," was the name of a film released in 1960 by Italian film director Federico Fellini.

SLOVENIA

AUSTRIA

Udine

Trieste

St Mark's basilica

Venice

Ibex

The Alps

Bolzano

White wine

Trento

Verona

Arena (Roman amphitheatre)

Ferrari factory • Ferrara

Po

Modena

Bologna

SWITZERLAND

St Bernard rescue dog

Bergamo

Parma ham

Parma

Piacenza

Lake Como

Milan cathedral

Milan

Rice

Olive oil

Genoa

La Spezia

Apennines

Florence cathedral

Florence

Red wine

Siena

Town Hall, Siena

Arno

Leaning Tower of Pisa

Pisa

Grosseto

Tuscan cowboy

Elba

Lake Bolsena

Viterbo

Lake Trasimeno

Arezzo

Perugia

Frasassi caves

Basilica of St Francis of Assisi

Rocca at San Marino

SAN MARINO

Forlì

Rimini

Ancona

Adriatic Sea

Brown bear

Aquila

Terni

Tiber

Giglio

ITALY

Novara

Turin

Soccer

Cuneo

Red wine

Aosta

Mt Blanc

Castle

FRANCE

Savona

Cruise boat

Ligurian Sea

Sardines

Corsica
(France)

Pescara

Anchovies

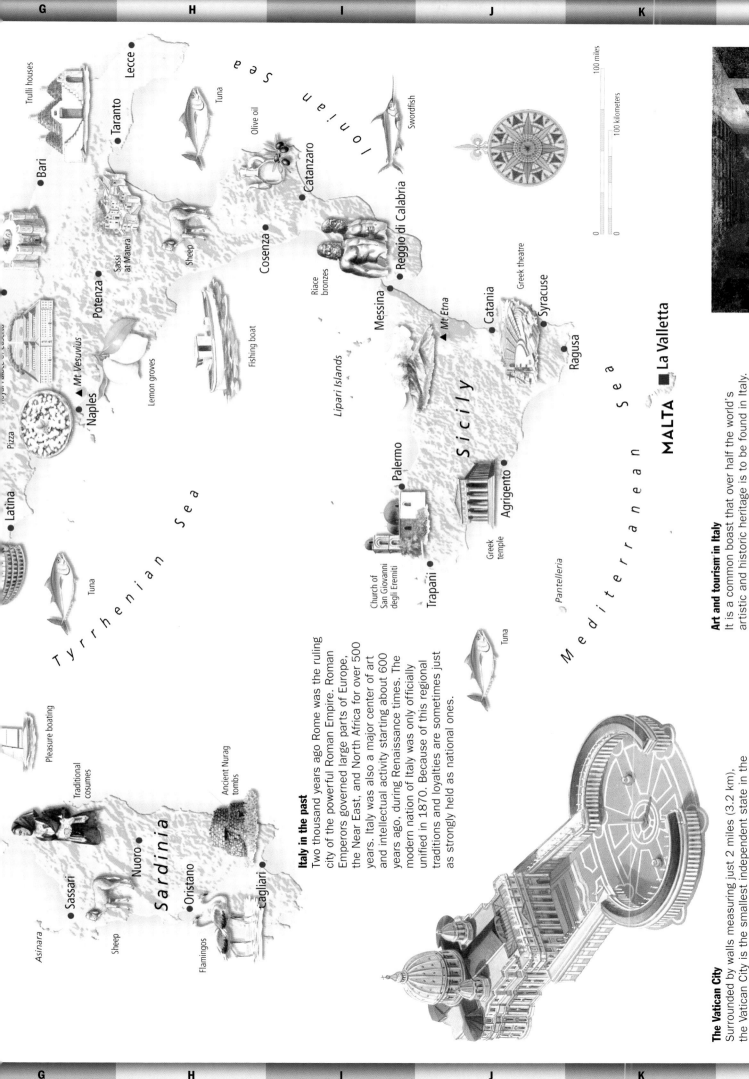

Trulli houses

Lecce

Taranto

Bari

Tuna

Olive oil

Ionian Sea

Catanzaro

Swordfish

100 miles

100 kilometers

Sassi
at Matera

Sheep

Potenza

Cosenza

Riace
bronzes

Reggio di Calabria

Greek theatre

Messina

Lipari Islands

▲ *Mt Etna*

Catania

Syracuse

Latina

Fishing boat

▲ *Mt Vesuvius*

Naples

Lemon groves

Pizza

Tyrrhenian Sea

Sicily

Ragusa

MALTA ■ **La Valletta**

Palermo

Agrigento

Mediterranean Sea

Church of
San Giovanni
degli Eremiti

Trapani

Greek
temple

Pantelleria

Tuna

Tuna

Asinara

Sheep

Pleasure boating

Traditional
costumes

Sardinia

Sassari

Nuoro

Ancient Nurag
tombs

Oristano

Cagliari

Flamingos

Italy in the past

Two thousand years ago Rome was the ruling city of the powerful Roman Empire. Roman Emperors governed large parts of Europe, the Near East, and North Africa for over 500 years. Italy was also a major center of art and intellectual activity starting about 600 years ago, during Renaissance times. The modern nation of Italy was only officially unified in 1870. Because of this regional traditions and loyalties are sometimes just as strongly held as national ones.

Art and tourism in Italy

It is a common boast that over half the world's artistic and historic heritage is to be found in Italy. More than 55 million tourists visit every year to see great works of art and architecture, such as Leonardo da Vinci's *Last Supper* in Milan, (right), Brunelleschi's magnificent dome on Florence Cathedral, St. Peters in Rome, and much, much more. Delicious Italian food and wine also draw tourists, as do its beautiful beaches and landscapes.

The Vatican City

Surrounded by walls measuring just 2 miles (3.2 km), the Vatican City is the smallest independent state in the world. It is located on a hill in the center of Rome and is the home of the pope and world headquarters of the Roman Catholic Church. The tiny city is comprised of Saint Peter's Basilica (above), the Sistine Chapel, the Vatican Museums, the Vatican Library, and the pope's residence. The pope is the head of state and the spiritual leader of the world's 950 million Roman Catholics.

71

Southeastern Europe

The countries of southeastern Europe embrace a patchwork of peoples, religions, languages, and states. As a group they are often referred to as the Balkans (the Turkish word for mountain), after the rugged mountain range that runs east-west across Bulgaria. The land is a mix of forested mountains, deep fertile valleys and plains, many lakes, and long coastlines skirting the Adriatic, Ionian, Aegean, and Black Seas. The summers are hot and dry. The Danube River, the second longest in Europe, forms the border between Romania and Bulgaria and is surrounded by rich, fertile farmlands. Both of these countries were controlled by the Soviet Union until they became independent in 1989–1990. They both joined the European Union (EU) on January 1, 2007. Tiny Slovenia, in the northwest, has been a member of the EU since 2004, while Greece joined much earlier, in 1981. Greece is the southernmost part of the Balkan Peninsula and is mainly mountainous, with a rocky coast and over 1,400 islands, the largest of which is Crete.

Right: Built in the 16th century, the famous Mostar Bridge collapsed in November 1993 after bombardment during the Bosnian war between the city's Muslims and Croats. Its re-opening in 2004 was regarded as a moment of reconciliation.

Above: A kalderash Rom or "gypsy." There are many Roma people living in Romania and Bulgaria.

Mouths of the Danube

The Danube River, which flows into the Black Sea, has Europe's largest delta. It is home to more than 300 bird species and 160 kinds of fish.

Map labels:

MOLDOVA
UKRAINE
HUNGARY
AUSTRIA
ITALY
ROMANIA
BULGARIA
SERBIA
CROATIA
SLOVENIA
BOSNIA & HERZEGOVINA
MONTENEGRO
KOSOVO

Carpathian Mountains
Transylvanian Mountains
Balkan Mountains

White spoonbill
White pelican
White-headed duck
Tulcea
Constanta
Dobrich
Varna
Martenitsa dolls
Burgas
Sirvachkari ceremony
Sliven
Stara Zagora
Shipka Memorial Tower
Rila Monastery
Alexander Newski Cathedral
Sofia
Pleven
Ruse
Pharmaceuticals
Craiova
Wheat
Danube
Oltu
Peles Castle
Triumphal Arch
Bucharest
Ploiesti
Wine
Roses and rose oil
Wels catfish
Brasov
Bran Castle
Braila
Sibiu
Tirgu Mures
Cluj
Roma people
Bacau
Sheep
Iasi
Shepherd
Traditional costume
Maramures wooden church
Oradea
Oil
Arad
Timisoara
Timisoara Catholic Cathedral
Donkey cart
Nis
National costume
Kragujevac
Belgrade
Novi Pazar
Mitrovice
Pristina
Prizren
Shkoder
Uzice
Pljevlja
Niksic
Podgorica
Budva
Dubrovnik
Corn
Sava
Danube
Novi Sad
Subotica
Potatoes
Osijek
Vukovar
Brcko
Cevapcici
Zenica
Sarajevo
Prijedor
Bihac
Timber
Mostar
Mostar bridge
Tourism
Split
Sibenik
Diocletian's Palace
Zadar
Traditional dance
Rijeka
Zagreb
St. Mark's Church
Maribor
Celje
Bled Island
Grapes
Sava
Ljubljana
Koper
Jesenice
Old Town
Adriatic Sea

72

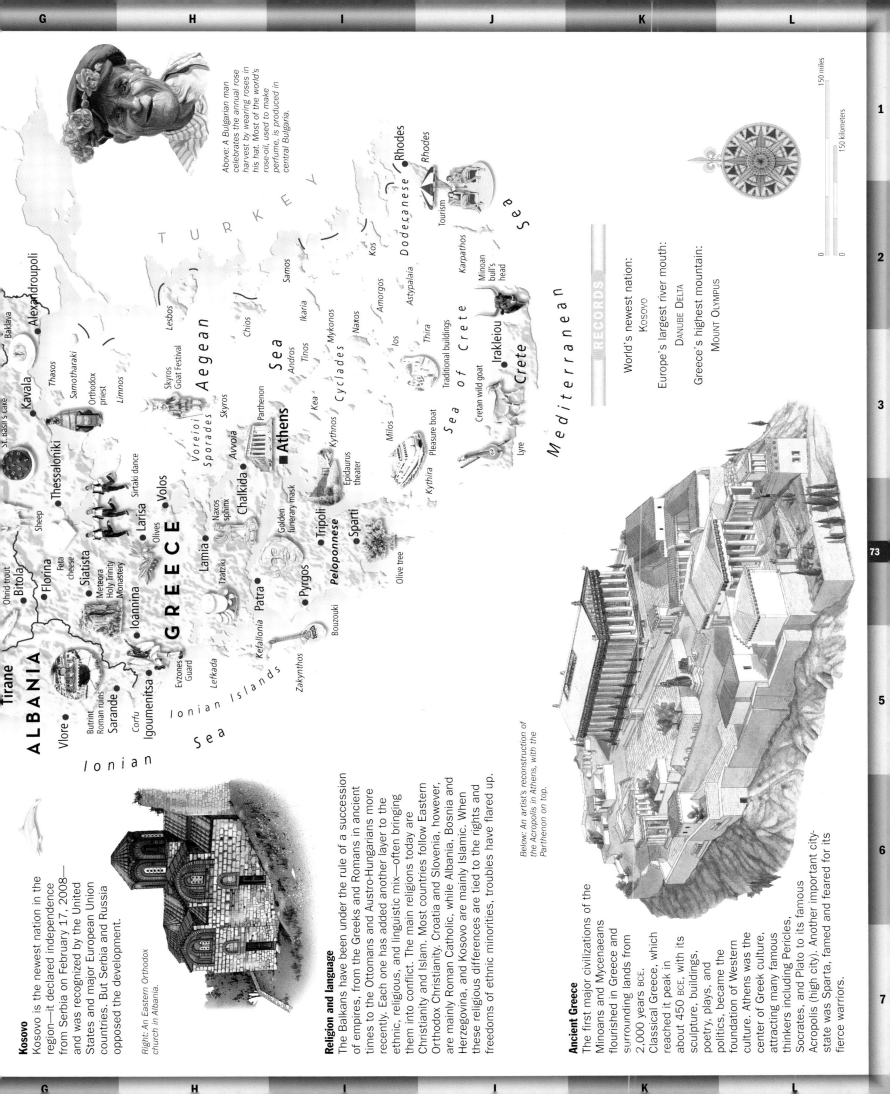

Above: A Bulgarian man celebrates the annual rose harvest by wearing roses in his hat. Most of the world's rose-oil, used to make perfume, is produced in central Bulgaria.

RECORDS

World's newest nation:
KOSOVO

Europe's largest river mouth:
DANUBE DELTA

Greece's highest mountain:
MOUNT OLYMPUS

150 miles
150 kilometers

Map labels:

Baklava
Alexandroupoli
Kavala
St. Basil's cake
Thasos
Samothraki
Orthodox priest
Limnos
Lesbos
Skyros Goat Festival
Skyros
Voreioi Sporades
Thessaloniki
Sheep
Ohrid trout
Bitola
Florina
Feta cheese
Siatista
Meteora Holy Trinity Monastery
Larisa
Sirtaki dance
Volos
Olives
Olive tree
Ioannina
Lamia
Naxos sphinx
Chalkida
Avvoia
Golden funerary mask
Parthenon
Athens
Kea
Kythnos
Epidaurus theater
Milos
Tripoli
Peloponnese
Sparti
GREECE
Tzatziki
Patra
Bouzouki
Pyrgos
Kefallonia
Lefkada
Evzones Guard
Zakynthos
Igoumenitsa
Corfu
Ionian Sea Islands
Ionian Sea
Butrint Roman ruins
Sarande
Vlore
ALBANIA
Tirane

Cyclades
Andros
Tinos
Mykonos
Ikaria
Chios
Samos
Kos
Amorgos
Ios
Thira
Astypalaia
Naxos
Kythira
Pleasure boat
Aegean Sea
Dodecanese
Rhodes
Tourism
Karpathos
Minoan bull's head
Sea of Crete
Irakleiou
Crete
Cretan wild goat
Lyre
Traditional buildings
Mediterranean Sea
TURKEY

Kosovo

Kosovo is the newest nation in the region—it declared independence from Serbia on February 17, 2008—and was recognized by the United States and major European Union countries. But Serbia and Russia opposed the development.

Right: An Eastern Orthodox church in Albania.

Religion and language

The Balkans have been under the rule of a succession of empires, from the Greeks and Romans in ancient times to the Ottomans and Austro-Hungarians more recently. Each one has added another layer to the ethnic, religious, and linguistic mix—often bringing them into conflict. The main religions today are Christianity and Islam. Most countries follow Eastern Orthodox Christianity. Croatia and Slovenia, however, are mainly Roman Catholic, while Albania, Bosnia and Herzegovina, and Kosovo are mainly Islamic. When these religious differences are tied to the rights and freedoms of ethnic minorities, troubles have flared up.

Below: An artist's reconstruction of the Acropolis in Athens, with the Parthenon on top.

Ancient Greece

The first major civilizations of the Minoans and Mycenaeans flourished in Greece and surrounding lands from 2,000 years BCE. Classical Greece, which reached it peak in about 450 BCE, with its sculpture, buildings, poetry, plays, and politics, became the foundation of Western culture. Athens was the center of Greek culture, attracting many famous thinkers including Pericles, Socrates, and Plato to its famous Acropolis (high city). Another important city-state was Sparta, famed and feared for its fierce warriors.

73

Central Europe

This region encompasses the Baltic States in the north, Poland, and the landlocked countries of the Czech Republic, Slovakia, and Hungary to the south. These countries all have enjoyed strong economic growth and they all joined the European Union on May 1, 2004. The Carpathians are the tallest mountains in the region, with peaks rising more than 8,500 feet (2,600 m) in the Tatras between Poland and Slovakia. Stretching for almost 1,000 miles (1,500 km), they are the longest mountain chain in Europe. Just over half of Hungary lies in the plains formed by the Carpathian Basin. North of the Carpathians, Poland has almost 10,000 lakes, second only to Finland on the European continent. Forests cover almost 30 percent of Poland and more than half is dedicated to farming.

Right: Well educated, skilled workers increase the potential for economic growth.

Industry

Poland and the Czech Republic are major producers of iron, steel, cars, ships, industrial machinery, and beer. Poland is a major exporter of coal and metals. It is also rich in natural mineral resources, including rock salt. Miners in the Wieliczka salt mine, which has been worked since the 13th century, have a tradition of carving statues from the salt and the mine now contains entire churches, a museum, many statues, and a sanatorium—all carved from salt! The mine is now on the UNESCO World Heritage List and receives more than one million visitors every year.

Bohemian glass

Bohemia, now part of the Czech Republic, has been famous for its decorative glass since Renaissance times. Hand-blown and cut figurines and glassware are important export items.

The Baltic Tigers

Estonia, Latvia, and Lithuania all border the Baltic Sea and are known together as the Baltic States. They are also known as the Baltic Tigers because they had the strongest economic growth in Europe during the first few years of the 21st century. The three countries have distinct, yet overlapping cultures and traditions.

Above: Considered sacred in pagan times, the oak tree still holds a special place in the minds of people in the Baltic States.

Above: The Europa Tower, in Vilnius, stands 486 feet (148 m) tall. The tallest skyscraper in the Baltic States, it is a symbol of economic rebirth in the region.

RUSSIAN FEDERATION

BELARUS

Gulf of Finland

Narva
Kunda
Alexander Nevsky Cathedral
Tallinn
Lake Peipus
Tartu
Valga
Easter eggs
Timber
E S T O N I A
Haapsalu
Hiiumaa
Muhu
Saaremaa
Windmill
Parnu
Gulf of Riga

Aluksne
Rezekne
European hare
Daugavpils
Dvina
Valmiera
House of Blackheads
Jekabpils
Riga
Western
L A T V I A
Ventspils
Mining
Amber
Potatoes
Liepaja

Utena
Beets
Europa Tower
Vilnius
Panevezys
Kelme
Mazeikiai
Jelgava
Kaunas
L I T H U A N I A
Mariampole
Klaipeda

Zubr (European

Easter palms
Bialystok

Baltic Sea

RUSSIAN FEDERATION

Kaliningrad
Gdynia
Gdansk
Elblag
Olsztyn
Queen of the Harvest Festival
Malbork
Teutonic Castle
Grudziadz
Koszalin
Vodka
Gdansk port
Amber
Farming
Swinoujscie
Szczecin

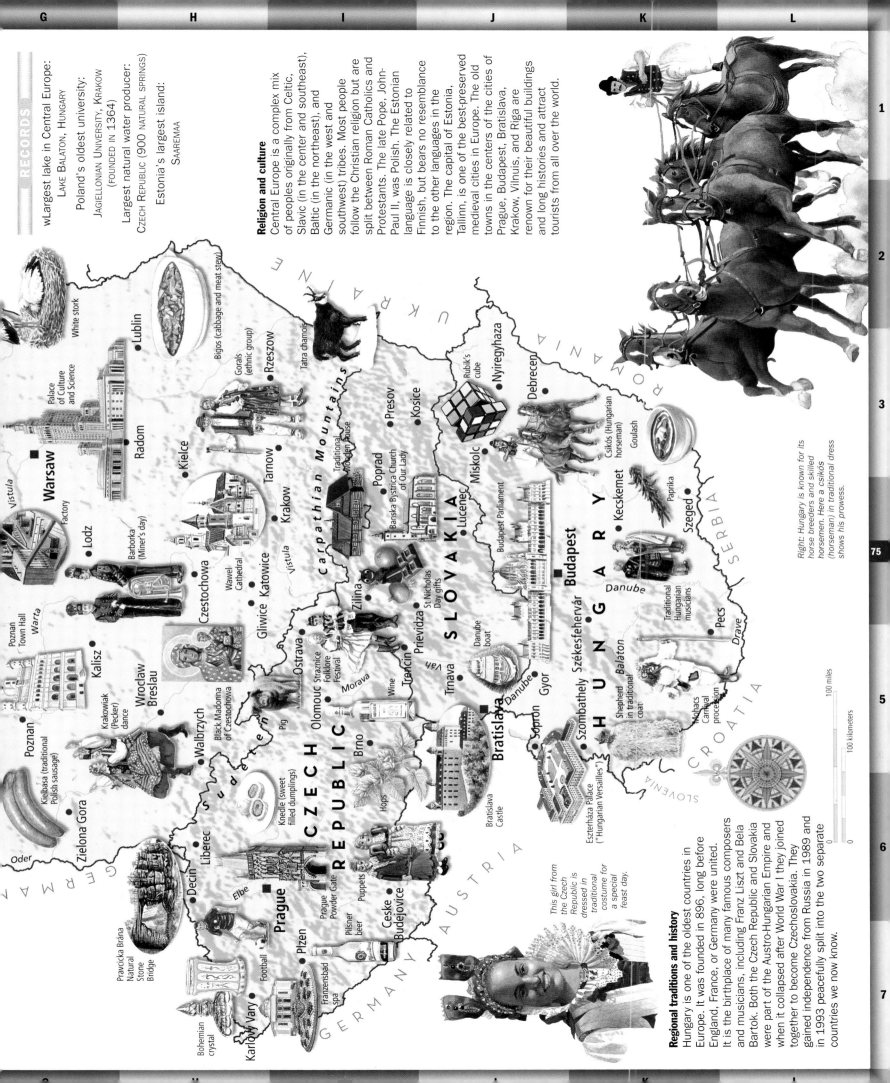

RECORDS

Largest lake in Central Europe:
LAKE BALATON, HUNGARY

Poland's oldest university:
JAGIELLONIAN UNIVERSITY, KRAKOW (FOUNDED IN 1364)

Largest natural water producer:
CZECH REPUBLIC (900 NATURAL SPRINGS)

Estonia's largest island:
SAAREMAA

Religion and culture

Central Europe is a complex mix of peoples originally from Celtic, Slavic (in the center and southeast), Baltic (in the northeast), and Germanic (in the west and southwest) tribes. Most people follow the Christian religion but are split between Roman Catholics and Protestants. The late Pope, John-Paul II, was Polish. The Estonian language is closely related to Finnish, but bears no resemblance to the other languages in the region. The capital of Estonia, Tallinn, is one of the best-preserved medieval cities in Europe. The old towns in the centers of the cities of Prague, Budapest, Bratislava, Krakow, Vilnuis, and Riga are renowned for their beautiful buildings and long histories and attract tourists from all over the world.

Regional traditions and history

Hungary is one of the oldest countries in Europe. It was founded in 896, long before England, France, or Germany were united. It is the birthplace of many famous composers and musicians, including Franz Liszt and Bela Bartok. Both the Czech Republic and Slovakia were part of the Austro-Hungarian Empire and when it collapsed after World War I they joined together to become Czechoslovakia. They gained independence from Russia in 1989 and in 1993 peacefully split into the two separate countries we now know.

This girl from the Czech Republic is dressed in traditional costume for a special feast day.

Right: Hungary is known for its horse breeders and skilled horsemen. Here a csikós (horseman) in traditional dress shows his prowess.

75

Map labels

White stork

Lublin

Bigos (cabbage and meat stew)

Gorals (ethnic group)

Rzeszow

Tatra chamois

U K R A I N E

R O M A N I A

Palace of Culture and Science

Radom

Kielce

Tarnow

Barborka (Miner's day)

Krakow

Wawel Cathedral

Czestochowa

Katowice

Gliwice

Vistula

Presov

Kosice

Rubik's cube

Nyiregyhaza

Debrecen

Miskolc

Traditional Wooden House

Poprad

Banska Bystrica Church of Our Lady

St Nicholas Day gifts

Csikós (Hungarian horseman)

Goulash

Warsaw

Vistula

Factory

Lodz

Black Madonna of Czestochowa

Poznan Town Hall

Warta

Kalisz

Wroclaw Breslau

Krakowiak (Pecker) dance

Poznan

Kielbasa (traditional Polish sausage)

Zielona Gora

Oder

Walbrzych

Knedle (sweet filled dumplings)

Pig

S u d e t e n

Olomouc

Strażnice Folklore Festival

Zilina

Trencin

Prievidza

Morava

Wine

C a r p a t h i a n M o u n t a i n s

S L O V A K I A

Budapest Parliament

Kecskemet

Paprika

Szeged

S E R B I A

Budapest

Danube

Traditional Hungarian musicians

Pecs

Drave

Danube boat

Trnava

Vah

Bratislava

Danube

Gyor

Sopron

Szekesfehervar

Szombathely

H U N G A R Y

Balaton

Shepherd in traditional coat

Mohacs Carnival procession

C R O A T I A

S L O V E N I A

Ostrava

Brno

Hops

C Z E C H R E P U B L I C

Bratislava Castle

Eszterháza Palace ("Hungarian Versailles")

Pravcicka Brana Natural Stone Bridge

Liberec

Decin

Elbe

Prague

Prague Powder Gate

Puppets

Pilsner beer

Ceske Budejovice

Plzen

Karlovy Vary

Franzensbad spa

Football

Bohemian crystal

G E R M A N Y

A U S T R I A

100 miles

100 kilometers

Eastern Europe

Eastern Europe today consists of the Russian Federation, only a quarter of which lies in Europe, (the rest is on the Asian continent), and the independent states of Belarus, Ukraine, and Moldova. The region stretches from the Crimea in the south, where the summers are hot and the winters mild, to the freezing Arctic north. Most of the land is steppe (fertile rolling grasslands) and forests, with vast areas of tundra in the north. The Ural Mountains divide the European steppes and forests of the Russian Federation from the tundra and forests of Siberia (see pages 84–85). The economy of the Ukraine—Europe's second largest country—declined steeply after the collapse of the Soviet Union, but it is now growing steadily despite political instability and corruption. Steel is the Ukraine's top export product. Moldova has fertile farmlands and it exports agricultural products and wine to Russia and other European countries. Belarus maintains strong economic ties with Russia.

The new Russia

Over 70 percent of Russians—about 100 million people—live in the European part of Russia where there is a milder climate, more fertile farmlands, and better economic conditions than in Siberia. Many live in the large cities of St. Petersburg and Moscow. Russia was once the leader of the Soviet Union, which had 15 countries under Communist rule. This broke up in 1991, and Russia, along with the other states, is now an independent republic. Russia has immense natural resources and has the world's largest reserves of energy, minerals, and timber. Industries include mining, chemicals, aircraft and space vehicles, electronics, and machinery. The Russian economy is growing quickly, although growth is mainly concentrated around Moscow and other large cities.

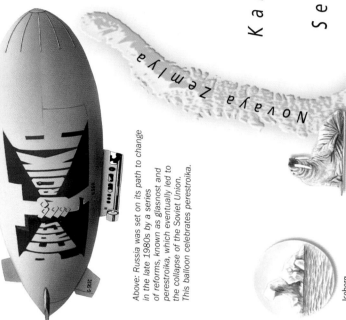

Above: Russia was set on its path to change in the late 1980s by a series of reforms, known as glasnost and perestroika, which eventually led to the collapse of the Soviet Union. This balloon celebrates perestroika.

Willow ptarmigan

Birch bark trinket box

Ural Mountain

Kara Sea

Novaya Zemlya

Amderma

Vorkuta

Pechora

National costume

Barnacle goose

Nar'yan Mar

Ukhta

Brown bear

Syktyvkar

Matrioska dolls

Samovar

Gray wolf

Walrus

Barents Sea

Kotlas

Iceberg

Mezen'

Northern Dvina

Vel'sk

Ice breaker

Salmon

Arkhangel'sk

Wooden church on Kizhi Island (Lake Onega)

Murmansk

White Sea

Belomorsk

St Petersburg Winter Palace

Ermine

Lake Onega

Lemming

Petrozavodsk

NORWAY

Lake Ladoga

FINLAND

Vyborg

Gulf of Finland

R U S S I A N   F E D E R A T I O N

Orsk

Orenburg

Ufa

Mining

Chess set

Kazan'

Kama

Ul'yanovsk

Samara

Car factories

Saransk

Kuznetsk

Saratov

Penza

Volga

Nizhniy Novgorod

Balalaika

Tambov

Vladimir

Vodka

VODKA

Russian Orthodox priest

Ryazan'

Moscow

Volga

Tula

Dacha

Bolshoi Theater

Voronezh

Kursk

Don

Bryansk

Smolensk

Chernihiv

Velikiy Novgorod

Pskov

Polotsk

B E L A R U S

Minsk

Homyel'

Black bread

Sumy

Kiev

Painted Easter eggs

Kharkiv

Poltava

Dnieper

U K R A I N E

Dnipropetrovs'k

Kirovograd

Donets'k

Rostov-na-Donu

Don

Berdyans'k

Sea of Azov

Cherries

Kherson

Odessa

Swallow's Nest Castle

Crimea Kerch

Sevastopol'

Yalta

Black Sea

Draniki

St. Sophia Cathedral

Chernobyl

Rivne

Balti

Chişinău

MOLDOVA

Tiraspol

Cahul

Borscht

Dniester

L'viv

Wine Festival

VALOGHI

Uzhhorod

R O M A N I A

P O L A N D

Kaliningrad **RUSSIAN FEDERATION**

LITHUANIA

Church of St. Simon and St. Helena

Kamenets White Tower

Hrodna

Brest

Pinsk

LATVIA

Baltic S...

Volga

K A Z A K H S T A N

Caspian gold
The Caspian Sea is Europe's largest enclosed body of water and, despite its name, many people consider it to be a lake. It stretches 750 miles (1,200 km), north to south, though its average width is only 200 miles (320 km). It is famous for its many sturgeon fish which lay eggs that are made into caviar—one of the world's most expensive foods. However, huge untapped oil and gas reserves are now more important to the world and in 2005 a new pipeline started carrying this "black gold" to Europe.

Caspian Sea

Astrakhan'

Caspian Depression

Volga

Volga cruise boat

Volgograd

Oil refinery

Grozny

Armavir

Elbrus

C a u c a s u s

G E O R G I A

A Z E R B A I J A N

Icon showing St. George (Patron Saint of Russia)

Novorossiysk

The Russian Orthodox Church
The Russian landscape is dotted with churches, monasteries, and former fortresses belonging to the Orthodox tradition of Christianity. They are easily recognizable by their golden or other brightly decorated mushroom-shaped domes. This religion—which is separate from the Roman Catholic Church under the Pope—was adopted by the first Russian state around Kiev in the 11th century. The Orthodox Church is also famous for its icons—flat panel paintings of holy beings or objects, often on wood or metal, and sometimes etched with gold.

Above: A fisherman at Astrakhan, at the mouth of the Volga River, shakes out a net full of sturgeon fish.

400 miles

400 kilometers

Right: This detail from an icon shows the first two Russian saints, Borsi and Gleb.

77

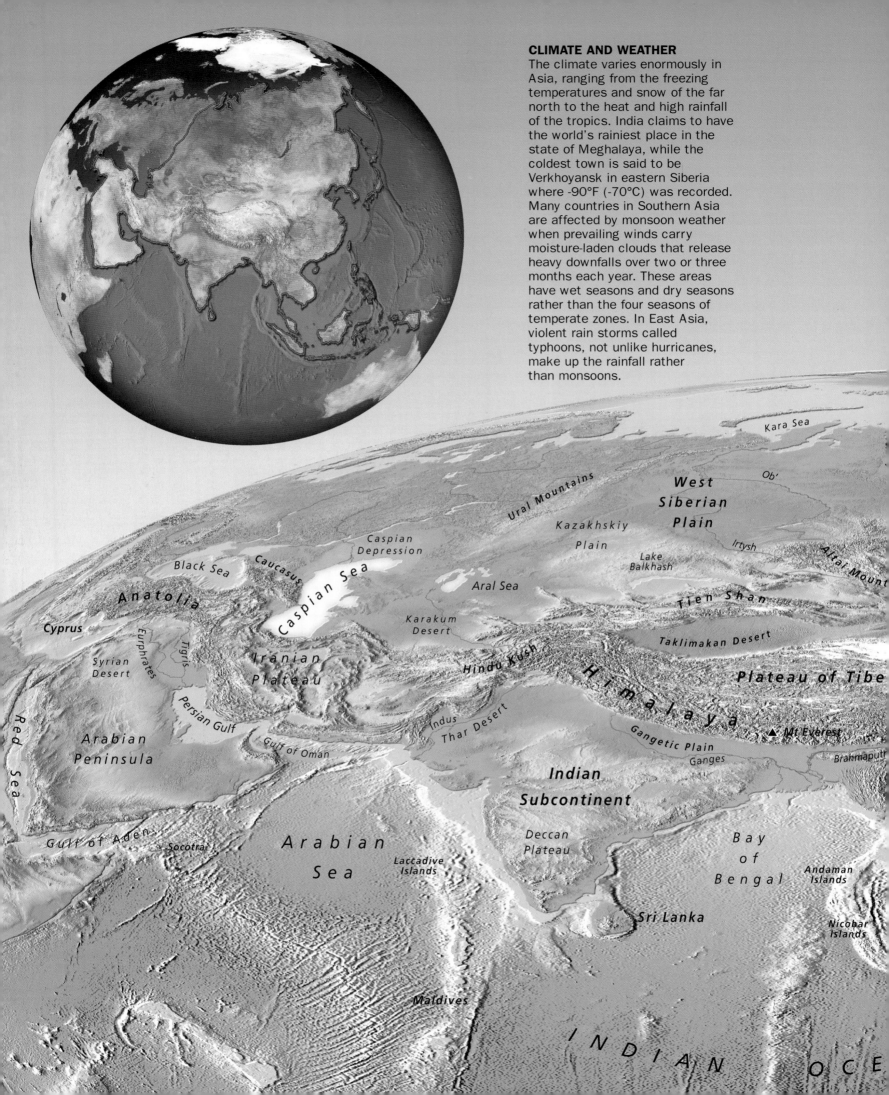

CLIMATE AND WEATHER

The climate varies enormously in Asia, ranging from the freezing temperatures and snow of the far north to the heat and high rainfall of the tropics. India claims to have the world's rainiest place in the state of Meghalaya, while the coldest town is said to be Verkhoyansk in eastern Siberia where -90°F (-70°C) was recorded. Many countries in Southern Asia are affected by monsoon weather when prevailing winds carry moisture-laden clouds that release heavy downfalls over two or three months each year. These areas have wet seasons and dry seasons rather than the four seasons of temperate zones. In East Asia, violent rain storms called typhoons, not unlike hurricanes, make up the rainfall rather than monsoons.

Kara Sea

Ob'

West
Siberian
Plain

Ural Mountains

Irtysh

Kazakhskiy
Plain

Altai Mount

Caspian
Depression

Lake
Balkhash

Black Sea

Caucasus

Aral Sea

Tien Shan

Anatolia

Caspian Sea

Taklimakan Desert

Cyprus

Karakum
Desert

Euphrates

Tigris

Iranian
Plateau

Hindu Kush

H i m a l a y a

Plateau of Tibe

Syrian
Desert

Persian Gulf

Indus

Gangetic Plain

▲ Mt Everest

Red
Sea

Arabian
Peninsula

Gulf of Oman

Thar Desert

Ganges

Brahmaput

Gulf of Aden

Socotra

Arabian

Sea

Indian

Subcontinent

Deccan
Plateau

Bay
of
Bengal

Laccadive
Islands

Andaman
Islands

Sri Lanka

Nicobar
Islands

Maldives

I N D I A N   O C E

ASIA

The largest continent in the world, Asia lies next to Europe but is four times bigger and takes up almost one-third of the world's total land area. It is a continent of extremes, with the world's tallest mountain—Mount Everest—and 90 of the planet's 100 highest peaks. It also has the world's lowest point—the Dead Sea—and its largest lake—the Caspian Sea. Like North America, it stretches from the freezing Arctic Circle down to the humid tropics and the Equator. In the north lies Siberia with its huge belt of conifer forests, called the taiga. The climate here is harsh and cold, with little seasonal variation. Above the forests, on the northern fringe of Asia, the tundra is a kind of freezing desert. South of the forests the vast Central Asian steppe (grasslands) sweeps across the continent, then gradually gives way to deserts, high plateaus, and some of the greatest mountain ranges in the world, including the Himalayas, the Tan Shan, and the Hindu Kush. Further south, there are large fertile plains as well as tropical forests in China and India. Southeast Asia is a region of tropical rain forest and volcanic islands—Indonesia alone has more than 17,000 islands.

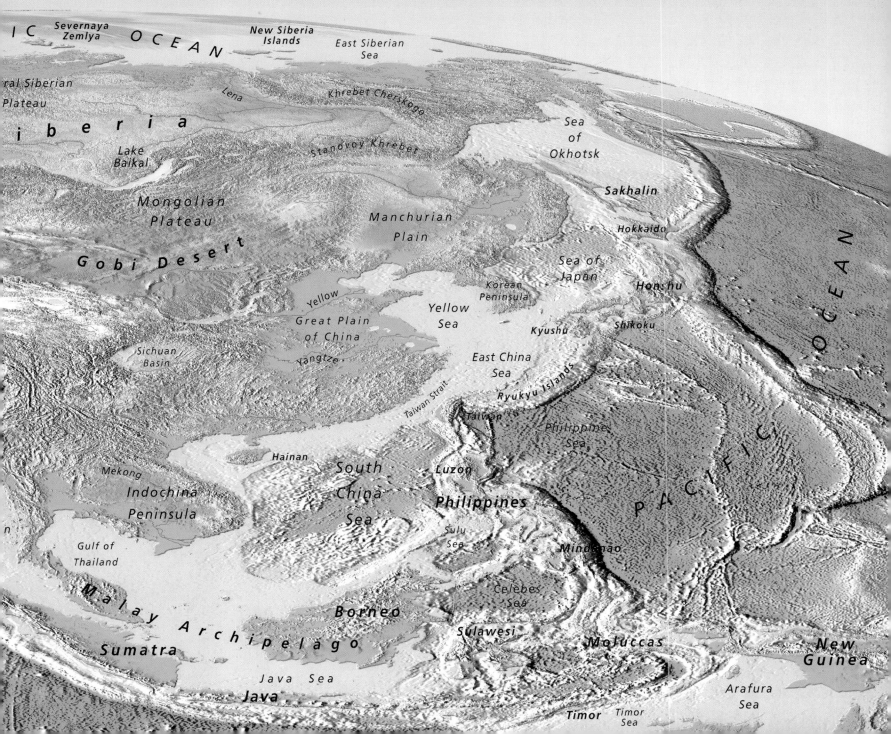

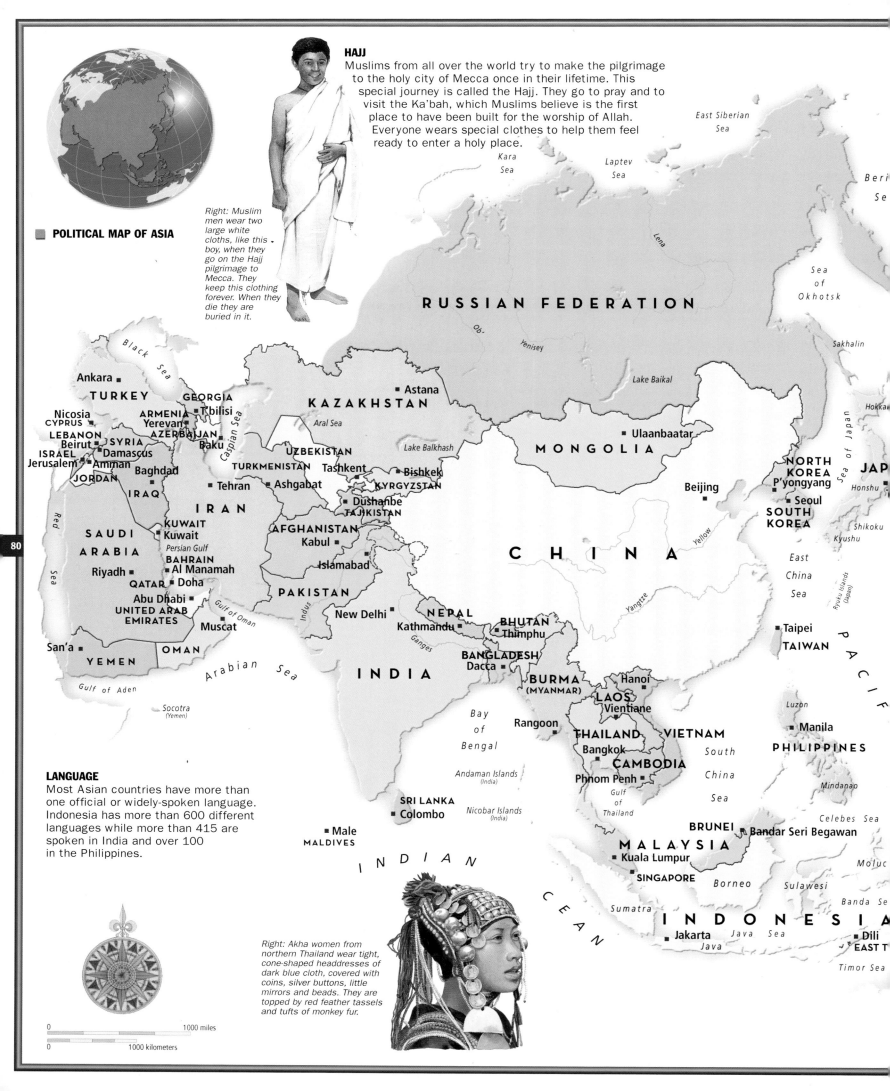

HAJJ

Muslims from all over the world try to make the pilgrimage to the holy city of Mecca once in their lifetime. This special journey is called the Hajj. They go to pray and to visit the Ka'bah, which Muslims believe is the first place to have been built for the worship of Allah. Everyone wears special clothes to help them feel ready to enter a holy place.

Right: Muslim men wear two large white cloths, like this boy, when they go on the Hajj pilgrimage to Mecca. They keep this clothing forever. When they die they are buried in it.

POLITICAL MAP OF ASIA

LANGUAGE

Most Asian countries have more than one official or widely-spoken language. Indonesia has more than 600 different languages while more than 415 are spoken in India and over 100 in the Philippines.

Right: Akha women from northern Thailand wear tight, cone-shaped headdresses of dark blue cloth, covered with coins, silver buttons, little mirrors and beads. They are topped by red feather tassels and tufts of monkey fur.

East Siberian Sea

Kara Sea

Laptev Sea

Beri Se

RUSSIAN FEDERATION

Ob'

Yenisey

Lena

Lake Baikal

Sea of Okhotsk

Sakhalin

Black Sea

Ankara ■

TURKEY

GEORGIA
ARMENIA ■ T'bilisi
Nicosia Yerevan
CYPRUS ■ **AZERBAIJAN**
LEBANON **SYRIA** Baku
Beirut ■ Damascus
ISRAEL
Jerusalem ■ Amman
JORDAN Baghdad
IRAQ

IRAN

KAZAKHSTAN

■ Astana

Aral Sea

UZBEKISTAN
Tashkent
TURKMENISTAN ■ Bishkek
Ashgabat **KYRGYZSTAN**
■ Dushanbe
Tehran **TAJIKISTAN**

AFGHANISTAN
Kabul ■

Lake Balkhash

MONGOLIA
■ Ulaanbaatar

Caspian Sea

Beijing

Sea of Japan

NORTH KOREA
P'yongyang

JAP
Honshu

■ Seoul
SOUTH KOREA

Shikoku
Kyushu

Hokka

Red Sea

SAUDI ARABIA
KUWAIT
■ Kuwait
Riyadh ■ **BAHRAIN**
■ Al Manamah
QATAR ■ Doha
Abu Dhabi ■
UNITED ARAB EMIRATES
■ Muscat

Persian Gulf

Islamabad

PAKISTAN

Indus

CHINA

Yellow

Yangtze

East China Sea

Ryuku Islands (Japan)

■ Taipei
TAIWAN

San'a

YEMEN **OMAN**

Gulf of Oman

Gulf of Aden

Socotra (Yemen)

Arabian Sea

New Delhi ■

INDIA

NEPAL
Kathmandu ■ **BHUTAN**
■ Thimphu

Ganges

BANGLADESH
Dacca ■

BURMA (MYANMAR)

Hanoi ■

LAOS
■ Vientiane

Rangoon ■

THAILAND **VIETNAM**
Bangkok ■ South China Sea

CAMBODIA
Phnom Penh ■

Gulf of Thailand

Luzon

■ Manila

PHILIPPINES

Mindanao

PACIF

Bay of Bengal

Andaman Islands (India)

SRI LANKA
■ Colombo

Nicobar Islands (India)

■ Male
MALDIVES

INDIAN

OCEAN

BRUNEI
■ Bandar Seri Begawan

MALAYSIA
■ Kuala Lumpur
■ **SINGAPORE**

Borneo

Sumatra

Celebes Sea

Moluc

Sulawesi

Banda Se

INDONESIA

■ Jakarta
Java Java Sea

■ Dili
EAST T

Timor Sea

0 ——— 1000 miles

0 ——— 1000 kilometers

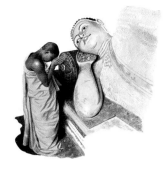
Above: A monk bends prayerfully toward a reclining Buddha statue in Sri Lanka.

Asia

With over four billion inhabitants (more than 60 percent of the world's population), Asia is by far the most populous continent. It encompasses a huge variety of peoples, economies, and belief systems, from the oil-rich Islamic states of the Middle East, to Southern Asia with its Hindu and Muslim mix, and from communist China and unique Japan in East Asia, to the burgeoning economies of Southeast Asia. Most Asians live in the east and south; population density in Siberia in the north is about 2.7 people per square kilometer, whereas there are 1,045 people per square kilometer in Bangladesh and 18,428 in Macau! Recent decades have seen strong economic growth in many parts of Asia, beginning with Japan and then spreading to South Korea, Hong Kong, Singapore, and Taiwan (the so-called Asian Tigers), and more recently to China and India. Annual growth of GDP (gross domestic product) has averaged eight percent in China for more than two decades, while Indian GDP growth rate reached nine percent in 2007.

Right: The Chinese are famous for four great inventions: paper, printing, gunpowder, and the compass. This clock tower, built in 1090, used a chain drive—another Chinese invention—to function.

RELIGION
Asia is the birthplace of almost all the world's major religions, including Hinduism, Taoism, Confucianism, Buddhism, Shinto, Judaism, Christianity, Islam, and Sikhism, as well as many smaller, local religions. Today, Islam is the main religion in the region, from Arabia to Indonesia. Most people in India and Nepal are Hindus, while Buddishm is predominant in Thailand, Cambodia, and Bura (Myanmar). Orthodox Christianity is the main religion in Armenia and Georgia, while Judaism is practised in Israel.

EVIRONMENTAL ISSUES
As Asian countries grow richer more and more people own cars that pollute the air, work in factories that emit greenhouse gases that damage the atmosphere, and generally adopt more comfortable—and wasteful—Western ways of life. Given the size of the population of Asia this is a pressing issue and governments and environmental groups are working to try to reduce the impact wealthier lifestyles can have on the natural world.

GREAT CIVILIZATIONS
Many of the great civilizations of the past grew up in Asia. In the Near East, the Mesopotamians established large empires and were among the first to use a written language. Another complex civilization flourished in the Indus Valley, in what is now Pakistan. In the Far East, the Chinese began farming the river valleys more than 7,500 years ago. By the 21st century BCE they had invented a writing system, domesticated the horse, and were learning to smelt bronze.

Below: Many large Asian cities are very polluted. People often wear disposable paper masks over their mouths when they go out in heavy traffic.

Irian Jaya

fura
ea

TURKEY
Country name Republic of Turkey
Area 301,383 sq mi (780,580 sq km)
Population 71,892,807
Government Parliamentary republic
Capital Ankara
Currency Turkish lira
Languages Turkish, Kurdish, Dimli (or Zaza), Azeri, Kabardian, Arabic
Main religions Muslim 99.8% (mostly Sunni)
Literacy 87.4%
GDP per capita $12,900 (2007 est.)

GEORGIA
Country name Georgia
Area 26,911 sq mi (69,700 sq km)
Population 4,630,841
Government Parliamentary republic
Capital T'bilisi
Currency Lari
Languages Georgian, Russian, Armenian, Azeri, Abkhaz
Main religions Orthodox Christian 83.9%, Muslim 9.9%, Armenian-Gregorian 3.9%, Catholic 0.8%
Literacy 100%
GDP per capita $4,700 (2007 est.)

ARMENIA
Country name Republic of Armenia
Area 11,505 sq mi (29,800 sq km)
Population 2,968,586
Government Parliamentary republic
Capital Yerevan
Currency Dram
Languages Armenian, Yezidi, Russian
Main religions Armenian Apostolic 94.7%, other Christian 4%, Yezidi 1.3%
Literacy 99.4%
GDP per capita $4,900 (2007 est.)

AZERBAIJAN
Country name Republic of Azerbaijan
Area 33,436 sq mi (86,600 sq km)
Population 8,177,717
Government Parliamentary republic
Capital Baku
Currency Azerbaijani manat
Languages Azeri, Lezgi, Russian, Armenian
Main religions Muslim 93.4%, Russian Orthodox 2.5%, Armenian Orthodox 2.3%
Literacy 98.8%
GDP per capita $7,700 (2007 est.)

KAZAKSTAN
Country name Republic of Kazakh
Area 1,049,155 sq mi (2,717,300 sq km)
Population 15,340,533
Government Republic with authoritarian presidential rule
Capital Astana
Currency Tenge
Languages Kazakh, Russian, Ukranian, Uzbek, German
Main religions Muslim 47%, Russian Orthodox 44%, Protestant 2%
Literacy 99.5%
GDP per capita $11,100 (2007 est.)

UZBEKISTAN
Country name Republic of Uzbekistan
Area 172,742 sq mi (447,400 sq km)
Population 28,268,440
Government Republic with authoritarian presidential rule
Capital Tashkent
Currency Soum
Languages Uzbek, Russian, Tajik
Main religions Muslim 88% (mostly Sunni), Eastern Orthodox 9%
Literacy 99.3%
GDP per capita $2,300 (2007 est.)

TURKMENISTAN
Country name Turkmenistan
Area 188,456 sq mi (488,100 sq km)
Population 5,179,571
Government Republic with authoritarian presidential rule
Capital Ashgabat
Currency Turkmen manat
Languages Turkmen, Russian, Uzbek
Main religions Muslim 89%, Eastern Orthodox 9%
Literacy 98.8%
GDP per capita $5,200 (2007 est.)

KYRGYZSTAN
Country name Kyrgyz Republic
Area 76,641 sq mi (198,500 sq km)
Population 5,356,869
Government Republic
Capital Bishkek
Currency Som
Languages Kyrgyz, Russian, Uzbek, Dungun
Main religions Muslim 75%, Russian Orthodox 20%
Literacy 98.7%
GDP per capita $2,000 (2007 est.)

TAJIKISTAN

Country name Republic of Tajikistan
Area 55,251sq mi
(143,100 sq km)
Population 7,211,884
Government Republic
Capital Dushanbe
Currency Somoni
Languages Tajik, Russian
Main religions Sunni Muslim 85%,
Shi'a Muslim 5%
Literacy 99.5%
GDP per capita $1,800 (2007 est.)

SYRIA

Country name Syrian Arab Republic
Area 71,498 sq mi
(185,180 sq km)
Population 19,747,586
Government Republic
Capital Damascus
Currency Syrian pound
Languages Arabic, Kurdish,
Armenian, Aramaic, Circassian
Main religions Sunni Muslim 74%,
other Muslim 16%, Christian 10%
Literacy 79.6%
GDP per capita $4,500 (2007 est.)

LEBANON

Country name Lebanese Republic
Area 4,015 sq mi (10,400 sq km)
Population 3,971,941
Government Republic
Capital Beirut
Currency Lebanese pound
Languages Arabic, French, English,
Armenian
Main religions Muslim 59.7% (Shi'a,
Sunni, Druze, Isma'ilite, Alawite or
Nusayri), Christian 39%
Literacy 87.4%
GDP per capita $11,300 (2007 est.)

ISRAEL

Country name State of Israel
Area 8,019.34 sq mi
(20,770 sq km)
Population 7,112,359
Government Parliamentary republic
Capital Jerusalem
Currency New Israeli shekel
Languages Hebrew, Arabic, English
Main religions Jewish 76.4%,
Muslim 16%, Arab Christians 1.7%
Literacy 97.1%
GDP per capita $25,800 (2007 est.)

JORDAN

Country name Hashemite Kingdom
of Jordan
Area 35,637 sq mi (92,300 sq km)
Population 6,198,677
Government Constitutional monarchy
Capital Amman
Currency Jordanian dinar
Languages Arabic, English
Main religions Sunni Muslim 92%,
Christian 6% (majority Greek
Orthodox)
Literacy 89.9%
GDP per capita $4,900 (2007 est.)

SAUDI ARABIA

Country name Kingdom of Saudi
Arabia
Area 829,999 sq mi
(2,149,690 sq km)
Population 28,161,417
Government Monarchy
Capital Riyadh
Currency Saudi riyal
Languages Arabic
Main religions Muslim 100%
Literacy 78.8%
GDP per capita $23,200 (2007 est.)

KUWAIT

Country name State of Kuwait
Area 6,880 sq mi (17,820 sq km)
Population 2,596,799
Government Constitutional emirate
Capital Kuwait
Currency Kuwaiti dinar
Languages Arabic, English
Main religions Muslim 85% (Sunni
70%, Shi'a 30%)
Literacy 93.3%
GDP per capita $39,300 (2007 est.)

BAHRAIN

Country name Kingdom of Bahrain
Area 257 sq mi (665 sq km)
Population 718,306
Government Constitutional monarchy
Capital El Manamah
Currency Bahraini dinar
Languages Arabic, English, Farsi,
Urdu
Main religions Muslim (Shi'a and
Sunni) 81.2%, Christian 9%
Literacy 86.5%
GDP per capita $32,100 (2007 est.)

UNITED ARAB EMIRATES

Country name United Arab Emirates
Area 32,278 sq mi
(83,600 sq km)
Population 4,621,399
Government Federation of emirates
Capital Abu Dhabi
Currency Emirati dirham
Languages Arabic, Persian, English,
Hindi, Urdu
Main religions Muslim 96% (Shi'a
16%), other (includes Christian,
Hindu) 4%
Literacy 77.9%
GDP per capita $37,300 (2007 est.)

QATAR

Country name State of Qatar
Area 4,415 sq mi
(11,437 sq km)
Population 928,635
Government Emirate
Capital Doha
Currency Qatari rial
Languages Arabic, English
Main religions Muslim 77.5%,
Christian 8.5%
Literacy 89%
GDP per capita $80,900 (2007 est.)

YEMEN

Country name Republic of Yemen
Area 203,850,356 sq mi
(527,970 sq km)
Population 23,013,376
Government Republic
Capital Sanaa
Currency Yemeni rial
Languages Arabic
Main religions Muslim including
Shaf'i (Sunni) and Zaydi (Shi'a),
small numbers of Jewish, Christian,
and Hindu
Literacy 50.2%
GDP per capita $2,300 (2007 est.)

OMAN

Country name Sultanate of Oman
Area 8,2031,264 sq mi
(212,460 sq km)
Population 3,311,640
Government Monarchy
Capital Muscat
Currency Omani rial
Languages Arabic, English, Baluchi,
Urdu, Indian dialects
Main religions Ibadhi Muslim 75%,
other (includes Sunni Muslim,
Shi'a Muslim, Hindu) 25%
Literacy 81.4%
GDP per capita $24,000 (2007 est.)

IRAQ

Country name Republic of Iraq
Area 168,754.44 sq mi
(437,072 sq km)
Population 28,221,181
Government Parliamentary democracy
Capital Baghdad
Currency New Iraqi dinar
Languages Arabic, Kurdish,
Turkoman, Assyrian, Armenian
Main religions Muslim 97% (Shi'a
60%-65%, Sunni 32%-37%)
Literacy 74.1%
GDP per capita $3,600 (2007 est.)

IRAN

Country name Islamic Republic of Iran
Area 636,296.36 sq mi
(1,648,000 sq km)
Population 65,875,223
Government Theocratic republic
Capital Tehran
Currency Iranian rial
Languages Persian and Persian dialects,
Turkic languages, Luri Kurdish, Pashto,
Balochi, Gilaki, Mazandarami, Arabic
Main religions Muslim 98% (Shi'a
89%, Sunni 9%)
Literacy 77%
GDP per capita $10,600 (2007 est.)

AFGHANISTAN

Country name Islamic Republic
of Afghanistan
Area 250,001,147 sq mi
(647,500 sq km)
Population 32,738,376
Government Islamic republic
Capital Kabul
Currency Afghani
Languages Afghan Persian or Dari,
Pashto, Turkic languages, 30 minor
languages
Main religions Sunni Muslim 80%,
Shi'a Muslim 19%
Literacy 28.1%
GDP per capita $1,000 (2007 est.)

PAKISTAN

Country name Islamic Republic
of Pakistan
Area 310,402 sq mi
(803,940 sq km)
Population 167,762,040
Government Federal republic
Capital Islamabad
Currency Pakistani rupee
Languages Urdu, English, Punjabi,
Sindhi, Siraiki (a Punjabi variant),
Pashtu, Balochi, Hindko, Brahui,
Burushaski
Main religions Muslim 97% (Sunni
77%, Shi'a 20%)
Literacy 49.9%
GDP per capita $2,600 (2007 est.)

MALDIVES

Country name Republic of Maldives
Area 116 sq mi (300 sq km)
Population 379,174
Government Republic
Capital Male
Currency Rufiyaa
Languages Maldivian Dhivehi,
English
Main religions Sunni Muslim
Literacy 96.3%
GDP per capita $4,600 (2007 est.)

INDIA

Country name Republic of India
Area 1,269,345 sq mi
(3,287,590 sq km)
Population 1,147,995,898
Government Federal republic
Capital New Delhi
Currency Indian rupee
Languages Hindi, English, Assamese,
Bengali, Bodo, Dogri, Gujarati, Kannada,
Kashmiri, Maithili, Malayalam, Manipuri,
Marathi, Nepali, Oriya, Punjabi, Sanscrit,
Santhali, Sindhi, Tamil, Telugu, Urdu
Main religions Hindu 80.5%, Muslim
13.4%, Christian 2.3%, Sikh 1.9%
Literacy 61%
GDP per capita $2,700 (2007 est.)

NEPAL

Country name Nepal
Area 56,826 sq mi
(147,181 sq km)
Population 29,519,114
Government Parliamentary republic
Capital Kathmandu
Currency Nepalese rupee
Languages Nepali, Maithali,
Bhojpuri, Tharu (Dagaura/Rana),
Tamang, Newar, Magar, Awadhi
Main religions Hindu 80.6%,
Buddhist 10.7%, Muslim 4.2%,
Kirant 3.6%
Literacy 48.6%
GDP per capita $1,200 (2007 est.)

BHUTAN

Country name Kingdom of Bhutan
Area 18,146 sq mi
(47,000 sq km)
Population 682,321
Government In transition to
constitutional monarchy
Capital Thimphu
Currency Ngultrum, Indian rupee
Languages Dzongkha, Tibetan and
Nepalese dialects
Main religions Lamaistic Buddhist
75%, Indian- and Nepalese-
influenced Hinduism 25%
Literacy 47%
GDP per capita $5,200 (2007 est.)

SRI LANKA

Country name Democratic Socialist Republic of Sri Lanka
Area 25,332 sq mi (65,610 sq km)
Population 21,128,773
Government Republic
Capital Colombo
Currency Sri Lankan rupee
Languages Sinhala, Tamil, English
Main religions Buddhist 69.1%, Muslim 7.6%, Hindu 7.1%, Christian 6.2%
Literacy 90.7%
GDP per capita $4,100 (2007 est.)

BANGLADESH

Country name People's Republic of Bangladesh
Area 55,598 sq mi (144,000 sq km)
Population 153,546,901
Government Parliamentary republic
Capital Dacca
Currency Taka
Languages Bengali, English
Main religions Muslim 83%, Hindu 16%
Literacy 43.1%
GDP per capita $1,300 (2007 est.)

MYANMAR (BURMA)

Country name Union of Burma
Area 261,970 sq mi (678,500 sq km)
Population 47,758,181
Government Military junta
Capital Rangoon
Currency kyat
Languages Burmese
Main religions Buddhist 89%, Christian 4%, Muslim 4%, animist 1%
Literacy 89.9%
GDP per capita $1,900 (2007 est.)

LAOS

Country name Lao People's Democratic Republic
Area 91,429 sq mi (236,800 sq km)
Population 6,677,534
Government Communist state
Capital Vientiane
Currency Kip
Languages Lao, French, English, and various ethnic languages
Main religions Buddhist 65%, animist 32.9%, Christian 1.3%
Literacy 68.7%
GDP per capita $2,100 (2007 est.)

THAILAND

Country name Kingdom of Thailand
Area 198,456 sq mi (514,000 sq km)
Population 65,493,298
Government Constitutional monarchy
Capital Bangkok
Currency Baht
Languages Thai, Chinese, Malai, Khmer, English
Main religions Buddhist 94.6%, Muslim 4.6%, Christian 0.7%
Literacy 92.6%
GDP per capita $7,900 (2007 est.)

MALAYSIA

Country name Malaysia
Area 127,317 sq mi (329,750 sq km)
Population 25,274,133
Government Constitutional monarchy
Capital Kuala Lumpur
Currency Ringgit
Languages Bahasa Malaysia, English, Chinese dialects, Tamil, Telugu, Malayalam, Panjabi, Thai
Main religions Muslim 60.4%, Buddhist 19.2%, Christian 9.1%, Hindu 6.3%
Literacy 88.7%
GDP per capita $13,300 (2007 est.)

CAMBODIA

Country name Kingdom of Cambodia
Area 69,899 sq mi (181,040 sq km)
Population 14,241,640
Government Multiparty democracy under a constitutional monarchy
Capital Phnom Penh
Currency Riel
Languages Khmer, French, English
Main religions Theravada Buddhist 95%
Literacy 73.6%
GDP per capita $1,800 (2007 est.)

SINGAPORE

Country name Republic of Singapore
Area 267 sq mi (692.7 sq km)
Population 4,608,167
Government Parliamentary republic
Capital Singapore
Currency Singapore dollar
Languages Mandarin, English, Malay, Hokkien, Cantonese, Teochew, Tamil
Main religions Buddhist 42.5%, Muslim 14.9%, Taoist 8.5%
Literacy 92.5%
GDP per capita $49,700 (2007 est.)

BRUNEI

Country name Brunei Darussalam
Area 2,228 sq mi (5,770 sq km)
Population 381,371
Government Constitutional sultanate
Capital Bandar Seri Begawan
Currency Bruneian dollar
Languages Malay, English, Chinese
Main religions Muslim 67%, Buddhist 13%, Christian 10%
Literacy 92.7%
GDP per capita $51,000 (2007 est.)

PHILIPPINES

Country name Republic of the Philippines
Area 115,831 sq mi (300,000 sq km)
Population 92,681,453
Government Republic
Capital Manila
Currency Philippine peso
Languages Filipino, English; many dialects
Main religions Roman Catholic 80.9%, Muslim 5%
Literacy 92.6%
GDP per capita $3,400 (2007 est.)

INDONESIA

Country name Republic of Indonesia
Area 741,099 sq mi (1,919,440 sq km)
Population 237,512,355
Government Republic
Capital Jakarta
Currency Indonesian rupiah
Languages Bahasa Indonesia, English, Dutch, Javanese and other dialects
Main religions Muslim 86.1%, Protestant 5.7%, Roman Catholic 3%, Hindu 1.8%, Buddhist 1%
Literacy 90.4%
GDP per capita $3,700 (2007 est.)

EAST TIMOR

Country name Democratic Republic of Timor-Leste
Area 5,794 sq mi (15,007 sq km)
Population 1,108,777
Government Republic
Capital Dili
Currency US dollar
Languages Tetum, Portuguese, Indonesian, English, other native languages
Main religions Roman Catholic 98%, Muslim 1%, Protestant 1%
Literacy 58.6%
GDP per capita $2,500 (2007 est.)

VIETNAM

Country name Socialist Republic of Vietnam
Area 127,243 sq mi (329,560 sq km)
Population 86,116,559
Government Communist state
Capital Hanoi
Currency Dong
Languages Vietnamese, English, French, Chinese, Khmer
Main religions Buddhist 9.3%, Catholic 6.7%, Hoa Hao 1.5%, Cao Dai 1.1%
Literacy 90.3%
GDP per capita $2,600 (2007 est.)

MONGOLIA

Country name Mongolia
Area 603,908 sq mi (1,564,116 sq km)
Population 2,996,081
Government Republic
Capital Ulaanbaatar
Currency Togrog/Tugrik
Languages Mongol, Turkic, Chinese, Russian
Main religions Buddhist Lamaist 50%, Shamanist and Christian 6%, Muslim 4%, none 40%
Literacy 97.8%
GDP per capita $3,200 (2007 est.)

CHINA

Country name People's Republic of China
Area 3,705,407 sq mi (9,596,960 sq km)
Population 1,330,044,605
Government Communist state
Capital Beijing
Currency Renminbi
Languages Mandarin, Yue, Wu, Minbei, Minnan, Xiang, Gan, Hakka dialects
Main religions Officially atheist; Taoism, Buddhism, Christian 3–4%, Muslim 1–2%
Literacy 90.9%
GDP per capita $5,300 (2007 est.)

Logo of the 2008 Beijing Olympics.

SPORTS

In August 2008 China hosted the Olympic Games in Beijing. The Olympic Games are held once every four years. The 2012 Games will be held in London. Tokyo is a top contender for the 2016 Games.

TAIWAN

Country name Taiwan
Area 13,891 sq mi (35,980 sq km)
Population 22,920,946
Government Parliamentary republic
Capital Taipei
Currency New Taiwan dollar
Languages Mandarin Chinese, Taiwanese, Hakka dialects
Main religions Mixture of Buddhist and Taoist 93%, Christian 4.5%
Literacy 96.1%
GDP per capita $30,100 (2007 est.)

NORTH KOREA

Country name Democratic People's Republic of Korea
Area 46,540 sq mi (120,540 sq km)
Population 23,479,089
Government Communist dictatorship
Capital Pyongyang
Currency North Korean won
Languages Korean
Main religions Traditionally Buddhist and Confucianist, some Christian and syncretic Chondogyo
Literacy 99%
GDP per capita $1,900 (2007 est.)

SOUTH KOREA

Country name Republic of Korea
Area 38,023 sq mi (98,480 sq km)
Population 49,232,844
Government Parliamentary republic
Capital Seoul
Currency South Korean won
Languages Korean, English
Main religions Christian 26.3%, Buddhist 23.2%
Literacy 97.9%
GDP per capita $24,800 (2007 est.)

JAPAN

Country name Japan
Area 145,882 sq mi (377,835 sq km)
Population 127,288,419
Government Constitutional monarchy
Capital Tokyo
Currency Yen
Languages Japanese
Main religions Shinto and Buddhist observed together by 84%
Literacy 99%
GDP per capita $33,600 (2007 est.)

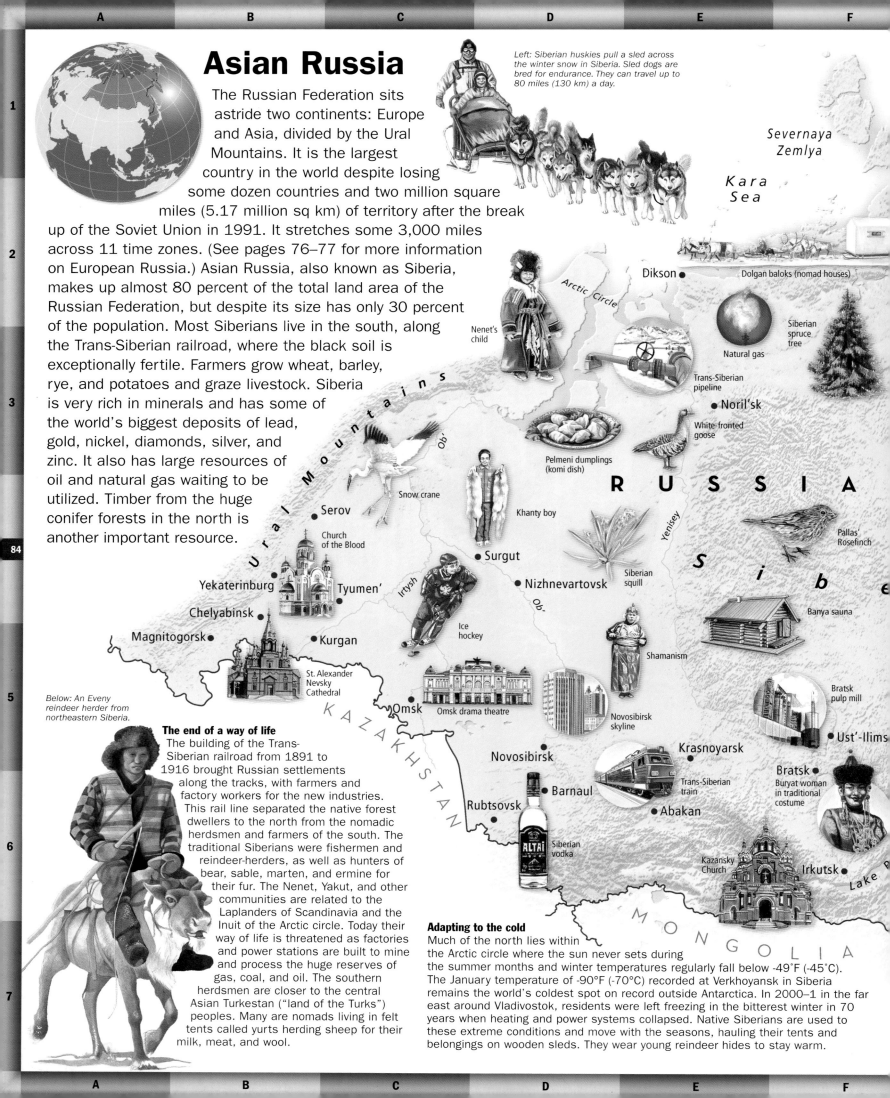

Asian Russia

The Russian Federation sits astride two continents: Europe and Asia, divided by the Ural Mountains. It is the largest country in the world despite losing some dozen countries and two million square miles (5.17 million sq km) of territory after the break up of the Soviet Union in 1991. It stretches some 3,000 miles across 11 time zones. (See pages 76–77 for more information on European Russia.) Asian Russia, also known as Siberia, makes up almost 80 percent of the total land area of the Russian Federation, but despite its size has only 30 percent of the population. Most Siberians live in the south, along the Trans-Siberian railroad, where the black soil is exceptionally fertile. Farmers grow wheat, barley, rye, and potatoes and graze livestock. Siberia is very rich in minerals and has some of the world's biggest deposits of lead, gold, nickel, diamonds, silver, and zinc. It also has large resources of oil and natural gas waiting to be utilized. Timber from the huge conifer forests in the north is another important resource.

Left: Siberian huskies pull a sled across the winter snow in Siberia. Sled dogs are bred for endurance. They can travel up to 80 miles (130 km) a day.

Severnaya Zemlya

Kara Sea

Dikson

Dolgan baloks (nomad houses)

Arctic Circle

Nenet's child

Natural gas

Siberian spruce tree

Trans-Siberian pipeline

Noril'sk

White-fronted goose

Pelmeni dumplings (komi dish)

R U S S I A

Yenisey

Pallas' Rosefinch

Snow crane

Ob'

Khanty boy

Siberian squill

S i b e

Serov

Church of the Blood

Surgut

Nizhnevartovsk

Banya sauna

Yekaterinburg

Tyumen'

Irtysh

Ice hockey

Ob'

Shamanism

Chelyabinsk

Magnitogorsk

Kurgan

St. Alexander Nevsky Cathedral

Omsk

Omsk drama theatre

Novosibirsk skyline

Bratsk pulp mill

Ust'-Ilims

Below: An Eveny reindeer herder from northeastern Siberia.

Krasnoyarsk

Novosibirsk

Bratsk

Buryat woman in traditional costume

The end of a way of life
The building of the Trans-Siberian railroad from 1891 to 1916 brought Russian settlements along the tracks, with farmers and factory workers for the new industries. This rail line separated the native forest dwellers to the north from the nomadic herdsmen and farmers of the south. The traditional Siberians were fishermen and reindeer-herders, as well as hunters of bear, sable, marten, and ermine for their fur. The Nenet, Yakut, and other communities are related to the Laplanders of Scandinavia and the Inuit of the Arctic circle. Today their way of life is threatened as factories and power stations are built to mine and process the huge reserves of gas, coal, and oil. The southern herdsmen are closer to the central Asian Turkestan ("land of the Turks") peoples. Many are nomads living in felt tents called yurts herding sheep for their milk, meat, and wool.

Barnaul

Trans-Siberian train

Abakan

ALTAI

Siberian vodka

Kazansky Church

Irkutsk

Lake B

K A Z A K H S T A N

M O N G O L I A

Adapting to the cold
Much of the north lies within the Arctic circle where the sun never sets during the summer months and winter temperatures regularly fall below -49°F (-45°C). The January temperature of -90°F (-70°C) recorded at Verkhoyansk in Siberia remains the world's coldest spot on record outside Antarctica. In 2000–1 in the far east around Vladivostok, residents were left freezing in the bitterest winter in 70 years when heating and power systems collapsed. Native Siberians are used to these extreme conditions and move with the seasons, hauling their tents and belongings on wooden sleds. They wear young reindeer hides to stay warm.

U r a l   M o u n t a i n s

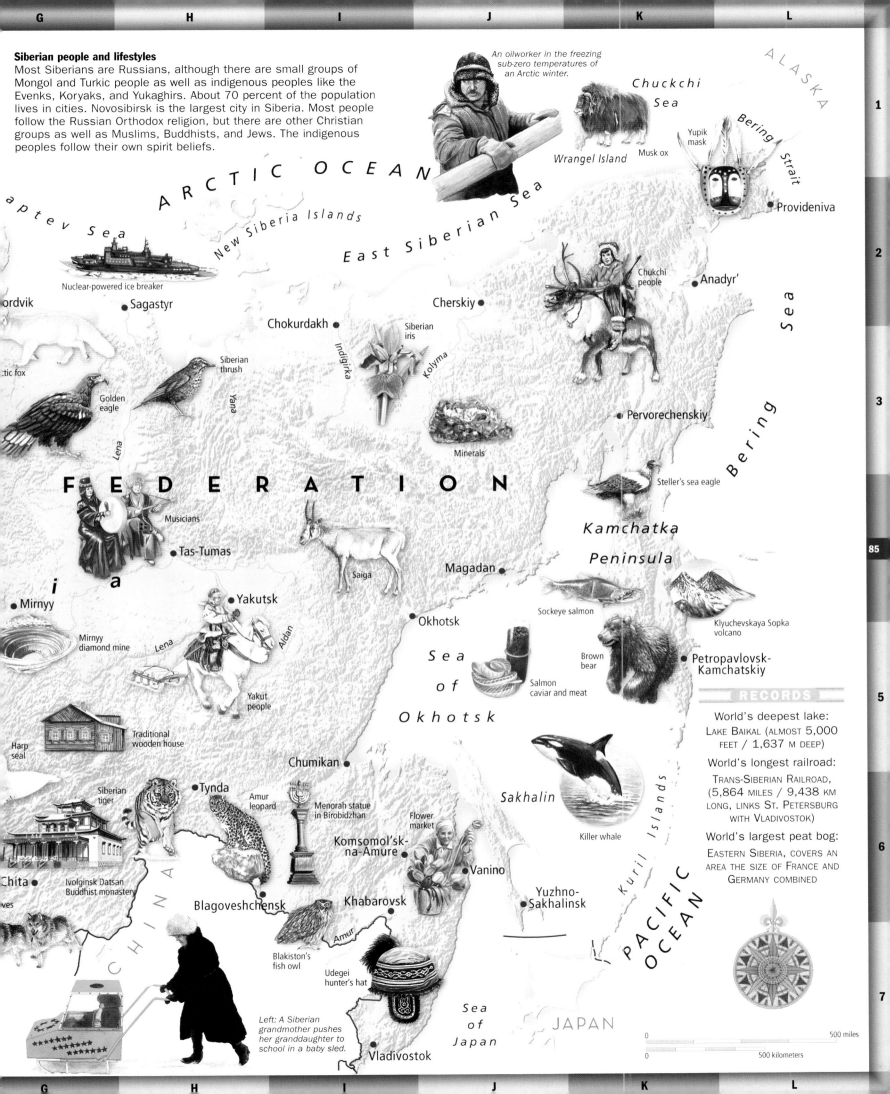

Siberian people and lifestyles

Most Siberians are Russians, although there are small groups of Mongol and Turkic people as well as indigenous peoples like the Evenks, Koryaks, and Yukaghirs. About 70 percent of the population lives in cities. Novosibirsk is the largest city in Siberia. Most people follow the Russian Orthodox religion, but there are other Christian groups as well as Muslims, Buddhists, and Jews. The indigenous peoples follow their own spirit beliefs.

An oilworker in the freezing sub-zero temperatures of an Arctic winter.

ALASKA

Chuckchi Sea

ARCTIC OCEAN

Wrangel Island

Musk ox

Yupik mask

Bering Strait

ProvidenIva

aptev Sea

New Siberia Islands

East Siberian Sea

Nuclear-powered ice breaker

ordvik

Sagastyr

Cherskiy

Chukchi people

Anadyr′

Chokurdakh

Siberian iris

Indigirka

Kolyma

tic fox

Siberian thrush

Golden eagle

Yana

Lena

Minerals

Pervorechenskiy

Bering Sea

F E D E R A T I O N

Musicians

Steller's sea eagle

Kamchatka Peninsula

i a

Tas-Tumas

Saiga

Magadan

Sockeye salmon

Klyuchevskaya Sopka volcano

Mirnyy

Yakutsk

Okhotsk

Brown bear

Petropavlovsk-Kamchatskiy

Mirnyy diamond mine

Lena

Aldan

Salmon caviar and meat

Harp seal

Yakut people

Sea of Okhotsk

Traditional wooden house

RECORDS

World's deepest lake:
LAKE BAIKAL (ALMOST 5,000 FEET / 1,637 M DEEP)

World's longest railroad:
TRANS-SIBERIAN RAILROAD, (5,864 MILES / 9,438 KM LONG, LINKS ST. PETERSBURG WITH VLADIVOSTOK)

World's largest peat bog:
EASTERN SIBERIA, COVERS AN AREA THE SIZE OF FRANCE AND GERMANY COMBINED

Chumikan

Siberian tiger

Tynda

Amur leopard

Menorah statue in Birobidzhan

Flower market

Sakhalin

Killer whale

Chita

Ivolginsk Datsan Buddhist monastery

Komsomol'sk-na-Amure

Vanino

ves

Blagoveshchensk

Khabarovsk

Yuzhno-Sakhalinsk

CHINA

Blakiston's fish owl

Amur

Udegei hunter's hat

Kuril Islands

PACIFIC OCEAN

Left: A Siberian grandmother pushes her granddaughter to school in a baby sled.

Sea of Japan

JAPAN

Vladivostok

0　　　　　　500 miles

0　　　　　　500 kilometers

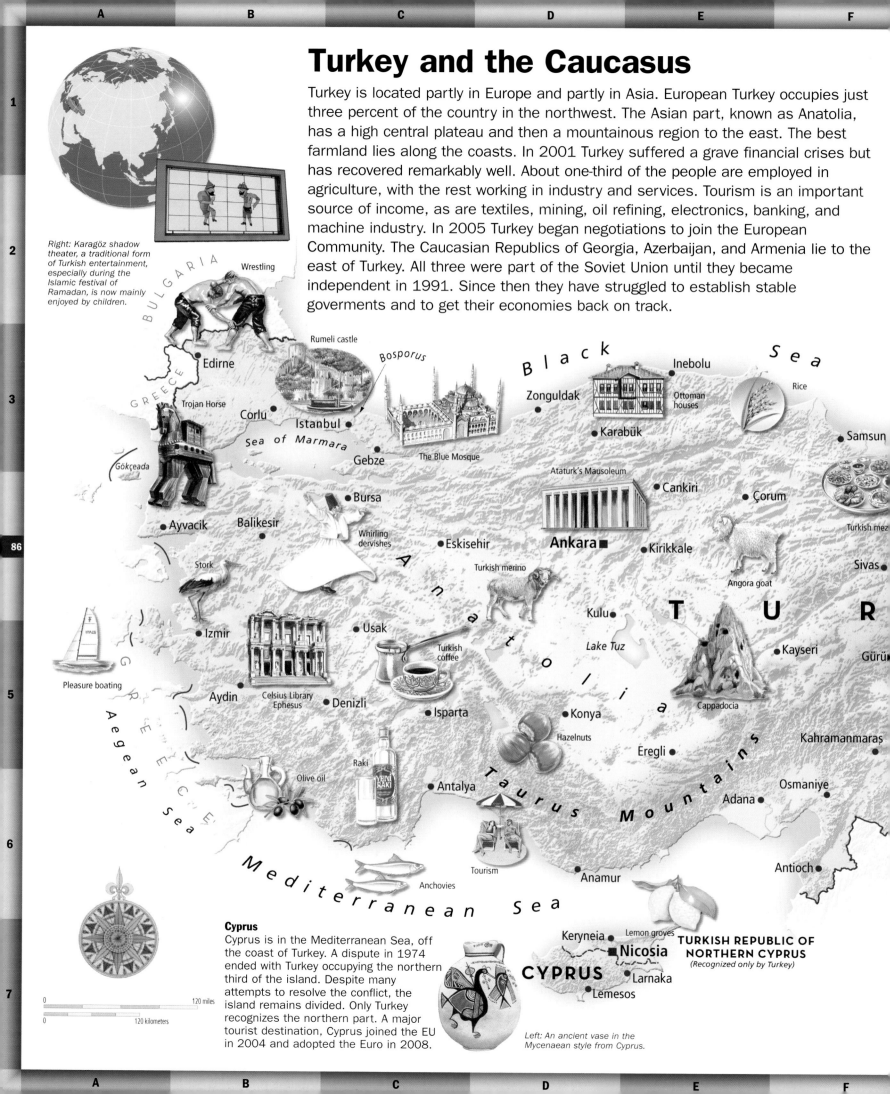

Turkey and the Caucasus

Turkey is located partly in Europe and partly in Asia. European Turkey occupies just three percent of the country in the northwest. The Asian part, known as Anatolia, has a high central plateau and then a mountainous region to the east. The best farmland lies along the coasts. In 2001 Turkey suffered a grave financial crises but has recovered remarkably well. About one-third of the people are employed in agriculture, with the rest working in industry and services. Tourism is an important source of income, as are textiles, mining, oil refining, electronics, banking, and machine industry. In 2005 Turkey began negotiations to join the European Community. The Caucasian Republics of Georgia, Azerbaijan, and Armenia lie to the east of Turkey. All three were part of the Soviet Union until they became independent in 1991. Since then they have struggled to establish stable goverments and to get their economies back on track.

Right: Karagöz shadow theater, a traditional form of Turkish entertainment, especially during the Islamic festival of Ramadan, is now mainly enjoyed by children.

Wrestling

BULGARIA

GREECE

Edirne

Rumeli castle

Bosporus

Black Sea

Inebolu

Rice

Zonguldak

Ottoman houses

Samsun

Trojan Horse

Corlu

Istanbul

Karabük

Sea of Marmara

The Blue Mosque

Gebze

Ataturk's Mausoleum

Cankiri

Çorum

Gökçeada

Bursa

Ankara ■

Kirikkale

Turkish mez

Ayvacik

Balikesir

Whirling dervishes

Eskisehir

Anatolia

Stork

Turkish merino

Kulu

Sivas

Angora goat

T U R

Izmir

Usak

Lake Tuz

Kayseri

Turkish coffee

Cappadocia

Gürü

Pleasure boating

GREECE

Aydin

Celsius Library Ephesus

Denizli

Isparta

Konya

Kahramanmaraş

Hazelnuts

Eregli

Taurus Mountains

Osmaniye

Raki

Adana

Olive oil

Antalya

Aegean Sea

Anchovies

Tourism

Antioch

Mediterranean Sea

Anamur

Cyprus
Cyprus is in the Mediterranean Sea, off the coast of Turkey. A dispute in 1974 ended with Turkey occupying the northern third of the island. Despite many attempts to resolve the conflict, the island remains divided. Only Turkey recognizes the northern part. A major tourist destination, Cyprus joined the EU in 2004 and adopted the Euro in 2008.

Keryneia

Lemon groves

TURKISH REPUBLIC OF NORTHERN CYPRUS
(Recognized only by Turkey)

Nicosia

CYPRUS

Larnaka

Lemesos

Left: An ancient vase in the Mycenaean style from Cyprus.

0   120 miles

0   120 kilometers

Istanbul

The great city of Istanbul sits astride the narrow Bosphorus Strait in western Turkey, half in Europe and half in Asia. Istanbul has long been a crossroads and a meeting point for East and West. In Ancient Roman times it was called Byzantium, until the emperor Constantine made it the capital of the Eastern Roman Empire in 330 CE and it came to be known as Constantinople. It was the center of the Ottoman Empire for more than 450 years until Mustafa Atatürk, the founder of modern Turkey, moved the capital to Ankara in 1923.

Left: This miniature shows Istanbul when it was still known as Constantinople. The city is a striking mixture of architectural styles and buildings and millions of tourists come to visit the city every year.

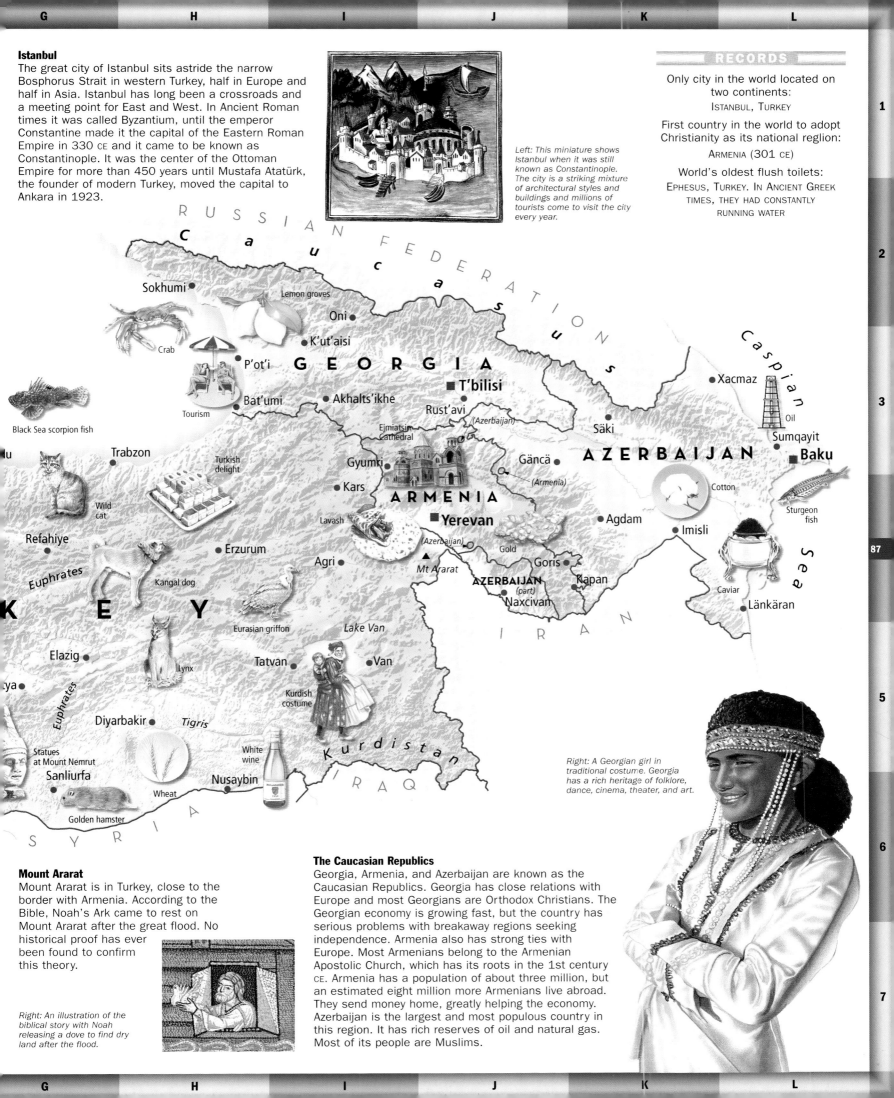

RUSSIAN FEDERATION

Caucasus

Sokhumi

Lemon groves

Crab

Black Sea scorpion fish

Oni

K'ut'aisi

P'ot'i

GEORGIA

T'bilisi

Akhalts'ikhe

Rust'avi

(Azerbaijan)

Xacmaz

Caspian

Oil

Sumqayit

Bat'umi

Tourism

Ejmiatsin Cathedral

Säki

AZERBAIJAN

Baku

Trabzon

Turkish delight

Gyumri

Gäncä

(Armenia)

Cotton

Wild cat

Kars

ARMENIA

Sturgeon fish

Refahiye

Lavash

Yerevan

Agdam

Imisli

Erzurum

(Azerbaijan)

Gold

Goris

Caviar

Euphrates

Kangal dog

Agri

Mt Ararat

AZERBAIJAN (part)

Kapan

Länkäran

T U R K E Y

Eurasian griffon

Lake Van

Naxcivan

I R A N

Sea

Elazig

Lynx

Tatvan

Van

Kurdish costume

Diyarbakir

Tigris

Kurdistan

White wine

Statues at Mount Nemrut

Sanliurfa

Wheat

Nusaybin

I R A Q

Golden hamster

S Y R I A

Right: A Georgian girl in traditional costume. Georgia has a rich heritage of folklore, dance, cinema, theater, and art.

Mount Ararat

Mount Ararat is in Turkey, close to the border with Armenia. According to the Bible, Noah's Ark came to rest on Mount Ararat after the great flood. No historical proof has ever been found to confirm this theory.

Right: An illustration of the biblical story with Noah releasing a dove to find dry land after the flood.

The Caucasian Republics

Georgia, Armenia, and Azerbaijan are known as the Caucasian Republics. Georgia has close relations with Europe and most Georgians are Orthodox Christians. The Georgian economy is growing fast, but the country has serious problems with breakaway regions seeking independence. Armenia also has strong ties with Europe. Most Armenians belong to the Armenian Apostolic Church, which has its roots in the 1st century CE. Armenia has a population of about three million, but an estimated eight million more Armenians live abroad. They send money home, greatly helping the economy. Azerbaijan is the largest and most populous country in this region. It has rich reserves of oil and natural gas. Most of its people are Muslims.

Central Asia

Central Asia is a vast area of rugged mountains, deserts, and steppe where the people traditionally lived as nomadic herders. The north has good farmland, producing plenty of grain and livestock. South of the steppes there is scorching desert. Further south again, and to the east, snowy mountains rise up, making travel and communications difficult. Much of Central Asia is far from water, so the winters are cold and dry and the summers are hot and dry. The ancient Silk Road, which linked China and Europe, had several routes across Central Asia, making the area a crossroads of people, trade, and cultures. Great market cities, such as Tashkent, Samarkand, and Bukhara, grew prosperous through trade. After the Russian Revolution in 1917 most of Central Asia (except for Pakistan and Afghanistan) was incorporated into the Soviet Union and only regained independence in 1991. Since then these countries have struggled to modernize their economies and to introduce democratic government, with varying measures of success.

Religious beliefs

Islam is the most common religion in Central Asia. The majority are Sunnite Muslims, but there are also many Shi'ites, especially in Afghanistan and Pakistan. There are many striking mosques and religious buildings in the region, including the Registan in Samarkand, and the Blue Mosque in Mazar-e Sharif, in Afghanistan. These buildings have huge, colored domes and glittering decoration on their outside walls. Many Russian Orthodox Christians live in Kazakhstan.

Above: The Ulugbek Madrassah in Registan Square, Samarkand, Uzbekistan. A Madrassah is an Islamic religious school.

RECORDS

World's two tallest dams:
ROGUN DAM (WILL BE 1,098 FEET / 335 M HIGH WHEN COMPLETED) AND NUREK DAM (1980; 984 FEET / 300 M HIGH); BOTH ON THE RIVER VAKHSH, TAJIKISTAN

World's longest irrigation canal:
KARAKUM CANAL, TURKMENISTAN; (870 MILES / 1,400 KM LONG)

World's largest dry steppe region:
NORTH KAZAKHSTAN

Map labels

RUSSIAN FEDERATION

KAZAKHSTAN
KYRGYZSTAN
UZBEKISTAN

Kazakh hunter
Golden Warrior Prince costume
Semipalatinsk
Zenkov Cathedral
Almaty
Ysyk-Köl
Kara-Say
Kirghiz storyteller
Cooking manti (mutton dumplings)
Taldykorgan
Lake Balkhash
Bishkek
Cotton farmer
Bobac
Pyramid of Peace
Astana
Astana tower
Karaganda
Traditional costume
Chromium
Shymkent
Tashkent
Zhezkazgan
Petropavlovsk
Saiga antelope
Bajkonur Space Center
Kyzylorda
Palov
Kostanay
Kazakh doll
Nan bread
Demoiselle crane
Aral'sk
Aral Sea
Rafting
Nukus
UZBEKISTAN
Aktyubinsk
Apples
Watermelons
Akhalteke horse
Kazakh horse
Ural
Wheat
Yurt with child
Karshi
Ural'sk
Pallas' cat
Atyrau
Aktau
Oil
Beluga sturgeon fish
Caspian Sea

88

Traditional cultures

Travel by horse is a good way of crossing open steppe and mountainous areas and Central Asia has been famous for its skilled horsemen for thousands of years. In the past, great armies of fast-galloping warriors fought to control this region. This is also a way of life that goes back thousands of years, although it is declining now. Some Central Asian people are nomads. They move from place to place, looking for fresh pastures for their animals to graze. Nomads keep animals and live in yurts.

Central Asian economies

Some countries in Central Asia have found it difficult to develop their economies since becoming independent from the Soviet Union. Others, such as Afghanistan and Pakistan, have been held back by political problems and wars. Kazakhstan is rich in metals, minerals, and farmland. It exports oil, grains, textiles, and livestock. Uzbekistan relies on cotton production—it is the world's second-largest cotton exporter.

Left: Cotton is an important export for many countries in Central Asia.

Wildlife

Much of the steppe is treeless and dry with large sandy areas. It is freezing cold and high winds sweep across the area in winter. Despite the harsh climate the steppe is home to many animals, including deer, foxes, badgers, wolves, and the very rare saiga. In the mountainous areas there are ibex, wild boars, and brown bears, as well as the highly endangered snow leopard.

Right: A dangerous and competitive game called buzkashi is played in Afghanistan. Skilled riders play the sport by carrying the body of a headless calf to scoring areas. Games can last for several days and are usually held to celebrate weddings or other ceremonial events.

Left: The snow leopard is native to the mountains of Central Asia. Only a few thousand of these large wild cats remain in the wild.

Map labels

CHINA

(Claimed by Pakistan. Administered by China)

(Claimed by India. Administered by Pakistan)

Carpet making

Lapis lazuli

Khorugh

Hindu Kush

Gilgit

Badshah mosque

500 miles

500 kilometers

Cotton factory

Rabab

Mazar-e Sharif

Blue Mosque

Registan Square

Peshawar

Kabul

Islamabad

Gujranwala

Lahore

Faisalabad

Multan

Bahawalpur

Indus Valley statue

Shepherd

Wakhi girl

Yurt

PAKISTAN

INDIA

Indus

Bus

Karakul sheep

Woman in burkha

Buzkashi

Herat

AFGHANISTAN

Minaret e-Jam

Sweet pumpkin with yogurt

Kandahar

Quetta

Shikarpur

Hyderabad

Karachi

Jinnah Mausoleum

Black cobra

Central Makran Range

Mouths of the Indus

Dalbandin

Turbat

Pasni

Arabian Sea

Aksakal (respected elder)

Mary

Neutrality

Sulphur mining

Fruit vendor

IRAN

Ashgabat

Okarem

Central Asian cobra

Dushanbe

Left. The city of Jerusalem, in Israel, shown here in an 18th century illustration, is holy for Jews, Christians, and Muslins.

Birthplace of religions

The Jewish faith is the world's oldest religion based on the belief in just one God. It was developed here by the Hebrews who, according to the Bible, were led to the "promised land" by the prophet Moses in about 1200 BCE. Christianity also began in this region with Jesus Christ who lived in Roman-occupied Palestine before he was tried and executed. Mecca, in Saudi Arabia, was the prophet Muhammad's birthplace and is the holiest city of Islam to which every Muslim tries to make a pilgrimage, called the hajj, once in his or her lifetime. All three major religions come together, not always happily, in the city of Jerusalem—a holy place for Christians, Muslims, and Jews. The Church of the Holy Sepulchre is built where Christians believe Jesus was buried. The gold-topped Dome of the Rock is a mosque erected where Muslims believe Muhammad ascended to heaven (and also where Jews believe that Abraham prepared to sacrifice his son). The Wailing Wall, where Jews go to pray, is all that remains of the Jewish Temple built by King Herod in the 1st century BCE. Other minority religions include Zoroastrianism, Druze, Bahá'í, and Yazdanism.

Right: The ancient Mesopotamians made marks in clay tablets to record their stores of barley and other produce. This gradually evolved into one of the earliest forms of writing.

The origins of civilization

The lands between the Tigris and Euphrates rivers, known as Mesopotamia (which is Greek for "land between two rivers"), and those along the Mediterranean Sea, were home to some of the world's first known settlements, including the oldest city in the world, Jericho. Important towns such as Damascus, Babylon, and Mari also developed along trade routes in the region. Irrigation from the rivers ensured that citrus fruits, olives, dates, pomegranates, and wheat could be grown. These lands were home to a succession of ancient empires and cultures, including the Sumerians, Assyrians, Babylonians, Hittites, Persians, Phoenicians, and Hebrews. The Sumerians built some of the world's earliest cities, including Ur and Uruk, as well as ancient pyramids called ziggurats.

The Middle East

The region that stretches from the Red Sea to the Persian Gulf and Iran is known as the Middle East. It is a crossroads of three continents—Africa, Europe, and Asia—and because many important ancient civilizations have thrived here it is sometimes called the "cradle of civilization." Apart from the Mediterranean coast, with its regular rainfall, and the lands around the Euphrates and Tigris rivers which have been irrigated for thousands of years, the land is parched, rocky, and mostly desert-covered. The Arabian Desert covers 95 percent of Saudi Arabia, which is the biggest country in the region. Not only is the land inhospitable; parts of it have suffered endless wars and skirmishes, boundary disputes, ethnic tensions, and religious conflict. At the same time, other countries in the Middle East have enjoyed the benefits of sitting upon a quarter of the world's known oil reserves. The Gulf States, including Saudi Arabia, Bahrain, Kuwait, Oman, Qatar, and the United Arab Emirates, are very rich thanks to the production of oil. Some of these states provide free schooling and health care for their citizens.

RECORDS

Earth's lowest place:
THE DEAD SEA
(1,312 FEET / 400 M BELOW SEA LEVEL)

World's oldest city:
JERICHO (FOUNDED ABOUT 8000 BCE)

World's tallest building:
THE MILE-HIGH TOWER TO BE BUILT IN JEDDAH
BY 2012 WILL BE 1 MILE (1609 M) TALL

Among the world's biggest producers
of luxury foods:
IRAN (CAVIAR, PISTACHIOS, SAFFRON)

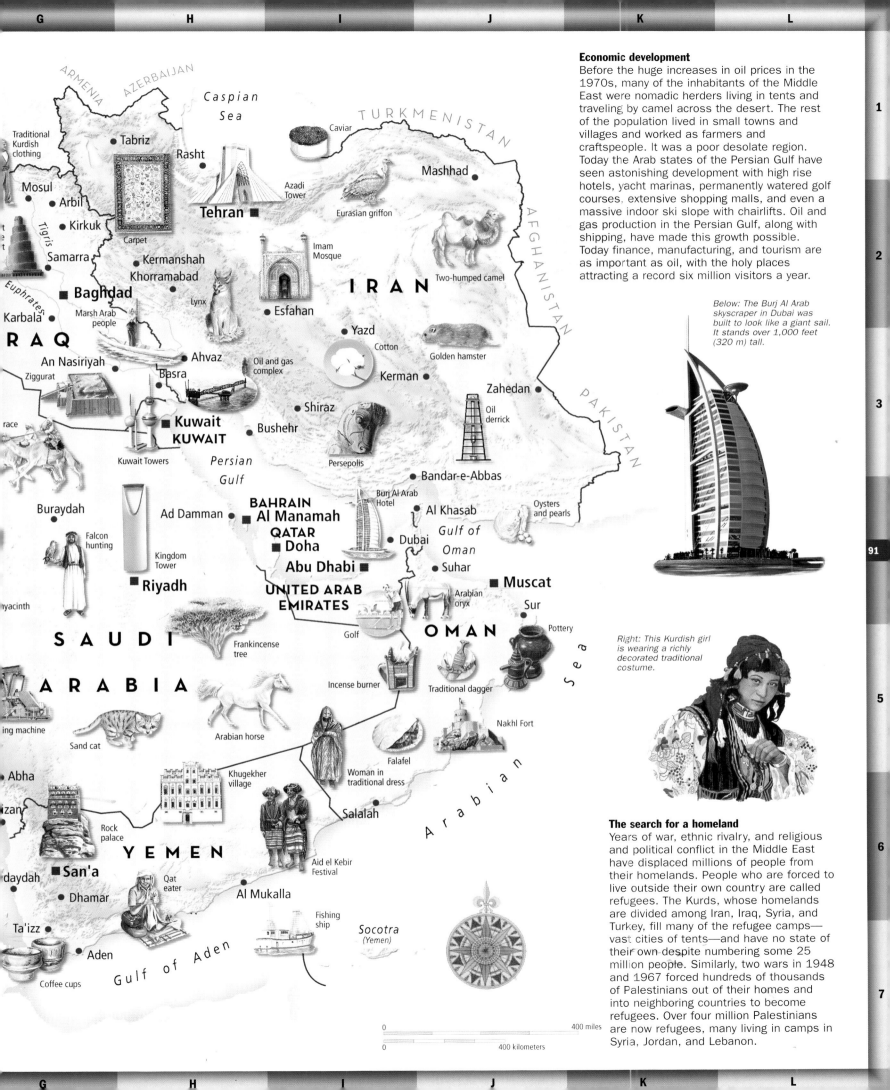

1

2

3

5

6

7

Economic development

Before the huge increases in oil prices in the 1970s, many of the inhabitants of the Middle East were nomadic herders living in tents and traveling by camel across the desert. The rest of the population lived in small towns and villages and worked as farmers and craftspeople. It was a poor desolate region. Today the Arab states of the Persian Gulf have seen astonishing development with high rise hotels, yacht marinas, permanently watered golf courses, extensive shopping malls, and even a massive indoor ski slope with chairlifts. Oil and gas production in the Persian Gulf, along with shipping, have made this growth possible. Today finance, manufacturing, and tourism are as important as oil, with the holy places attracting a record six million visitors a year.

Below: The Burj Al Arab skyscraper in Dubai was built to look like a giant sail. It stands over 1,000 feet (320 m) tall.

Right: This Kurdish girl is wearing a richly decorated traditional costume.

The search for a homeland

Years of war, ethnic rivalry, and religious and political conflict in the Middle East have displaced millions of people from their homelands. People who are forced to live outside their own country are called refugees. The Kurds, whose homelands are divided among Iran, Iraq, Syria, and Turkey, fill many of the refugee camps—vast cities of tents—and have no state of their own despite numbering some 25 million people. Similarly, two wars in 1948 and 1967 forced hundreds of thousands of Palestinians out of their homes and into neighboring countries to become refugees. Over four million Palestinians are now refugees, many living in camps in Syria, Jordan, and Lebanon.

Map labels

ARMENIA
AZERBAIJAN
Caspian Sea
TURKMENISTAN
Caviar
Traditional Kurdish clothing
Tabriz
Rasht
Mashhad
Azadi Tower
Mosul
Arbil
Kirkuk
Tehran
Eurasian griffon
Samarra
Carpet
Kermanshah
Khorramabad
Imam Mosque
IRAN
AFGHANISTAN
Baghdad
Lynx
Karbala
Marsh Arab people
Esfahan
Two-humped camel
RAQ
Yazd
Cotton
An Nasiriyah
Ahvaz
Oil and gas complex
Golden hamster
Ziggurat
Basra
Kerman
PAKISTAN
race
Shiraz
Zahedan
Kuwait
KUWAIT
Bushehr
Persepolis
Oil derrick
Kuwait Towers
Persian Gulf
Bandar-e-Abbas
Buraydah
Burj Al Arab Hotel
Al Khasab
Falcon hunting
Ad Damman
BAHRAIN
Al Manamah
Oysters and pearls
Kingdom Tower
QATAR
Doha
Dubai
Gulf of Oman
hyacinth
Riyadh
Abu Dhabi
Suhar
UNITED ARAB EMIRATES
Arabian oryx
Muscat
SAUDI
Frankincense tree
Golf
Sur
OMAN
Pottery
ARABIA
Incense burner
Traditional dagger
Nakhl Fort
ing machine
Sand cat
Arabian horse
Sea
Abha
Khugekher village
Woman in traditional dress
Falafel
zan
Woman in traditional dress
Arabian Sea
Rock palace
Salalah
daydah
YEMEN
Aid el Kebir Festival
San'a
Qat eater
Dhamar
Al Mukalla
Ta'izz
Fishing ship
Socotra (Yemen)
Aden
Coffee cups
Gulf of Aden

0   400 miles
0   400 kilometers

Southern Asia

Southern Asia looks like a giant triangle, pointing down into the warm Indian Ocean. Across the top of the triangle lie the towering Himalaya Mountains—the world's highest mountain range. Nestling against these peaks are the mountainous lands of Nepal and Bhutan. Hot, dry deserts are found in the northwest. To the east, where India meets Bangladesh, two great rivers called the Indus and the Brahmaputra have created a huge delta with rich farming land. This area is very densely populated. Moving south, toward India's tip, the climate becomes more tropical. India is by far the largest country in Southern Asia, bursting with color and variety. It is the world's seventh largest country and has the world's second largest population, after China. Although most Indians still live and work on the land, the service and industrial sectors are growing rapidly, making the Indian economy one of the fastest-growing in the world. India has many large cities, such as Mumbai, Delhi, and Bangalore. In the south, the tropical island of Sri Lanka lies off the east coast of India. A mainly Buddhist country, Sri Lanka has a newly industrialized economy based on textiles, food processing, and finance, as well as the export of coffee, tea, rubber, and coconuts. Sri Lanka has suffered an off-and-on civil war since 1983, which has damaged the economy and tourism.

Right: This beautifully painted Buddha from Bhutan is making a traditional Buddhist gesture with his hands.

Bhutan, Nepal, and Bangladesh

Bhutan and Nepal lie in the Himalayas to the north of India. Bhutan is one of the most isolated and least developed countries in the world. The government controls foreign influence and tries hard to protect the traditional Buddhist culture. Next door, in Nepal, a long civil war ended in 2006 and a democratic government was established the following year. In 2008 lawmakers abolished the monarchy, ending 239 years of royal rule. Nepal is a Hindu and Buddhist country, with most people working as farmers. Bangladesh lies to the east, facing the Bay of Bengal. Bangladesh became separate from India in 1947, at the same time as Pakistan. Until 1971 it was know as East Pakistan. The country is located in the Ganges-Brahmaputra delta and has fertile soils. But because it is so low-lying it is often flooded, with devastating results for the people living there.

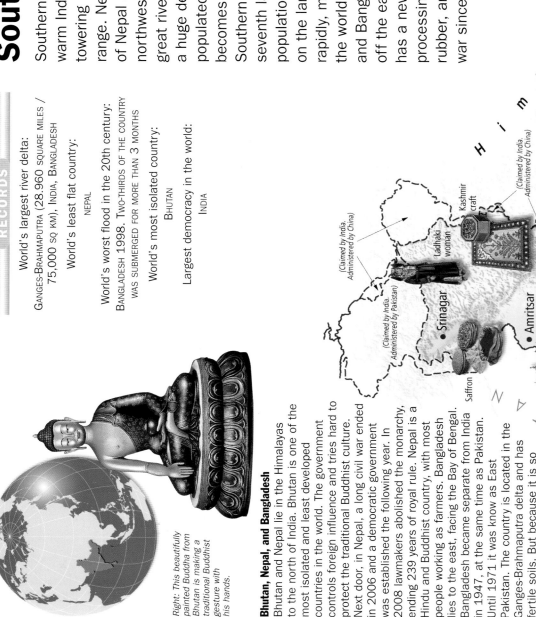

CHINA

BURMA

BHUTAN
■ Thimphu

BANGLADESH
Rajshahi
Dacca ■

Axis deer

Dibrugarh

Mridangam dancer

Yak

Traditional boots

Brahmaputra

Guwahati

Indian rhinoceros

Rangpur

Imphal

Bengal tiger

Mt Everest

Kathmandu

Biratnagar

Mahabodhi Temple

Kali Temple

Sherpa

NEPAL

Pokhara

Patna

Gavial

Varanasi

Bodnath Stupa

Lucknow

Ganges

Allahabad

Jumla

Kanpur

Indian star tortoise

Himalaya

Trekking

Kashmir craft

(Claimed by India.
Administered by China)

Ladhaki woman

Delhi

Agra

Taj Mahal

Jaipur

Bhopal

New Delhi

Diwali Festival

(Claimed by India.
Administered by China)

Srinagar

Amritsar

Ludhiana

Golden Temple

Sikh man

Hawa Mahal

Hindu wedding

Cricket

(Claimed by India.
Administered by Pakistan)

Saffron

PAKISTAN

Markhor

Jodhpur

Holi Festival

Ahmadabad

Wild dog

Hanuman langur

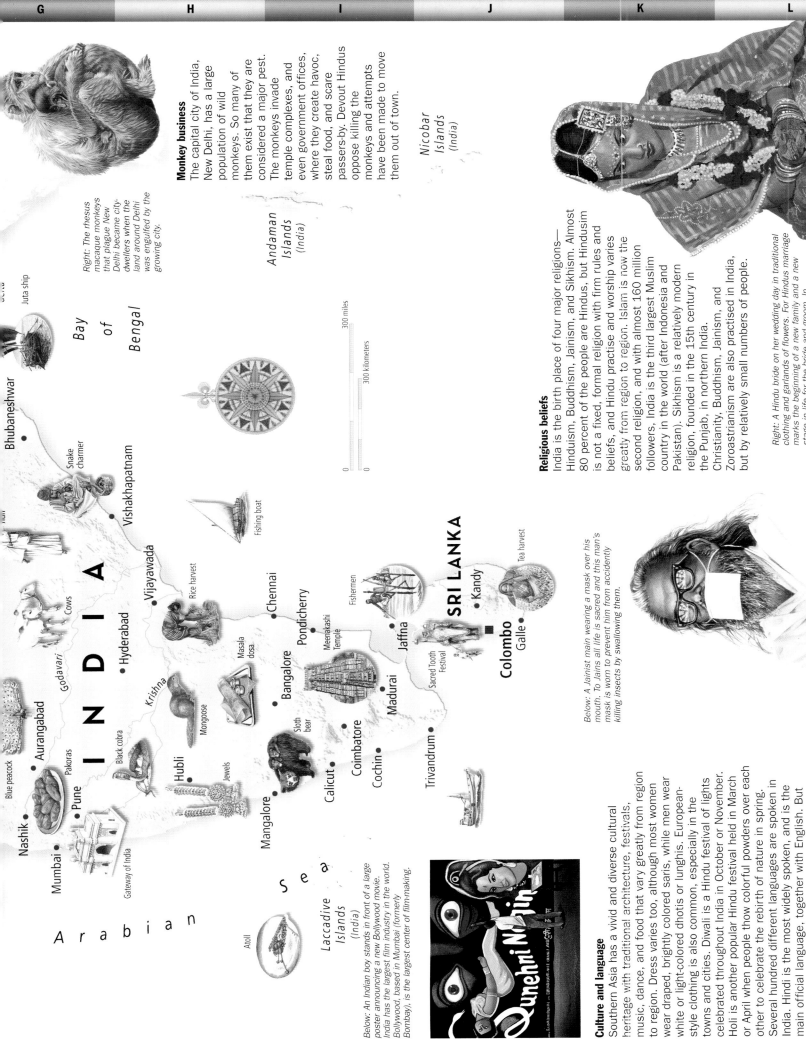

Monkey business

The capital city of India, New Delhi, has a large population of wild monkeys. So many of them exist that they are considered a major pest. The monkeys invade temple complexes, and even government offices, where they create havoc, steal food, and scare passers-by. Devout Hindus oppose killing the monkeys and attempts have been made to move them out of town.

Right: The rhesus macaque monkeys that plague New Delhi became city-dwellers when the land around Delhi was engulfed by the growing city.

Andaman Islands (India)

Nicobar Islands (India)

Juta ship

Bay of Bengal

Snake charmer

300 miles

300 kilometers

300 meters

0

0

Religious beliefs

India is the birth place of four major religions—Hinduism, Buddhism, Jainism, and Sikhism. Almost 80 percent of the people are Hindus, but Hindusim is not a fixed, formal religion with firm rules and beliefs, and Hindu practise and worship varies greatly from region to region. Islam is now the second religion, and with almost 160 million followers, India is the third largest Muslim country in the world (after Indonesia and Pakistan). Sikhism is a relatively modern religion, founded in the 15th century in the Punjab, in northern India. Christianity, Buddhism, Jainism, and Zoroastrianism are also practised in India, but by relatively small numbers of people.

Right: A Hindu bride on her wedding day in traditional clothing and garlands of flowers. For Hindus marriage marks the beginning of a new family and a new stage in life for the bride and groom. In many cases the couple do not know each other before the wedding day and the marriage is arranged by their families.

Below: A Jainist main wearing a mask over his mouth. To Jains all life is sacred and this man's mask is worn to prevent him from accidentally killing insects by swallowing them.

Bhubaneshwar

Vishakhapatnam

Fishing boat

Rice harvest

Vijayawada

Chennai

Pondicherry

Meenakashi Temple

Fishermen

SRI LANKA

Kandy

Tea harvest

Jaffna

Sacred Tooth Festival

Colombo

Galle

I N D I A

Hyderabad

Godavari

Cows

Krishna

Masala dosa

Bangalore

Madurai

Sloth bear

Mongoose

Coimbatore

Cochin

Trivandrum

Aurangabad

Black cobra

Pakoras

Blue peacock

Hubli

Jewels

Nashik

Pune

Mumbai

Gateway of India

Mangalore

Calicut

Arabian Sea

Atoll

Laccadive Islands (India)

Below: An Indian boy stands in front of a large poster announcing a new Bollywood movie. India has the largest film industry in the world. Bollywood, based in Mumbai (formerly Bombay), is the largest center of film-making.

Culture and language

Southern Asia has a vivid and diverse cultural heritage with traditional architecture, festivals, music, dance, and food that vary greatly from region to region. Dress varies too, although most women wear draped, brightly colored saris, while men wear white or light-colored dhotis or lunghis. European-style clothing is also common, especially in the towns and cities. Diwali is a Hindu festival of lights celebrated throughout India in October or November. Holi is another popular Hindu festival held in March or April when people thow colorful powders over each other to celebrate the rebirth of nature in spring. Several hundred different languages are spoken in India. Hindi is the most widely spoken, and is the main official language, together with English. But there are many millions of native speakers of other Indian languages, such as Bengali, Punjabi, Telugu, Marathi, and Tamil.

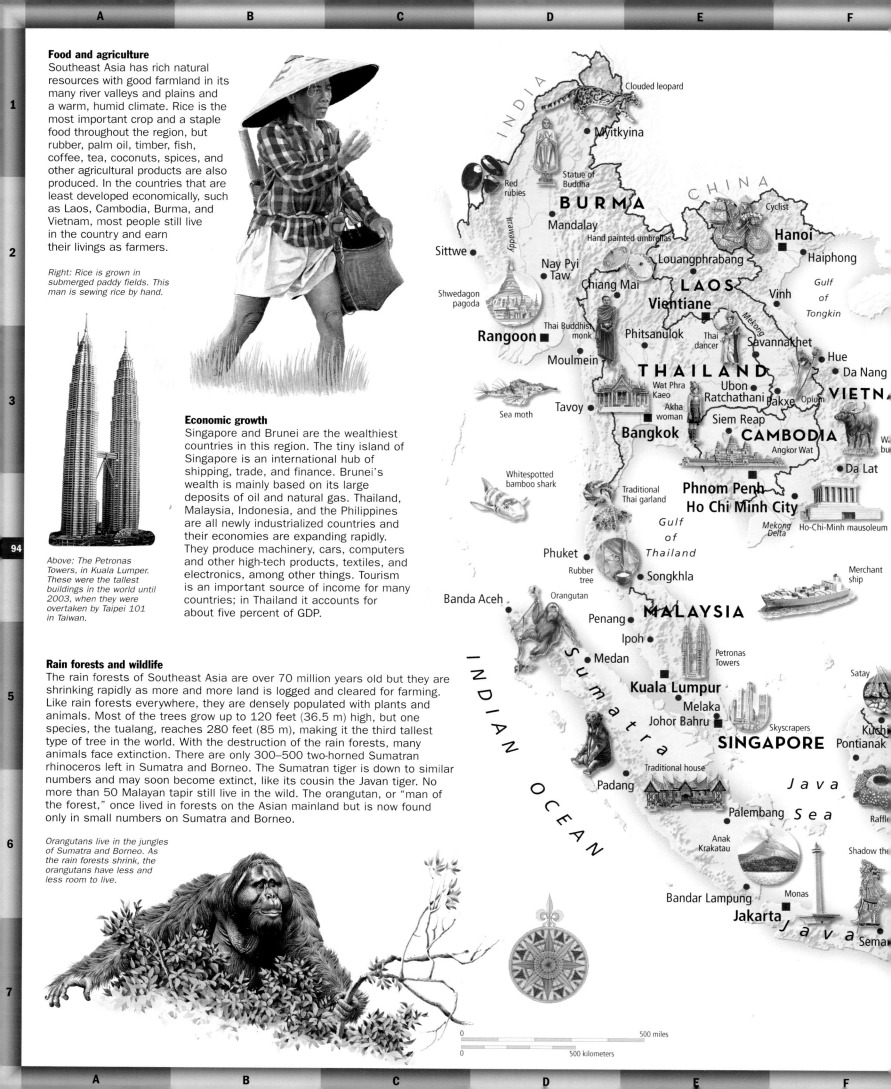

Food and agriculture

Southeast Asia has rich natural resources with good farmland in its many river valleys and plains and a warm, humid climate. Rice is the most important crop and a staple food throughout the region, but rubber, palm oil, timber, fish, coffee, tea, coconuts, spices, and other agricultural products are also produced. In the countries that are least developed economically, such as Laos, Cambodia, Burma, and Vietnam, most people still live in the country and earn their livings as farmers.

Right: Rice is grown in submerged paddy fields. This man is sewing rice by hand.

Above: The Petronas Towers, in Kuala Lumper. These were the tallest buildings in the world until 2003, when they were overtaken by Taipei 101 in Taiwan.

Economic growth

Singapore and Brunei are the wealthiest countries in this region. The tiny island of Singapore is an international hub of shipping, trade, and finance. Brunei's wealth is mainly based on its large deposits of oil and natural gas. Thailand, Malaysia, Indonesia, and the Philippines are all newly industrialized countries and their economies are expanding rapidly. They produce machinery, cars, computers and other high-tech products, textiles, and electronics, among other things. Tourism is an important source of income for many countries; in Thailand it accounts for about five percent of GDP.

Rain forests and wildlife

The rain forests of Southeast Asia are over 70 million years old but they are shrinking rapidly as more and more land is logged and cleared for farming. Like rain forests everywhere, they are densely populated with plants and animals. Most of the trees grow up to 120 feet (36.5 m) high, but one species, the tualang, reaches 280 feet (85 m), making it the third tallest type of tree in the world. With the destruction of the rain forests, many animals face extinction. There are only 300–500 two-horned Sumatran rhinoceros left in Sumatra and Borneo. The Sumatran tiger is down to similar numbers and may soon become extinct, like its cousin the Javan tiger. No more than 50 Malayan tapir still live in the wild. The orangutan, or "man of the forest," once lived in forests on the Asian mainland but is now found only in small numbers on Sumatra and Borneo.

Orangutans live in the jungles of Sumatra and Borneo. As the rain forests shrink, the orangutans have less and less room to live.

RECORDS

World's most densely populated island:
JAVA, INDONESIA

Country made up of the most islands:
INDONESIA. IT HAS MORE THAN 17,000, OF WHICH OVER 6,000 ARE UNINHABITED

World's largest flower:
RAFFLESIA.
IT BLOOMS IN THE RAIN FORESTS OF SOUTHEAST ASIA

Southeast Asia

Southeast Asia is made up of the countries on the Asian mainland that lie south of China and India and more than 24,000 islands scattered between the Indian and Pacific Oceans. The climate across the region is mainly tropical, with hot temperatures all year round and high rainfall during the wet season. The landscape is mountainous and was once almost completely covered in dense rain forest; in recent years a lot of the land has been cleared for timber and farmland. With more than 600 million people, the region is quite densely populated. Indonesia, made up of over 17,000 islands, is the fourth most populous state in the world. Jakarta, the capital city of Indonesia, is the biggest city in Southeast Asia and one of the largest in the world. There are several other very large cities, including Manila (capital city of the Philippines) and Bangkok (capital city of Thailand). These and other cities are growing very quickly as more and more people move to the towns. Many cities just don't have room for the new arrivals, and shantytowns and slums have grown up on the outskirts.

Religion

Most people in mainland Southeast Asia are Buddhists. In the islands they are mainly Muslim, except for the Philippines, where a majority are Roman Catholics. Buddhism and Hinduism were the dominant religions in early history, and there are wonderful ancient temples from this time. From the 9th to the 12th century Angkor Wat (in modern Cambodia) was the capital of the Khymer Empire, and its Hindu temple of five towers surrounded by a moated wall was discovered in thick jungle. In the same period a magnificent three-tiered Buddhist temple was established at Borobudur in central Java. Today many beautiful Buddhist temples and giant statues stand in Thailand and Burma.

Above: The Ananda stupa (temple) in Pagan, in Burma (Myanmar). It was built in the 11th century.

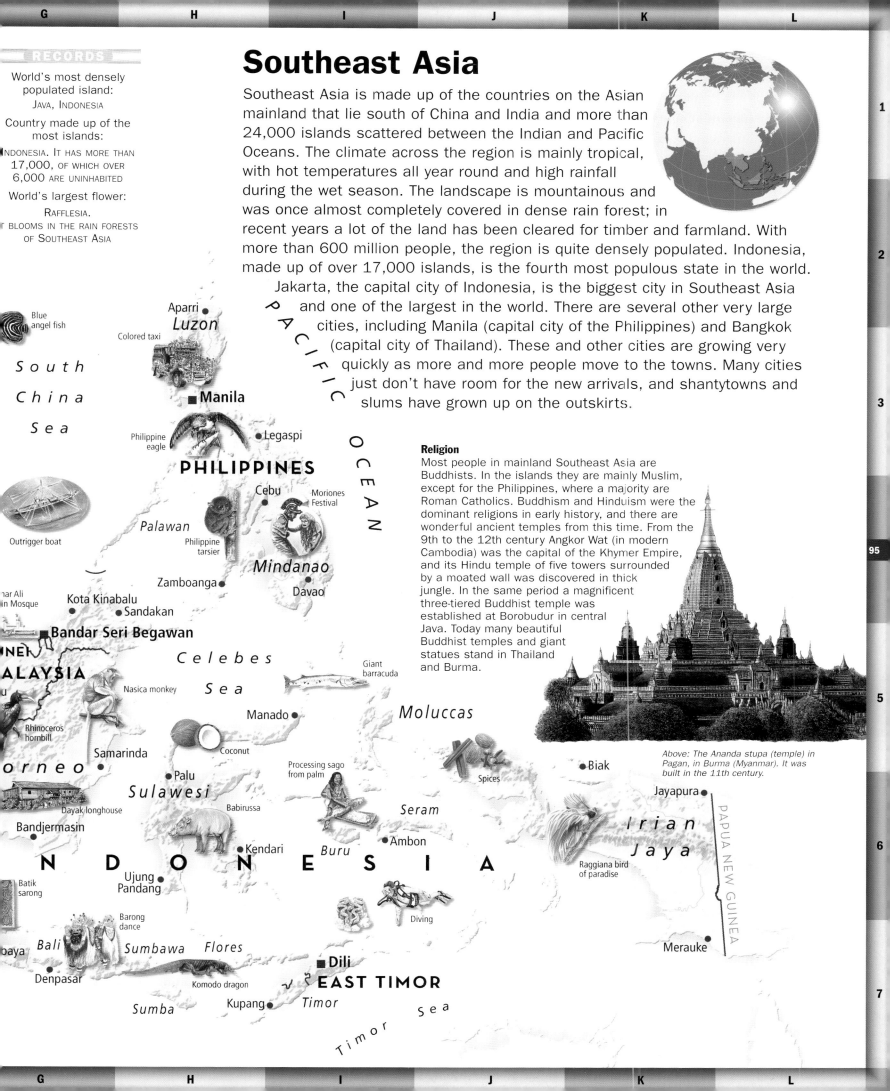

Blue angel fish

Aparri

Luzon

Colored taxi

South China Sea

PACIFIC OCEAN

Manila

Philippine eagle

Legaspi

PHILIPPINES

Cebu

Moriones Festival

Outrigger boat

Palawan

Philippine tarsier

Mindanao

Zamboanga

Davao

ar Ali in Mosque

Kota Kinabalu

Sandakan

Bandar Seri Begawan

NEI

ALAYSIA

Nasica monkey

Celebes

Sea

Giant barracuda

Moluccas

Rhinoceros hornbill

Manado

orneo

Samarinda

Coconut

Processing sago from palm

Spices

Biak

Dayak longhouse

Palu

Sulawesi

Babirussa

Seram

Jayapura

Irian

Jaya

Bandjermasin

N

D

O

Kendari

Buru

Ambon

S

I

A

Raggiana bird of paradise

PAPUA NEW GUINEA

Batik sarong

Ujung Pandang

Diving

Barong dance

baya

Bali

Sumbawa

Flores

Merauke

Denpasar

Komodo dragon

■Dili

EAST TIMOR

Sumba

Kupang

Timor

Sea

Timor

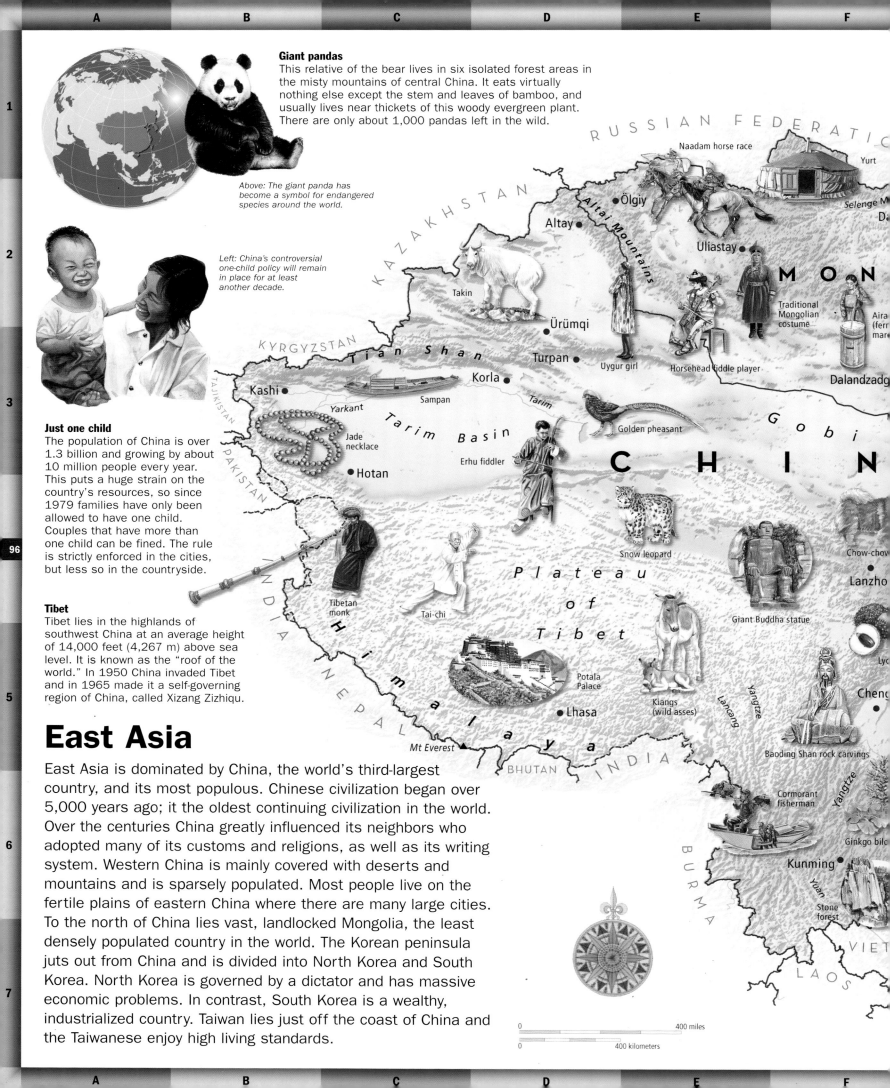

Giant pandas
This relative of the bear lives in six isolated forest areas in the misty mountains of central China. It eats virtually nothing else except the stem and leaves of bamboo, and usually lives near thickets of this woody evergreen plant. There are only about 1,000 pandas left in the wild.

Above: The giant panda has become a symbol for endangered species around the world.

Left: China's controversial one-child policy will remain in place for at least another decade.

Just one child
The population of China is over 1.3 billion and growing by about 10 million people every year. This puts a huge strain on the country's resources, so since 1979 families have only been allowed to have one child. Couples that have more than one child can be fined. The rule is strictly enforced in the cities, but less so in the countryside.

Tibet
Tibet lies in the highlands of southwest China at an average height of 14,000 feet (4,267 m) above sea level. It is known as the "roof of the world." In 1950 China invaded Tibet and in 1965 made it a self-governing region of China, called Xizang Zizhiqu.

East Asia

East Asia is dominated by China, the world's third-largest country, and its most populous. Chinese civilization began over 5,000 years ago; it the oldest continuing civilization in the world. Over the centuries China greatly influenced its neighbors who adopted many of its customs and religions, as well as its writing system. Western China is mainly covered with deserts and mountains and is sparsely populated. Most people live on the fertile plains of eastern China where there are many large cities. To the north of China lies vast, landlocked Mongolia, the least densely populated country in the world. The Korean peninsula juts out from China and is divided into North Korea and South Korea. North Korea is governed by a dictator and has massive economic problems. In contrast, South Korea is a wealthy, industrialized country. Taiwan lies just off the coast of China and the Taiwanese enjoy high living standards.

RUSSIAN FEDERATION

KAZAKHSTAN

KYRGYZSTAN

TAJIKISTAN

PAKISTAN

INDIA

NEPAL

BHUTAN

BURMA

INDIA

LAOS

VIET

Naadam horse race
Yurt
Ölgiy
Altay
Altai Mountains
Selenge
Uliastay
M O N G
Traditional Mongolian costume
Airag (ferm mare
Dalandzadg
Dalandzadgad
Takin
Ürümqi
Uygur girl
Horsehead fiddle player
Turpan
Korla
Tarim
Gobi
Kashi
Sampan
Yarkant
Tarim Basin
Golden pheasant
C H I N
Jade necklace
Erhu fiddler
Hotan
Snow leopard
Chow-chow
Lanzho
Plateau
of
Tibet
Giant Buddha statue
Tibetan monk
Tai-chi
Potala Palace
Kiangs (wild asses)
Cheng
Lhasa
Baoding Shan rock carvings
Mt Everest
Lancang
Yangtze
Yangtze
Cormorant fisherman
Ginkgo bilo
Kunming
Yuan
Stone forest
Himalaya

0			400 miles
0			400 kilometers

96

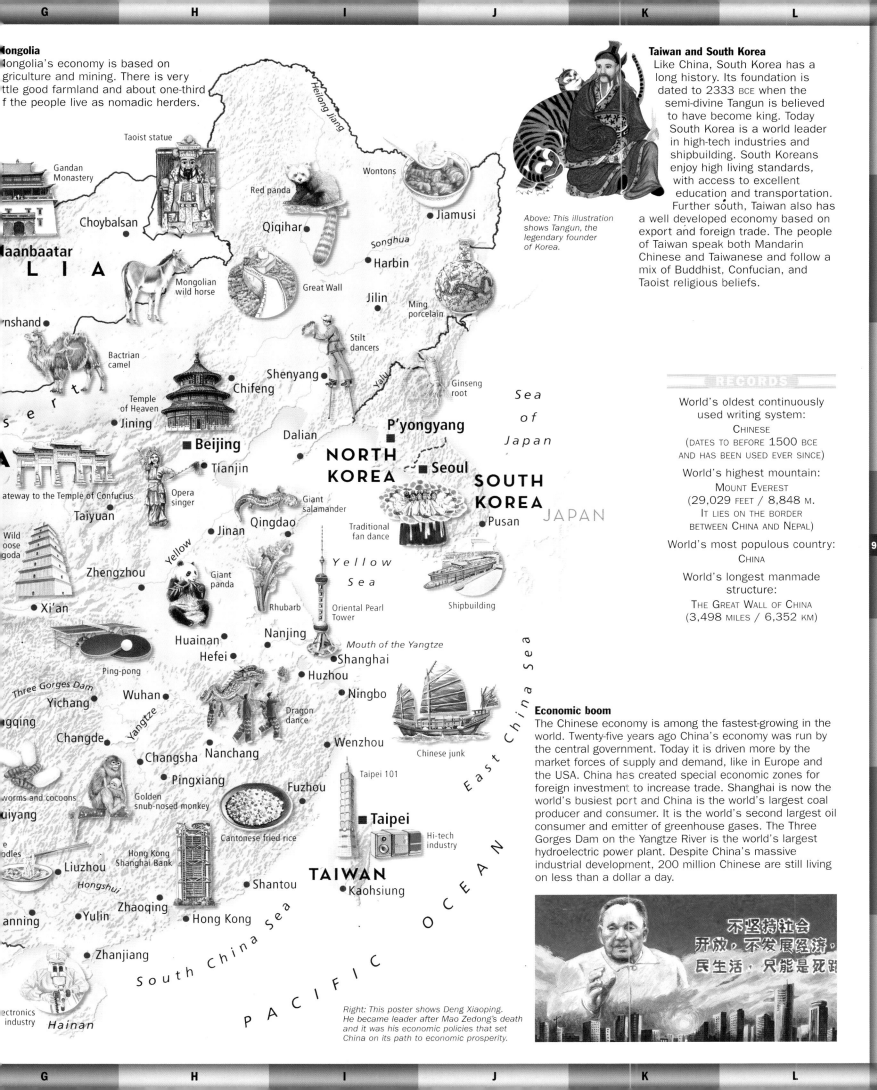

Mongolia

Mongolia's economy is based on agriculture and mining. There is very little good farmland and about one-third of the people live as nomadic herders.

Gandan Monastery

Taoist statue

Choybalsan

Red panda

Wontons

Jiamusi

Qiqihar

Ulaanbaatar

M O N G O L I A

Songhua

Mongolian wild horse

Harbin

Great Wall

Jilin

Heilong Jiang

Ming porcelain

Tianshand

Bactrian camel

Desert

Temple of Heaven

Shenyang

Chifeng

Stilt dancers

Yalu

Ginseng root

Sea of Japan

Jining

Dalian

P'yongyang

Beijing

Tianjin

Opera singer

NORTH KOREA

Seoul

SOUTH KOREA

JAPAN

Gateway to the Temple of Confucius

Taiyuan

Giant salamander

Traditional fan dance

Pusan

Wild Goose Pagoda

Jinan

Qingdao

Yellow Sea

Zhengzhou

Giant panda

Yellow

Rhubarb

Oriental Pearl Tower

Shipbuilding

Xi'an

Ping-pong

Huainan

Nanjing

Mouth of the Yangtze

Hefei

Shanghai

Huzhou

Three Gorges Dam

Yichang

Wuhan

Ningbo

Chongqing

Yangtze

Dragon dance

Changde

Wenzhou

East China Sea

Changsha

Nanchang

Chinese junk

Golden snub-nosed monkey

Pingxiang

Fuzhou

Taipei 101

Guiyang

silkworms and cocoons

Cantonese fried rice

Hi-tech industry

noodles

Liuzhou

Hong Kong Shanghai Bank

Taipei

TAIWAN

Hongshui

Shantou

Kaohsiung

Nanning

Zhaoqing

Yulin

Hong Kong

South China Sea

Zhanjiang

electronics industry

Hainan

P A C I F I C   O C E A N

Taiwan and South Korea

Like China, South Korea has a long history. Its foundation is dated to 2333 BCE when the semi-divine Tangun is believed to have become king. Today South Korea is a world leader in high-tech industries and shipbuilding. South Koreans enjoy high living standards, with access to excellent education and transportation. Further south, Taiwan also has a well developed economy based on export and foreign trade. The people of Taiwan speak both Mandarin Chinese and Taiwanese and follow a mix of Buddhist, Confucian, and Taoist religious beliefs.

Above: This illustration shows Tangun, the legendary founder of Korea.

RECORDS

World's oldest continuously used writing system:
CHINESE
(DATES TO BEFORE 1500 BCE AND HAS BEEN USED EVER SINCE)

World's highest mountain:
MOUNT EVEREST
(29,029 FEET / 8,848 M.
IT LIES ON THE BORDER BETWEEN CHINA AND NEPAL)

World's most populous country:
CHINA

World's longest manmade structure:
THE GREAT WALL OF CHINA
(3,498 MILES / 6,352 KM)

Economic boom

The Chinese economy is among the fastest-growing in the world. Twenty-five years ago China's economy was run by the central government. Today it is driven more by the market forces of supply and demand, like in Europe and the USA. China has created special economic zones for foreign investment to increase trade. Shanghai is now the world's busiest port and China is the world's largest coal producer and consumer. It is the world's second largest oil consumer and emitter of greenhouse gases. The Three Gorges Dam on the Yangtze River is the world's largest hydroelectric power plant. Despite China's massive industrial development, 200 million Chinese are still living on less than a dollar a day.

不坚持社会
开放，不发展经济，
民生活，只能是死路

Right: This poster shows Deng Xiaoping. He became leader after Mao Zedong's death and it was his economic policies that set China on its path to economic prosperity.

97

Japan

Japan is made up of a long string of more than 3,000 islands in the Pacific Ocean off the coast of East Asia. Most of the population lives on the four main islands of Hokkaido, Honshu (the largest), Shikoku, and Kyushu. In Japan the sea and the mountains are never far apart and no point is farther than 100 miles (160 km) from the coast. Nearly three-quarters of the land is mountainous and wooded and there is little room for farming.

The biggest crop is rice, which is a staple food, along with fish. Japan takes a larger catch from the sea than any other nation and continues the much-opposed hunting of whales. Japan's islands are located on the Pacific Ring of Fire where three of the Earth's tectonic plates collide. So not only does the climate vary greatly from the chilly north to the tropical south, life in Japan is also punctuated with earthquakes, typhoons, and tsunamis. The coastline is amazingly varied with deep inlets and bays which make magnificent harbors. Mount Fujiyama on Honshu Island is the highest point at 12,338 feet (2,200 m). It is a beautiful dormant volcano, its peak covered with snow year round. It is also a sacred national symbol of Japan.

Left: The beautiful Japanese crane is a symbol of fidelity and luck.

RECORDS

World's largest bank (by assets):
JAPAN POST BANK

World's oldest pottery:
JOMON (FROM ABOUT 13,000 YEARS AGO)

Japan's largest trading partners:
USA, CHINA, EUROPE

World's oldest wooden building:
HORYU-JI TEMPLE, NARA

World's oldest living thing:
JOMONSUGU, CRYPTOMERIA TREE, YAKUSHIMA ISLAND
(MORE THAN 3,000 YEARS OLD)

World's best-selling motorcycle:
HONDA SUPER CUB (MORE THAN 50 MILLION SOLD)

The Ainu people of Hokkaido

The Ainu people live on the island of Hokkaido and further north on the Kuril Islands (The Kurils are administered by the Russian Federation but claimed by Japan). The Ainu have a different culture from the rest of Japan and their language does not appear to be related to any other known language. Only small numbers of Ainu survive, but in June 2008 they were officially recognized by the Japanese parliament as an indigenous minority group.

Right: This Ainu woman has traditional blue tattooing around her mouth. These tattoos are now very rare.

Sumo wrestling

Wrestling has been the national sport of Japan for centuries. The average Sumo wrestler weighs between 300–400 pounds (136–181 kg). The two contestants use their weight, power, and lightning speed to try to force each other to touch the ground or step out of the small ring. They wear only loin clothes, gripping each other by the belt.

Wildlife in Japan

With its very diverse climate zones, Japan has a great variety of wildlife, from brown bears in the north to tropical snakes in the south. The Japanese macaque is one of Japan's most famous mammals—no other monkey is found this far north. Other special Japanese animals include the beautiful crane, the Japanese deer, the fox (kitsune), and the raccoon dog (tanuki).

Below: Japanese macaque monkeys take steam baths in the hot thermal waters in the north of Honshu island. They also make snowballs and have snow fights.

RUSSIAN FEDERATION
(Administered by Russian Federation. Claimed by Japan.)

Ostrov Iturup

Ostrov Shikotan

Ostrov Kunashir

Kuril Islands

Sea of Okhotsk

PACIFIC OCEAN

Hokkaido

Wakkanai

Kitami

Kushiro

Sashimi

Obihiro

Sapporo

Muroran

Aomori

Akita

Sakata

Sendai

Japanese crane

Portable shrine

Japanese serow

Ainu man

Japanese sawshark

Woman cooking octopus

Sapporo Snow Festival

Setsuban festival

Dried calamari

Japanese macaque

Sake

Shinto priestess

Giant spider crab

Pufferfish

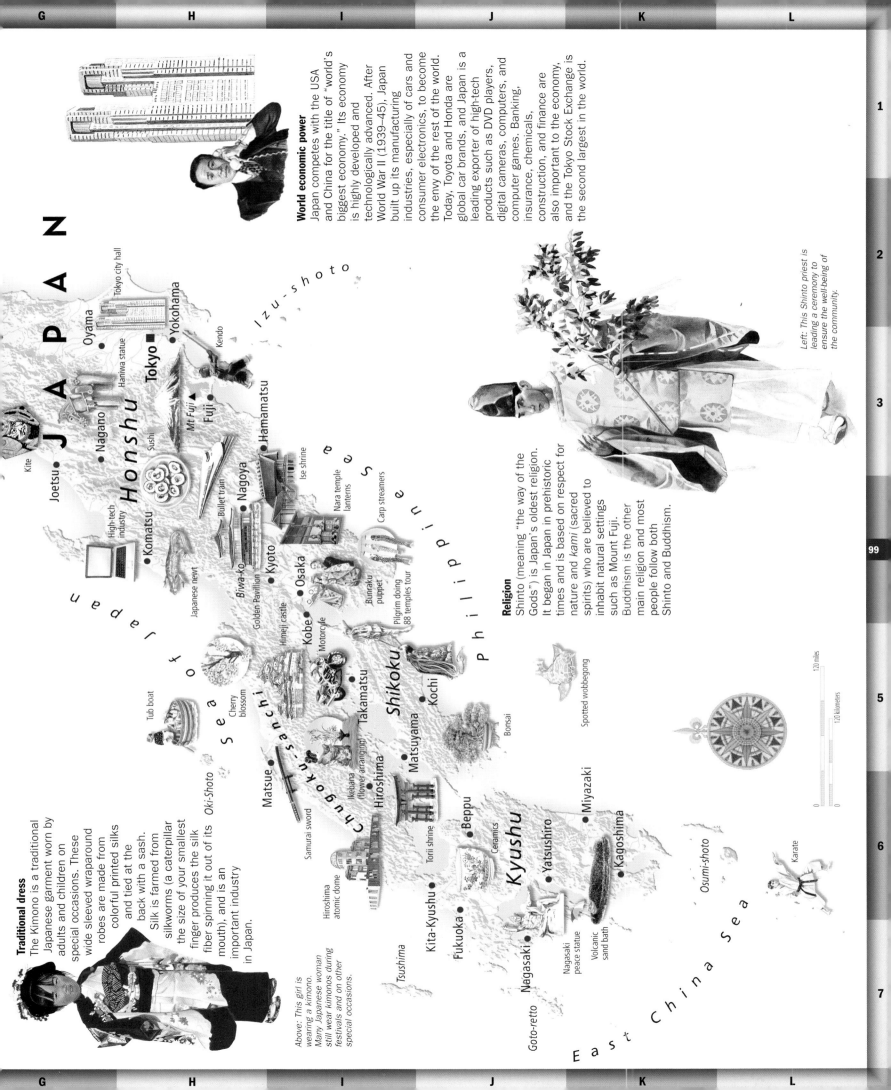

J A P A N

World economic power

Japan competes with the USA and China for the title of "world's biggest economy." Its economy is highly developed and technologically advanced. After World War II (1939–45), Japan built up its manufacturing industries, especially of cars and consumer electronics, to become the envy of the rest of the world. Today, Toyota and Honda are global car brands, and Japan is a leading exporter of high-tech products such as DVD players, digital cameras, computers, and computer games. Banking, insurance, chemicals, construction, and finance are also important to the economy, and the Tokyo Stock Exchange is the second largest in the world.

Left: This Shinto priest is leading a ceremony to ensure the well-being of the community.

Religion

Shinto (meaning "the way of the Gods") is Japan's oldest religion. It began in Japan in prehistoric times and is based on respect for nature and *kami* (sacred spirits) who are believed to inhabit natural settings such as Mount Fuji. Buddhism is the other main religion and most people follow both Shinto and Buddhism.

Traditional dress

The Kimono is a traditional Japanese garment worn by adults and children on special occasions. These wide sleeved wraparound robes are made from colorful printed silks and tied at the back with a sash. Silk is farmed from silkworms (a caterpillar the size of your smallest finger produces the silk fiber spinning it out of its mouth), and is an important industry in Japan.

Above: This girl is wearing a kimono. Many Japanese woman still wear kimonos during festivals and on other special occasions.

Izu-shoto

Tokyo city hall

Haniwa statue

Kendo

Oyama

Yokohama

Tokyo

Nagano

Fuji

Mt Fuji ▲

Hamamatsu

Kite

Joetsu

Honshu

Sushi

High-tech industry

Komatsu

Japanese newt

Bullet train

Ise shrine

Nagoya

Nara temple lanterns

Carp streamers

Kyoto

Golden Pavillion

Biwa-ko

Osaka

Kobe

Motorcyle

Himeji castle

Bunraku puppet

Pilgrim doing 88 temples tour

Spotted wobbegong

Bonsai

Chugoku-sanchi

Oki-Shoto

Tub boat

Cherry blossom

Samurai sword

Hiroshima atomic dome

Torii shrine

Matsue

Ikebana (flower arranging)

Hiroshima

Takamatsu

Shikoku

Matsuyama

Kochi

Philippine Sea

Sea of Japan

Tsushima

Kita-Kyushu

Fukuoka

Nagasaki

Nagasaki peace statue

Goto-retto

Volcanic sand bath

Yatsushiro

Ceramics

Kyushu

Beppu

Miyazaki

Kagoshima

Osumi-shoto

Karate

East China Sea

120 miles

120 kilometers

CLIMATE AND WEATHER

More than any other continent, Africa is a land of the tropics. Every day of the year the overhead sun sends its hot, vertical rays at midday. This also makes it the warmest of the continents, and the only difference in Africa's seasons is between rainy and dry periods. The far north and south have a milder Mediterranean climate, enabling grapes and other fruit to be grown, but the rest of Africa is tropical. In the central rain forest belt the climate is endlessly hot and humid with daily downpours. In the vast desert regions it often happens that not one drop of rain falls from one year to the next. You will find snow in Africa—but only on the peaks of the highest mountains.

Mediterranean

Atlas Mountains

S a h a r a

Niger

Lake Chad

S a h e l

Sénégal

Lake Volta

Mouths of the Niger

Gulf of Guinea

Congo

ATLANTIC OCEAN

Kalahari Desert

Cape of Good Hope

AFRICA

Only on one continent does the world's longest river cross the world's largest desert: Africa. This is the planet's second largest continent and second longest—its northernmost point (in Tunisia) is the same distance from the Equator (2,400 miles/3,862 km) as its southernmost tip (Cape Agulhas). Africa is so big you could fit 11 billion soccer pitches or three USAs easily onto its landmass. The Sahara Desert, with its exposed rock outcrops, shifting sand dunes, and camel trains, covers almost 30 percent of the continent. The Nile River brings vital water supplies to its desert shores near the end of its 4,160 mile (6,695 km) journey across Africa. To the east and south the Great Rift Valley with its vast tropical savanna (grasslands) is Africa's other key feature. Here huge herds of wildebeest, zebras, elephants, and giraffes graze, as do the lions, leopards, and hyenas that feed on them. The equator runs right through the center of the continent, with a belt of misty tropical rain forests, home to the endangered gorilla—the largest living primate in Africa.

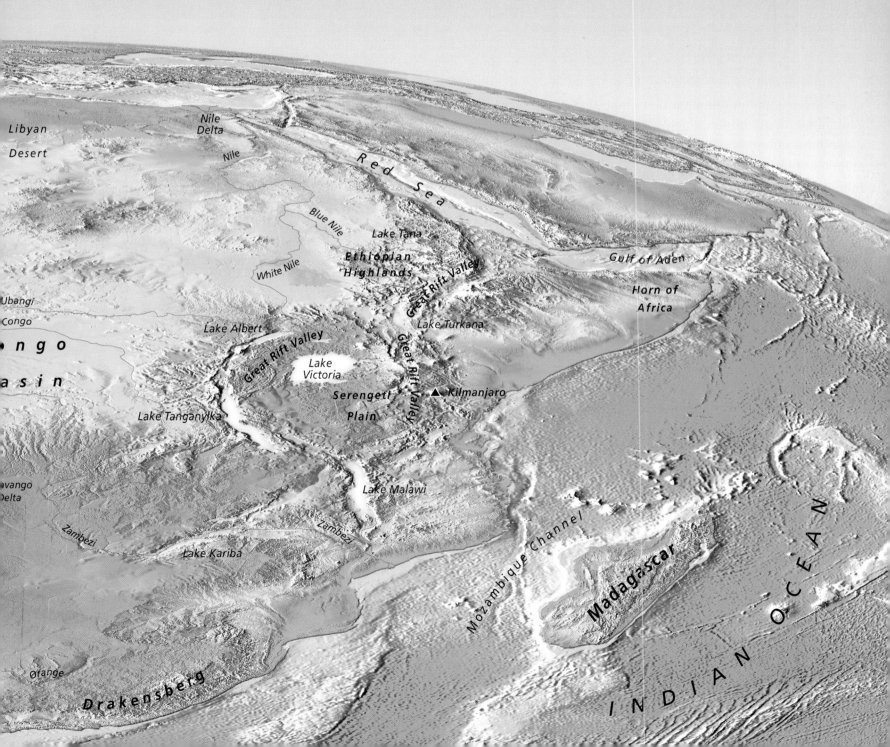

Libyan Desert

Nile Delta

Nile

Red Sea

Blue Nile

Lake Tana

White Nile

Ethiopian Highlands

Gulf of Aden

Ubangi

Congo

Horn of Africa

Great Rift Valley

Lake Albert

Lake Turkana

ongo

Great Rift Valley

Lake Victoria

asin

Great Rift Valley

▲ Kilmanjaro

Lake Tanganyika

Serengeti Plain

avango Delta

Lake Malawi

Zambezi

Zambezi

Mozambique Channel

Lake Kariba

Madagascar

INDIAN OCEAN

Orange

Drakensberg

HEALTH

Africa has been badly hit by the global AIDS (Acquired Immune Deficiency Syndrome) epidemic. In some countries more than 20 percent of the adult population suffers from HIV or AIDS. Most of those who are sick with HIV or AIDS cannot afford the drugs they need to treat the illness. Tuberculosis and malaria are just two other diseases that are widespread and lethal in Africa. African governments and international agencies are working hard to educate people about how to avoid these sicknesses and helping those who are already sick.

Above: in this magnified image a human immune-system cell is shown being attacked by the HIV virus that causes AIDS.

POLITICAL MAP OF AFRICA

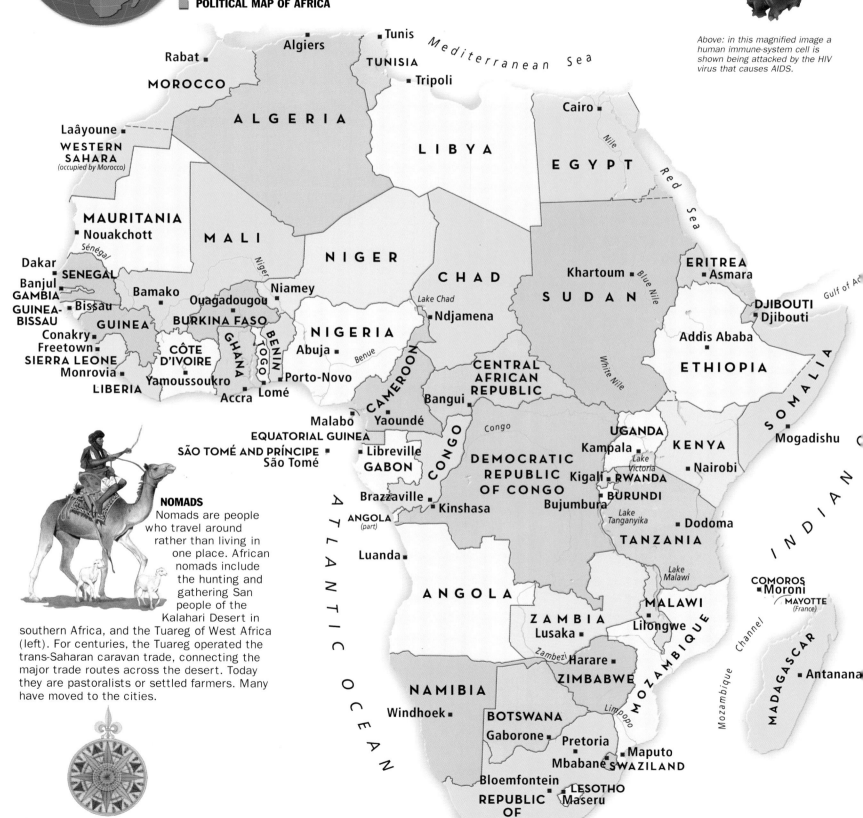

NOMADS

Nomads are people who travel around rather than living in one place. African nomads include the hunting and gathering San people of the Kalahari Desert in southern Africa, and the Tuareg of West Africa (left). For centuries, the Tuareg operated the trans-Saharan caravan trade, connecting the major trade routes across the desert. Today they are pastoralists or settled farmers. Many have moved to the cities.

Tunis
Algiers
Rabat
TUNISIA
Tripoli
MOROCCO
Mediterranean Sea
Laâyoune
ALGERIA
LIBYA
EGYPT
Cairo
WESTERN SAHARA (occupied by Morocco)
Nile
Red Sea
MAURITANIA
Nouakchott
MALI
NIGER
CHAD
Khartoum
Blue Nile
SUDAN
ERITREA
Asmara
Dakar
Sénégal
SENEGAL
Niger
Niamey
DJIBOUTI
Djibouti
Banjul
GAMBIA
Bamako
Ouagadougou
Lake Chad
Ndjamena
Bissau
GUINEA-BISSAU
BURKINA FASO
NIGERIA
Addis Ababa
Conakry
GUINEA
CÔTE D'IVOIRE
GHANA
TOGO
BENIN
Abuja
Benue
ETHIOPIA
Freetown
SIERRA LEONE
Porto-Novo
CAMEROON
CENTRAL AFRICAN REPUBLIC
White Nile
SOMALIA
Monrovia
Yamoussoukro
Lomé
Accra
LIBERIA
Bangui
Malabo
Yaoundé
Mogadishu
EQUATORIAL GUINEA
SÃO TOMÉ AND PRÍNCIPE
São Tomé
Libreville
GABON
CONGO
Congo
DEMOCRATIC REPUBLIC OF CONGO
UGANDA
Kampala
KENYA
Nairobi
Lake Victoria
Kigali
RWANDA
Brazzaville
Kinshasa
Bujumbura
BURUNDI
ANGOLA (part)
Dodoma
Lake Tanganyika
TANZANIA
Luanda
INDIAN OCEAN
Lake Malawi
COMOROS
Moroni
MAYOTTE (France)
ANGOLA
MALAWI
ZAMBIA
Lilongwe
Lusaka
MOZAMBIQUE
Mozambique Channel
Zambezi
Harare
MADAGASCAR
Antanana
ZIMBABWE
NAMIBIA
ATLANTIC OCEAN
Windhoek
Limpopo
BOTSWANA
Gaborone
Pretoria
Maputo
Mbabane
SWAZILAND
Bloemfontein
LESOTHO
Maseru
REPUBLIC OF SOUTH AFRICA
Cape Town

0   1000 miles

0   1000 kilometers

Above: This fossil, known as the Toumaï skull, was found in Chad in 2002. It may belong to one of our earliest hominid ancestors.

AFRICAN ORIGINS

Most scientists now believe that Africa is the original homeland of the hominid family, to which modern humans also belong. They have found fossils of early hominids (human-like creatures) dating to millions of years ago, as well as fossils of *Homo sapiens* (modern humans) from about 160,000 years ago. Most scientists think that modern humans began a long migration from Africa about 100,000 years ago and that from here they spread across the globe. All of the people in the world today are believed to descend from these early African migrants.

Africa

Africa includes 53 independent nations, ranging from the huge, mainly desert-covered lands of Sudan, Mali, and Algeria, to the tiny tropical islands of São Tomé and the Seychelles. At the end of the 19th century almost all of Africa was colonialized by European countries. They continued to rule until the 1950s and 1960s when most African nations regained their independence. Since then, many countries have experienced political instability with corrupt governments and frequent wars causing widespread poverty. People in many countries, especially in central and southern Africa, are still very poor with little or no access to education, health care, or even clean drinking water. However, Africa is rich in natural resources, with large reserves of oil, natural gas, diamonds and other minerals, as well as agricultural products. The African Economic Outlook 2008 reported record growth over the last five years with many countries exporting more than ever before.

Above: About 40 percent of African children do not attend school. As Africa changes and joins the global economy, young people will need basic skills to find jobs. In many poor countries children stay home to help their parents, and schools lack even basic facilities.

MOROCCO

Country name Kingdom of Morocco
Area 172,413 sq mi
(446,550 sq km)
Population 34,343,219
Government Constitutional monarchy
Capital Rabat
Currency Moroccan dirham
Languages Arabic, Berber languages, French, Spanish, English
Main religions Muslim 98.7%, Christian 1.1%, Jewish 0.2%
Literacy 52.3%
GDP per capita $4,100 (2007 est.)

ALGERIA

Country name People's Democratic Republic of Algeria
Area 919,594 sq mi
(2,381,740 sq km)
Population 33,769,669
Government Republic
Capital Algiers
Currency Algerian dinar
Languages Arabic, French, Berber languages
Main religions Sunni Muslim 99%, Christian and Jewish 1%
Literacy 69.9%
GDP per capita $6,500 (2007 est.)

TUNISIA

Country name Tunisian Republic
Area 63,170 sq mi
(163,610 sq km)
Population 10,383,577
Government Republic
Capital Tunis
Currency Tunisian dinar
Languages Arabic, French
Main religions Muslim 98% (official; mostly Sunni), Christian 1%
Literacy 74.3%
GDP per capita $7,500 (2007 est.)

LIBYA

Country name Great Socialist People's Libyan Arab Jamahiriya (Mass-State)
Area 679,362 sq mi
(1,759,540 sq km)
Population 6,173,579
Government Islamic Arabic Socialist "Mass-State"; in practise, an authoritarian state
Capital Tripoli
Currency Libyan dinar
Languages Arabic, Italian, English
Main religions Muslim 97% (official; mostly Sunni)
Literacy 82.6%
GDP per capita $12,300 (2007 est.)

CAPE VERDE ISLANDS

Country name Republic of Cape Verde
Area 1,557 sq mi
(4,033 sq km)
Population 426,998
Government Republic
Capital Praia
Currency Cape Verdean escudo
Languages Portuguese, Crioulo (a blend of Portuguese and West African words)
Main religions Roman Catholic (infused with Indigenous beliefs), Protestant (mostly Church of the Nazarene)
Literacy 76.6%
GDP per capita $3,200 (2007 est.)

CHAD

Country name Republic of Chad
Area 495,755 sq mi
(1,284,000 sq km)
Population 10,111,337
Government Republic
Capital Ndjamena
Currency CFA franc
Languages French, Arabic, Sara, more than 120 different languages and dialects
Main religions Muslim 53.1%, Catholic 20.1%, Protestant 14.2%, Animist 7.3%, Atheist 3.1%
Literacy 25.7%
GDP per capita $1,700 (2007 est.)

SUDAN

Country name Republic of the Sudan
Area 967,498 sq mi
(2,505,810 sq km)
Population 40,218,455
Government Republic with strong military influence
Capital Khartoum
Currency Sudanese pound
Languages Arabic, Nubian, Ta Bedawie, Nilotic dialects, Nilo-Hamitic, Sudanic languages, English
Main religions Sunni Muslim 70%, Indigenous beliefs 25%, Christian 5%
Literacy 61.1%
GDP per capita $2,200 (2007 est.)

ERITREA

Country name State of Eritrea
Area 46,841 sq mi
(121,320 sq km)
Population 5,028,475
Government In transition
Capital Asmara
Currency Nakfa
Languages Arabic, Tigrinya, Afar, Tigre and Kunama, other Cushitic languages
Main religions Muslim (50%), Coptic Christian, Roman Catholic, Protestant
Literacy 58.6%
GDP per capita $800 (2007 est.)

MALI

Country name Republic of Mali
Area 478,766 sq mi
(1,240,000 sq km)
Population 12,324,029
Government Republic
Capital Bamako
Currency CFA franc
Languages French, Bambara 80%, numerous African languages
Main religions Muslim 90%, Christian 1%, Indigenous beliefs 9%
Literacy 46.4%
GDP per capita $1,000 (2007 est.)

NIGER

Country name Republic of Niger
Area 489,191 sq mi
(1,267,000 sq km)
Population 13,272,679
Government Republic
Capital Niamey
Currency CFA franc
Languages French, Hausa, Djerma, Fulani
Main religions Muslim 80%
Literacy 28.7%
GDP per capita $700 (2007 est.)

MAURITANIA

Country name Islamic Republic of Mauritania
Area 397,955 sq mi
(1,030,700 sq km)
Population 3,364,940
Government Democratic Republic
Capital Nouakchott
Currency Ouguiya
Languages Arabic, Pulaar, Soninke, French, Hassaniya, Wolof
Main religions Muslim 100%
Literacy 51.2%
GDP per capita $2,000 (2007 est.)

EGYPT

Country name Arab Republic of Egypt
Area 386,662 sq mi
(1,001,450 sq km)
Population 81,713,517
Government Republic
Capital Cairo
Currency Egyptian pound
Languages Arabic, English, French
Main religions Muslim (mostly Sunni) 90%, Coptic 9%, Other Christian 1%
Literacy 71.4%
GDP per capita $5,500 (2007 est.)

BURKINA FASO

Country name Burkina Faso
Area 105,869 sq mi
(274,200 sq km)
Population 15,264,735
Government Parliamentary republic
Capital Ouagadougou
Currency CFA franc
Languages French, Sudanic languages 90%
Main religions Muslim 50%, Indigenous beliefs 40%, Christian (mainly Roman Catholic) 10%
Literacy 21.8%
GDP per capita $1,300 (2007 est.)

ETHIOPIA

Country name Federal Democratic Republic of Ethiopia

Area 435,186 sq mi (1,127,127 sq km)

Population 78,254,090

Government Federal republic

Capital Addis Ababa

Currency Birr

Languages Amharic, Oromigna, Tigrigna, Somaligna, Guaragigna, Sidamigna and over 200 other languages

Main religions Orthodox 50.6%, Protestant 10.2%, Muslim 32.8%, Animist 4.6%

Literacy 42.7%

GDP per capita $800 (2007 est.)

SIERRA LEONE

Country name Republic of Sierra Leone

Area 27,698 sq mi (71,740 sq km)

Population 6,294,774

Government Constitutional democracy

Capital Freetown

Currency Leone

Languages English, Mende (in the south), Temne (in the north), Krio (English-based Creole)

Main religions Muslim 60%, Christian 10%, Indigenous beliefs 30%

Literacy 35.1%

GDP per capita $700 (2007 est.)

CÔTE D'IVOIRE (IVORY COAST)

Country name Republic of Côte d'Ivoire

Area 12,4502 sq mi (322,460 sq km)

Population 18,373,060

Government Presidential republic. In transition.

Capital Yamoussoukro

Currency CFA franc

Languages French, 60 native dialects with Dioula the most widely spoken

Main religions Muslim 35–40%, Indigenous beliefs 25–40%, Christian 20–30%

Literacy 50.9%

GDP per capita $1,700 (2007 est.)

EQUATORIAL GUINEA

Country name Republic of Equatorial Guinea

Area 10,830 sq mi (28,051 sq km)

Population 616,459

Government Republic

Capital Malabo

Currency CFA franc

Languages Spanish, French, Fang, Bubi, English, Portuguese Creole, Ibo

Main religions nominally Christian and predominantly Roman Catholic, pagan practices

Literacy 85.7%

GDP per capita $12,900 (2007 est.)

GHANA

Country name Republic of Ghana

Area 92,456 sq mi (239,460 sq km)

Population 23,382,848

Government Constitutional democracy

Capital Accra

Currency Ghana cedi

Languages English, about 75 African languages, including Akan, Moshi-Dagomba, Ewe, and Ga

Main religions Christian 68.8%, Muslim 15.9%, traditional 8.5%

Literacy 57.9%

GDP per capita $1,400 (2007 est.)

GUINEA-BISSAU

Country name Republic of Guinea-Bissau

Area 13,946 sq mi (36,120 sq km)

Population 1,503,182

Government Republic

Capital Bissau

Currency CFA franc

Languages Portuguese, Crioulo, Indigenous languages

Main religions Indigenous beliefs 50%, Muslim 45%, Christian 5%

Literacy 42.4%

GDP per capita $500 (2007 est.)

GUINEA

Country name Republic of Guinea

Area 94,925 sq mi (245,857 sq km)

Population 10,211,437

Government Republic

Capital Conakry

Currency Guinean franc

Languages French; each ethnic group has its own language

Main religions Muslim 85%, Christian 8%, Indigenous beliefs 7%

Literacy 29.5%

GDP per capita $1,100 (2007 est.)

SOMALIA

Country name Somalia

Area 246,200 sq mi (637,657 sq km)

Population 9,558,666

Government No permanent national government; transitional

Capital Mogadishu

Currency Somali shilling

Languages Somali, Arabic, Italian, English

Main religions Sunni Muslim

Literacy 37.8%

GDP per capita $600 (2007 est.)

BENIN

Country name Republic of Benin

Area 43,482 sq mi (112,620 sq km)

Population 8,294,941

Government Republic

Capital Porto-Novo

Currency CFA franc

Languages French, Fon and Yoruba, various tribal languages

Main religions Christian 42.8%, Muslim 24.4%, Vodoun 17.3%

Literacy 34.7%

GDP per capita $1,500 (2007 est.)

GAMBIA

Country name Republic of The Gambia

Area 4,362 sq mi (11,300 sq km)

Population 1,735,464

Government Republic

Capital Banjul

Currency Dalasi

Languages English, Mandinka, Wolof, Fula, other indigenous languages

Main religions Muslim 90%, Christian 9%, Indigenous beliefs 1%

Literacy 40.1%

GDP per capita $1,300 (2007 est.)

LIBERIA

Country name Republic of Liberia

Area 43,000,197 sq mi (111,370 sq km)

Population 3,334,587

Government Republic

Capital Monrovia

Currency Liberian dollar

Languages English, about 20 ethnic group languages

Main religions Indigenous beliefs 40%, Christian 40%, Muslim 20%

Literacy 57.5%

GDP per capita $400 (2007 est.)

CENTRAL AFRICAN REPUBLIC

Country name Central African Republic

Area 240,535 sq mi (622,984 sq km)

Population 4,434,873

Government Republic

Capital Bangui

Currency CFA franc

Languages French, Sangho, Indigenous languages

Main religions Indigenous beliefs 35%, Protestant 25%, Roman Catholic 25%, Muslim 15%

Literacy 48.6%

GDP per capita $700 (2007 est.)

TOGO

Country name Togolese Republic

Area 21,924 sq mi (56,785 sq km)

Population 5,858,673

Government Republic under transition to multiparty democracy

Capital Lome

Currency CFA franc

Languages French, Ewe, Mina, Kabye, Dagomba

Main religions Indigenous beliefs 51%, Christian 29%, Muslim 20%

Literacy 60.9%

GDP per capita $800 (2007 est.)

GABON

Country name Gabonese Republic

Area 103,346 sq mi (267,667 sq km)

Population 1,485,832

Government Republic; multiparty presidential regime

Capital Libreville

Currency CFA franc

Languages French, Fang, Myene, Nzebi, Bapounou/Eschira, Bandjabi

Main religions Christian 55%–75%, animist, Muslim less than 1%

Literacy 63.2%

GDP per capita $14,100 (2007 est.)

CAMEROON

Country name Republic of Cameroon

Area 183,568 sq mi (475,440 sq km)

Population 18,467,692

Government Republic; multiparty presidential regime

Capital Yaounde

Currency CFA franc

Languages English, French, 24 African language groups

Main religions Indigenous beliefs 40%, Christian 40%, Muslim 20%

Literacy 67.9%

GDP per capita $2,100 (2007 est.)

SÃO TOMÉ AND PRÍNCIPE

Country name Democratic Republic of São Tomé and Príncipe

Area 386 sq mi (1,001 sq km)

Population 206,178

Government Republic

Capital São Tomé

Currency Dobra

Languages Portuguese, Creole, Fang

Main religions Roman Catholic 70.3%, Evangelical 3.4%, New Apostolic 2%, none 19.4%

Literacy 84.9%

GDP per capita $1,600 (2007 est.)

NIGERIA

Country name Federal Republic of Nigeria

Area 356,668 sq mi (923,768 sq km)

Population 138,283,240

Government Federal republic

Capital Abuja

Currency Naira

Languages English, Hausa, Yoruba, Igbo (Ibo), Fulani

Main religions Muslim 50%, Christian 40%, Indigenous beliefs 10%

Literacy 68%

GDP per capita $2,000 (2007 est.)

DJIBOUTI

Country name Republic of Djibouti

Area 8,880 sq mi (23,000 sq km)

Population 506,221

Government Republic

Capital Djibouti

Currency Djiboutian franc

Languages French, Arabic, Somali, Afar

Main religions Muslim 94%, Christian 6%

Literacy 67.9%

GDP per capita $2,300 (2007 est.)

SENEGAL

Country name Republic of Senegal

Area 75,749 sq mi (196,190 sq km)

Population 12,853,259

Government Republic

Capital Dakar

Currency CFA franc

Languages French, Wolof, Pulaar, Jola, Mandinka

Main religions Muslim 94%, Christian 5%, Indigenous beliefs 1%

Literacy 51.1%

GDP per capita $1,700 (2007 est.)

CONGO

Country name Republic of The Congo

Area 132,046 sq mi (342,000 sq km)

Population 3,903,318

Government Republic

Capital Brazzaville

Currency CFA franc

Languages French, Lingala, and Monokutuba, many local languages and dialects (main: Kikongo)

Main religions Christian 50%, Animist 48%, Muslim 2%

Literacy 83.8%

GDP per capita $3,700 (2007 est.)

DEMOCRATIC REPUBLIC OF CONGO (EX ZAIRE)

Country name Democratic Republic of The Congo
Area 905,567,863 sq mi (2,345,410 sq km)
Population 66,514,506
Government republic
Capital Kinshasa
Currency Congolese franc
Languages French, Lingala, Kingwana, Kikongo, Tshiluba
Main religions Roman Catholic 50%, Protestant 20%, Kimbanguist 10%, Muslim 10%
Literacy 67.2%
GDP per capita $300 (2007 est.)

UGANDA

Country name Republic of Uganda
Area 91,135 sq mi (236,040 sq km)
Population 31,367,972
Government Republic
Capital Kampala
Currency Ugandan shilling
Languages English, Ganda or Luganda, other Niger-Congo languages, Nilo-Saharan languages, Swahili, Arabic
Main religions Protestant 42%, Roman Catholic 41.9%, Muslim 12.1%
Literacy 66.8%
GDP per capita $900 (2007 est.)

MOZAMBIQUE

Country name Republic of Mozambique
Area 309,495,629 sq mi (801,590 sq km)
Population 21,284,701
Government Republic
Capital Maputo
Currency Metical
Languages Portuguese, Emakhuwa, Xichangana, Elomwe, Cisena, Echuwabo
Main religions Catholic 23.8%, Muslim 17.8%, Zionist Christian 17.5%, other 17.8%, none 23.1%
Literacy 47.8%
GDP per capita $800 (2007 est.)

RWANDA

Country name Republic of Rwanda
Area 10,169,158 sq mi (26,338 sq km)
Population 10,186,063
Government Presidential republic, multiparty system
Capital Kigali
Currency Rwandan franc
Languages Kinyarwanda, French, English, Kiswahili
Main religions Roman Catholic 56.5%, Protestant 26%, Adventist 11.1%, Muslim 4.6%
Literacy 70.4%
GDP per capita $900 (2007 est.)

TANZANIA

Country name United Republic of Tanzania
Area 364,900 sq mi (945,087 sq km)
Population 40,213,162
Government Republic
Capital Dodoma
Currency Tanzanian shilling
Languages Kiswahili, English, Arabic, many local languages
Main religions Muslim 35%, Indigenous beliefs 35%, Christian 30%; Zanzibar is more than 99% Muslim
Literacy 69.4%
GDP per capita $1,300 (2007 est.)

SOUTH AFRICA

Country name Republic of South Africa
Area 471,010,656 sq mi (1,219,912 sq km)
Population 43,786,115
Government Republic
Capitals Pretoria (adm.), Cape Town (leg.), Bloemfontein (jud.)
Currency Rand
Languages IsiZulu, IsiXhosa, Afrikaans, Sepedi, English, Setswana, Sesotho, Xitsonga, Ndebele, Pedi, Swazi
Main religions Christian 68.7%, Muslim 1.5%
Literacy 86.4%
GDP per capita $9,800 (2007 est.)

ANGOLA

Country name Republic of Angola
Area 481,353 sq mi (1,246,700 sq km)
Population 12,531,357
Government Republic; multiparty presidential regime
Capital Luanda
Currency Kwanza
Languages Portuguese, Bantu and other African languages
Main religions Indigenous beliefs 47%, Roman Catholic 38%, Protestant 15%
Literacy 67.4%
GDP per capita $5,600 (2007 est.)

ZAMBIA

Country name Republic of Zambia
Area 290,585 sq mi (752,614 sq km)
Population 11,669,534
Government Republic
Capital Lusaka
Currency Zambian kwacha
Languages English, Bemba, Kaonda, Lozi, Lunda, Luvale, Nyanja, Tonga, 70 others
Main religions Christian 50%–75%, Muslim and Hindu 24%–49%
Literacy 80.6%
GDP per capita $1,300 (2007 est.)

ZIMBABWE

Country name Republic of Zimbabwe
Area 150,803 sq mi (390,580 sq km)
Population 12,382,920
Government Parliamentary republic
Capital Harare
Currency Zimbabwean dollar
Languages English, Shona, Sindebele, numerous tribal dialects
Main religions syncretic (Christian-Indigenous mix) 50%, Christian 25%, Indigenous beliefs 24%
Literacy 90.7%
GDP per capita $200 (2007 est.)

MALAWI

Country name Republic of Malawi
Area 45,745 sq mi (118,480 sq km)
Population 13,931,831
Government Multiparty democracy
Capital Lilongwe
Currency Malawian kwacha
Languages Chichewa, Chinyanja, Chiyao, Chitumbuka, Chisena, Chilomwe, Chitonga
Main religions Christian 79.9%, Muslim 12.8%
Literacy 62.7%
GDP per capita $800 (2007 est.)

KENYA

Country name Republic of Kenya
Area 224,962,422 sq mi (582,650 sq km)
Population 37,953,838
Government Republic
Capital Nairobi
Currency Kenyan shilling
Languages English, Kiswahili, numerous Indigenous languages
Main religions Protestant 45%, Roman Catholic 33%, Muslim 10%, Indigenous beliefs 10%
Literacy 85.1%
GDP per capita $1,700 (2007 est.)

COMOROS

Country name Union of the Comoros
Area 837 sq mi (2,170 sq km)
Population 731,775
Government Republic
Capital Moroni
Currency Comoran franc
Languages Arabic, French, Shikomoro (blend of Swahili and Arabic)
Main religions Sunni Muslim 98%, Roman Catholic 2%
Literacy 56.5%
GDP per capita $1,100 (2007 est.)

LESOTHO

Country name Kingdom of Lesotho
Area 11,720 sq mi (30,355 sq km)
Population 2,128,180
Government Parliamentary constitutional monarchy
Capital Maseru
Currency Loti; South African rand
Languages Sesotho, English, Zulu, Xhosa
Main religions Christian 80%, Indigenous beliefs 20%
Literacy 84.8%
GDP per capita $1,300 (2007 est.)

MAURITIUS

Country name Republic of Mauritius
Area 787 sq mi (2,040 sq km)
Population 1,274,189
Government Parliamentary democracy
Capital Port Louis
Currency Mauritian rupee
Languages Creole, Bhojpuri, French, English
Main religions Hindu 48%, Roman Catholic 23.6%, Muslim 16.6%, Other Christian 8.6%
Literacy 84.4%
GDP per capita $11,200 (2007 est.)

SEYCHELLES

Country name Republic of Seychelles
Area 175 sq mi (455 sq km)
Population 82,247
Government Republic
Capital Victoria
Currency Seychelles rupee
Languages Creole, English, French
Main religions Roman Catholic 82.3%, Anglican 6.4%, Seventh Day Adventist 1.1%, other Christian 3.4%, Hindu 2.1%, Muslim 1.1%
Literacy 91.8%
GDP per capita $16,600 (2007 est.)

SWAZILAND

Country name Kingdom of Swaziland
Area 6,703,891 sq mi (17,363 sq km)
Population 1,128,814
Government Monarchy
Capital Mbabane
Currency Lilangeni
Languages English, siSwati
Main religions Zionist 40%, Roman Catholic 20%, Muslim 10%, Indigenous and other 30%
Literacy 81.6%
GDP per capita $4,800 (2007 est.)

BOTSWANA

Country name Republic of Botswana
Area 231,804 sq mi (600,370 sq km)
Population 1,842,323
Government Parliamentary republic
Capital Gaborone
Currency Pula
Languages English, SetswanaKalanga, Sekgalagadi
Main religions Christian 71.6%, Badimo 6%
Literacy 81.2%
GDP per capita $16,400 (2007 est.)

MADAGASCAR

Country name Republic of Madagascar
Area 226,657 sq mi (587,040 sq km)
Population 20,042,551
Government Republic
Capital Antananarivo
Currency Ariary
Languages English, French, Malagasy
Main religions Indigenous beliefs 52%, Christian 41%, Muslim 7%
Literacy 68.9%
GDP per capita $1,100 (2007 est.)

BURUNDI

Country name Republic of Burundi
Area 10,745 sq mi (27,830 sq km)
Population 8,691,005
Government Republic
Capital Bujumbura
Currency Burundi franc
Languages Kirundi, French, Swahili
Main religions Roman Catholic 62%, Indigenous beliefs 23%, Muslim 10%, Protestant 5%
Literacy 59.3%
GDP per capita $400 (2007 est.)

NAMIBIA

Country name Republic of Namibia
Area 318,695 sq mi (825,418 sq km)
Population 2,088,669
Government Presidential republic
Capital Windhoek
Currency Namibian dollar
Languages English, Afrikaans, German
Main religions Lutheran 50%, other Christian 30%, Indigenous beliefs 10%–20%, Indigenous languages
Literacy 85%
GDP per capita $5,200 (2007 est.)

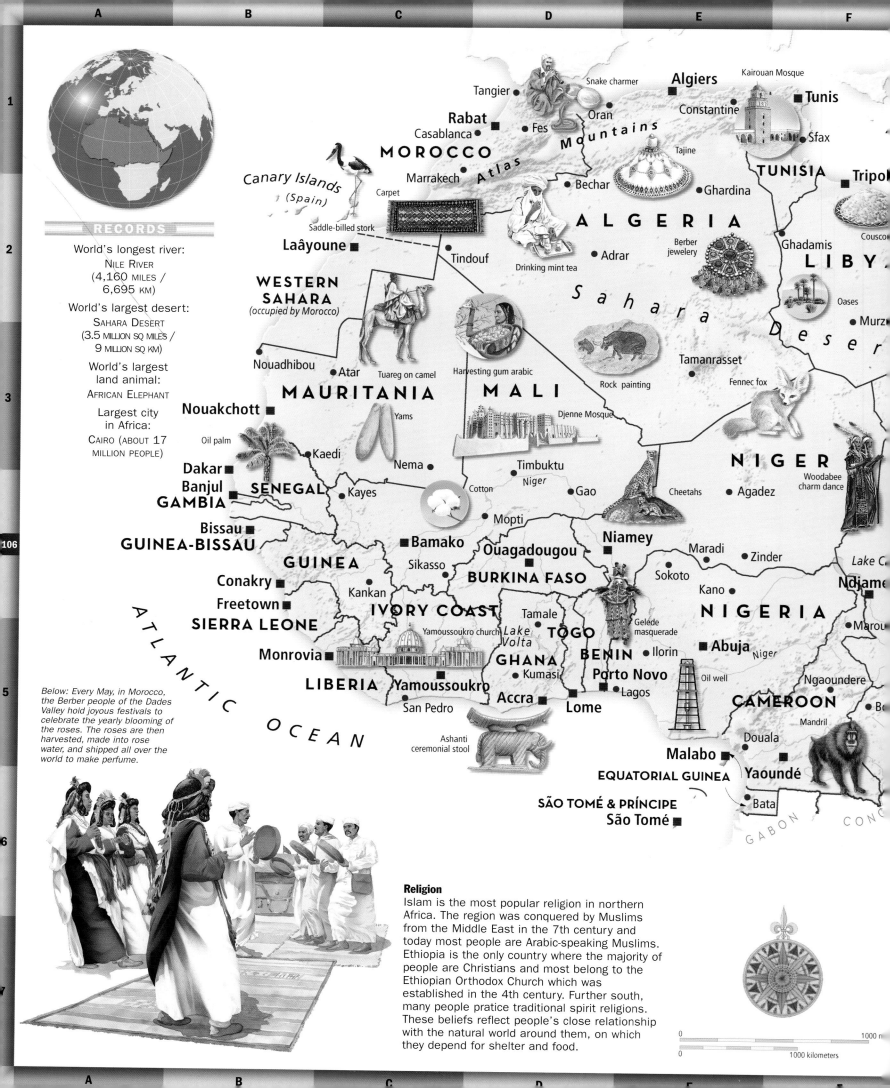

RECORDS

World's longest river:
NILE RIVER
(4,160 MILES /
6,695 KM)

World's largest desert:
SAHARA DESERT
(3.5 MILLION SQ MILES /
9 MILLION SQ KM)

World's largest
land animal:
AFRICAN ELEPHANT

Largest city
in Africa:
CAIRO (ABOUT 17
MILLION PEOPLE)

Tangier

Rabat
Casablanca
MOROCCO
Fes
Oran

Marrakech   *Atlas*   *Mountains*

Snake charmer

Algiers
Constantine
Kairouan Mosque
Tunis
Sfax

TUNISIA

Tripol

Canary Islands
(Spain)

Carpet

Saddle-billed stork

Laâyoune

Tindouf

**WESTERN
SAHARA**
(occupied by Morocco)

Bechar
Tajine
Ghardina

A L G E R I A

Adrar

Drinking mint tea

Berber
jewelery

Ghadamis

LIBY

Oases

Murz

Couscou

Sahara

Nouadhibou

Atar

Tuareg on camel

MAURITANIA

Yams

Oil palm

Kaedi

Nema

Harvesting gum arabic

M A L I

Rock painting

Tamanrasset

Fennec fox

Deser

Nouakchott

Timbuktu
Niger
Gao

Djenne Mosque

N I G E R

Woodabee
charm dance

Cheetahs

Agadez

Dakar
Banjul
GAMBIA
SENEGAL
Kayes
Cotton

Bissau
GUINEA-BISSAU

GUINEA

Bamako
Sikasso

Mopti

Ouagadougou

BURKINA FASO

Niamey

Maradi
Zinder

Sokoto

Lake C

Ndjame

Conakry
Freetown
SIERRA LEONE

Kankan

IVORY COAST
Tamale

Yamoussoukro church   *Lake
Volta*

TOGO

Gelede
masquerade

Kano

N I G E R I A

Marou

Monrovia

LIBERIA   **Yamoussoukro**
San Pedro

GHANA
Kumasi
Accra
Lome

Ashanti
ceremonial stool

BENIN
Porto Novo
Ilorin
Lagos

Abuja
Niger

Oil well

Ngaoundere

CAMEROON

Bo

Mandril

Malabo
EQUATORIAL GUINEA
Yaoundé

Douala

SÃO TOMÉ & PRÍNCIPE
São Tomé

Bata

GABON   *CONG*

*Below: Every May, in Morocco,
the Berber people of the Dades
Valley hold joyous festivals to
celebrate the yearly blooming of
the roses. The roses are then
harvested, made into rose
water, and shipped all over the
world to make perfume.*

A T L A N T I C

O C E A N

Religion

Islam is the most popular religion in northern
Africa. The region was conquered by Muslims
from the Middle East in the 7th century and
today most people are Arabic-speaking Muslims.
Ethiopia is the only country where the majority of
people are Christians and most belong to the
Ethiopian Orthodox Church which was
established in the 4th century. Further south,
many people pratice traditional spirit religions.
These beliefs reflect people's close relationship
with the natural world around them, on which
they depend for shelter and food.

0   1000 m

0   1000 kilometers

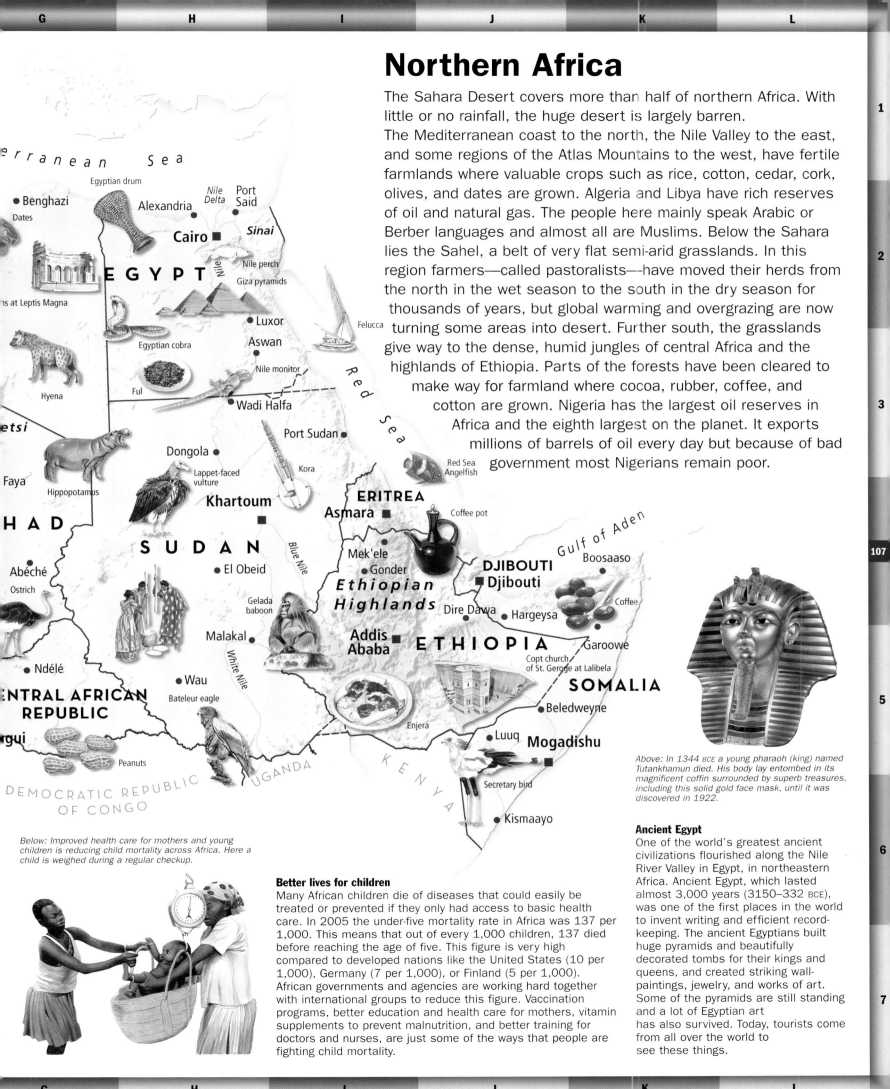

Northern Africa

The Sahara Desert covers more than half of northern Africa. With little or no rainfall, the huge desert is largely barren.

The Mediterranean coast to the north, the Nile Valley to the east, and some regions of the Atlas Mountains to the west, have fertile farmlands where valuable crops such as rice, cotton, cedar, cork, olives, and dates are grown. Algeria and Libya have rich reserves of oil and natural gas. The people here mainly speak Arabic or Berber languages and almost all are Muslims. Below the Sahara lies the Sahel, a belt of very flat semi-arid grasslands. In this region farmers—called pastoralists—-have moved their herds from the north in the wet season to the south in the dry season for thousands of years, but global warming and overgrazing are now turning some areas into desert. Further south, the grasslands give way to the dense, humid jungles of central Africa and the highlands of Ethiopia. Parts of the forests have been cleared to make way for farmland where cocoa, rubber, coffee, and cotton are grown. Nigeria has the largest oil reserves in Africa and the eighth largest on the planet. It exports millions of barrels of oil every day but because of bad government most Nigerians remain poor.

Mediterranean Sea

Benghazi
Dates
Egyptian drum
Alexandria
Nile Delta
Port Said
Cairo
Sinai
EGYPT
Nile
Nile perch
Giza pyramids
s at Leptis Magna
Egyptian cobra
Luxor
Aswan
Ful
Nile monitor
Hyena
Felucca
Wadi Halfa
Red Sea
Port Sudan
Dongola
Kora
Faya
Lappet-faced vulture
Hippopotamus
Khartoum
ERITREA
Asmara
Coffee pot
Red Sea Angelfish
HAD
SUDAN
Blue Nile
Mek'ele
Gonder
Gulf of Aden
Boosaaso
DJIBOUTI
Djibouti
Abéché
El Obeid
Ethiopian Highlands
Coffee
Ostrich
Gelada baboon
Dire Dawa
Hargeysa
Malakal
Addis Ababa
ETHIOPIA
Garoowe
Ndélé
White Nile
Copt church of St. Geroge at Lalibela
Wau
Bateleur eagle
SOMALIA
NTRAL AFRICAN REPUBLIC
Enjera
Beledweyne
gui
Luuq
Mogadishu
Peanuts
DEMOCRATIC REPUBLIC OF CONGO
UGANDA
KENYA
Secretary bird
Kismaayo

Above: In 1344 BCE a young pharaoh (king) named Tutankhamun died. His body lay entombed in its magnificent coffin surrounded by superb treasures, including this solid gold face mask, until it was discovered in 1922.

Below: Improved health care for mothers and young children is reducing child mortality across Africa. Here a child is weighed during a regular checkup.

Better lives for children

Many African children die of diseases that could easily be treated or prevented if they only had access to basic health care. In 2005 the under-five mortality rate in Africa was 137 per 1,000. This means that out of every 1,000 children, 137 died before reaching the age of five. This figure is very high compared to developed nations like the United States (10 per 1,000), Germany (7 per 1,000), or Finland (5 per 1,000). African governments and agencies are working hard together with international groups to reduce this figure. Vaccination programs, better education and health care for mothers, vitamin supplements to prevent malnutrition, and better training for doctors and nurses, are just some of the ways that people are fighting child mortality.

Ancient Egypt

One of the world's greatest ancient civilizations flourished along the Nile River Valley in Egypt, in northeastern Africa. Ancient Egypt, which lasted almost 3,000 years (3150–332 BCE), was one of the first places in the world to invent writing and efficient record-keeping. The ancient Egyptians built huge pyramids and beautifully decorated tombs for their kings and queens, and created striking wall-paintings, jewelry, and works of art. Some of the pyramids are still standing and a lot of Egyptian art has also survived. Today, tourists come from all over the world to see these things.

Southern Africa

The Great Rift Valley runs down the east coast of Africa, from Ethiopia to Mozambique. Here there are deep valleys and lakes and tall mountains, including Mount Kilamanjaro, the highest mountain in Africa. Further west, the Congo river system drains an area the size of Europe. It takes six months for the waters to flow from the headlands through dense rain forests to the Atlantic Ocean. To the south, there are high grasslands known as the veld and then two great deserts—the Kalahari and the Namib. Southern Africa is home to many different cultures and peoples. The Kkoisan peoples, including the San (or "Kalahari Bushmen"), and the "Pygmies," were the original inhabitants of the region. About 2,000 years ago Bantu-speaking peoples moved into the area and today most southern Africans are descended from them. During the colonial period European settlers came, as well as people of Indian descent. Botswana and South Africa are the richest nations in this region with their economies largely based on diamonds and other mining industries. Other countries in this area, such as Zimbabwe, Mozambique, and Malawi, are among the poorest in the world.

Right: Africa has more than 30 percent of the planet's mineral reserves and mining is an important industry in many countries. Diamonds, gold, cobalt, uranium, nickel, and bauxite are among the most important minerals.

African animals

Africa has a spectacular number of unique animals. The vast savannas are home to predators, such as cheetahs (the fastest animals on land), lions, leopards, hyenas, and wild dogs that feast on the grassland herbivores like zebras, gazelles, impala, wildebeest, and rhinoceros. Birds are also plentiful, including ostriches (the largest living bird), hornbills, parrots, flamingos, and pelicans. African forests hold a wide variety of primates, such as gorillas, chimpanzees, baboons, and mandrills, as well as large herbivores like forest elephants and okapi. Ferocious crocodiles live along river banks and around waterholes.

RECORDS

World's highest free-standing mountain:
MOUNT KILIMANJARO
(19,331 feet / 5,892 m)

Largest crack in the Earth's crust:
THE RIFT VALLEY
(6,000 MILES / 9,000 KM FROM LEBANON TO MOZAMBIQUE)

World's largest bird:
THE OSTRICH

World's fastest land animal:
CHEETAH (70 MPH / 112 KM/H)

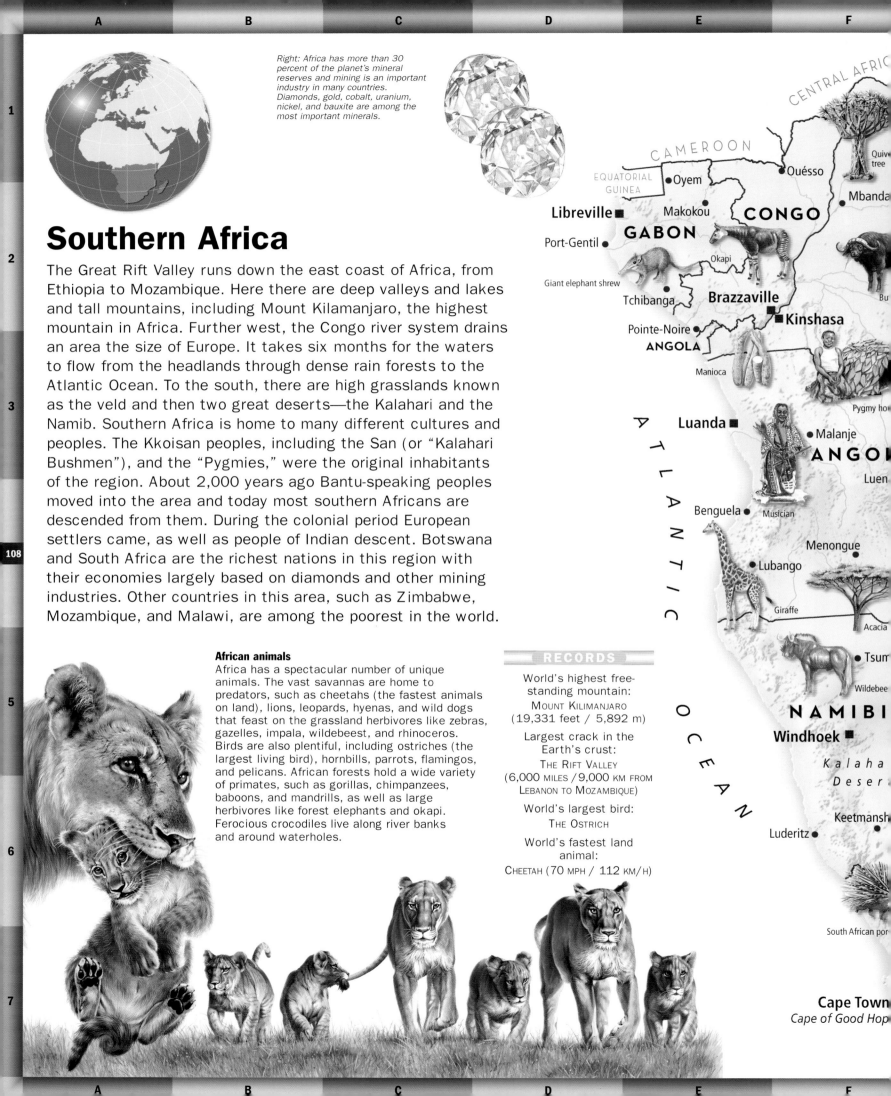

CENTRAL AFRIC

CAMEROON
EQUATORIAL GUINEA
Oyem
Ouésso
Mbanda
Libreville
Makokou
CONGO
GABON
Okapi
Port-Gentil
Giant elephant shrew
Tchibanga
Brazzaville
Bu
Pointe-Noire
Kinshasa
ANGOLA
Manioca
Pygmy ho
Luanda
Malanje
ANGO
Luen
Benguela
Musician
Menongue
Lubango
Giraffe
Acacia
Tsum
Wildebee
NAMIBI
Windhoek
Kalaha
Deser
Keetmansh
Luderitz
South African por
Cape Town
Cape of Good Hop
Quive tree

108

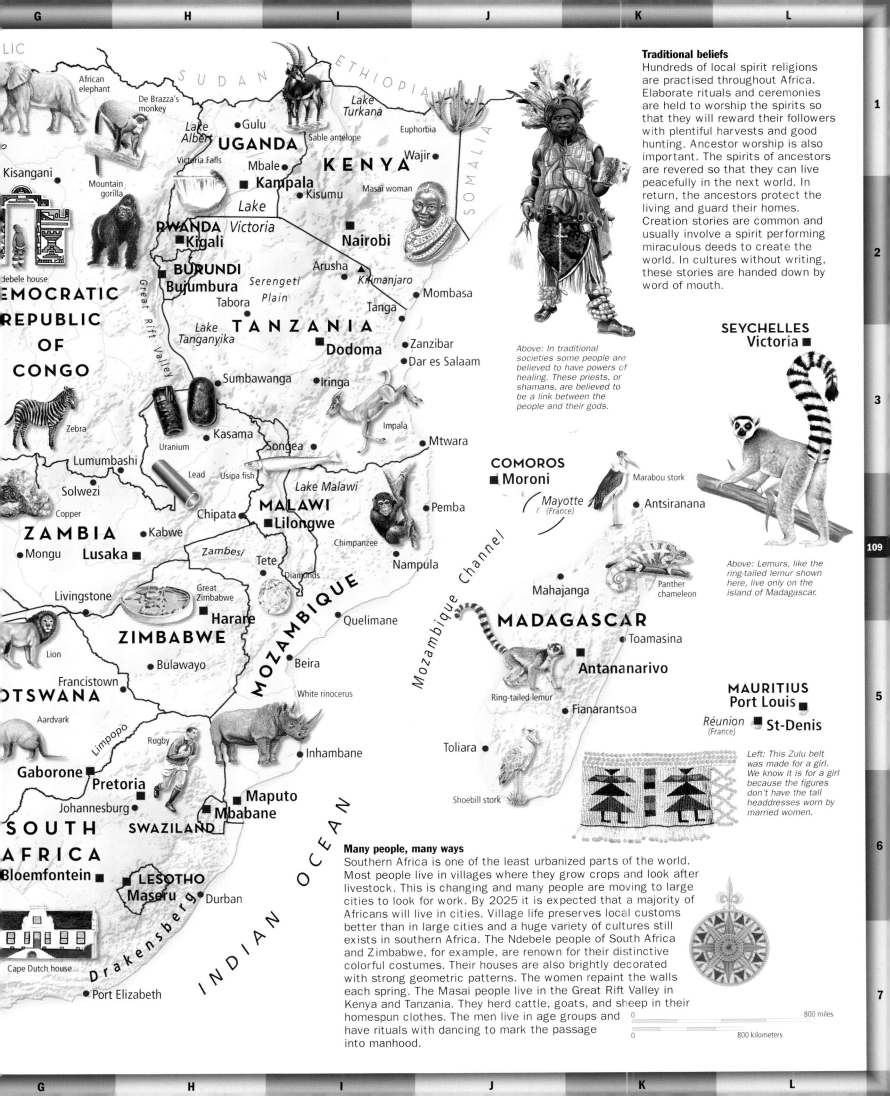

LIC

African elephant

SUDAN

De Brazza's monkey

Kisangani

Lake Albert

•Gulu

UGANDA

Mountain gorilla

Victoria Falls

Mbale

Kampala

Sable antelope

ETHIOPIA

Lake Turkana

Euphorbia

KENYA

Wajir

•Kisumu

Masai woman

SOMALIA

•debele house

DEMOCRATIC

REPUBLIC

OF

CONGO

RWANDA

Kigali

Lake Victoria

Nairobi

BURUNDI

Bujumbura

Great Rift Valley

Serengeti Plain

Arusha

▲ Kilimanjaro

Tabora•

T A N Z A N I A

•Mombasa

Tanga

Zebra

Lake Tanganyika

Sumbawanga•

Dodoma

•Zanzibar

Dar es Salaam

Uranium

•Iringa

Impala

Kasama•

Lumumbashi•

Lead

Usipa fish

Songea•

•Mtwara

Solwezi•

Copper

Lake Malawi

MALAWI

•Pemba

COMOROS

Moroni

Marabou stork

SEYCHELLES

Victoria ■

Z A M B I A

•Mongu

Lusaka ■

Kabwe•

Chipata•

Lilongwe

Chimpanzee

•Nampula

Mayotte (France)

Antsiranana•

Zambesi

Tete•

Panther chameleon

Diamonds

Great Zimbabwe

Livingstone•

Harare

Quelimane

Mahajanga•

Lion

ZIMBABWE

M O Z A M B I Q U E

Mozambique Channel

M A D A G A S C A R

Toamasina

•Bulawayo

Beira•

White rinocerus

Francistown•

Aardvark

Rugby

•Inhambane

Ring-tailed lemur

Antananarivo

Fianarantsoa•

MAURITIUS

Port Louis ■

OTSWANA

Limpopo

Gaborone ■

Pretoria ■

Réunion (France)

■ **St-Denis**

Johannesburg•

Maputo

Mbabane

Toliara•

SOUTH

SWAZILAND

Shoebill stork

AFRICA

Bloemfontein ■

LESOTHO

Maseru

•Durban

Cape Dutch house

Drakensberg

Port Elizabeth•

INDIAN OCEAN

Traditional beliefs

Hundreds of local spirit religions are practised throughout Africa. Elaborate rituals and ceremonies are held to worship the spirits so that they will reward their followers with plentiful harvests and good hunting. Ancestor worship is also important. The spirits of ancestors are revered so that they can live peacefully in the next world. In return, the ancestors protect the living and guard their homes. Creation stories are common and usually involve a spirit performing miraculous deeds to create the world. In cultures without writing, these stories are handed down by word of mouth.

Above: In traditional societies some people are believed to have powers of healing. These priests, or shamans, are believed to be a link between the people and their gods.

Above: Lemurs, like the ring-tailed lemur shown here, live only on the island of Madagascar.

Left: This Zulu belt was made for a girl. We know it is for a girl because the figures don't have the tall headdresses worn by married women.

Many people, many ways

Southern Africa is one of the least urbanized parts of the world. Most people live in villages where they grow crops and look after livestock. This is changing and many people are moving to large cities to look for work. By 2025 it is expected that a majority of Africans will live in cities. Village life preserves local customs better than in large cities and a huge variety of cultures still exists in southern Africa. The Ndebele people of South Africa and Zimbabwe, for example, are renown for their distinctive colorful costumes. Their houses are also brightly decorated with strong geometric patterns. The women repaint the walls each spring. The Masai people live in the Great Rift Valley in Kenya and Tanzania. They herd cattle, goats, and sheep in their homespun clothes. The men live in age groups and have rituals with dancing to mark the passage into manhood.

0   800 miles

0   800 kilometers

109

Meriana Islands
Saipan
Guam
Palau Islands
Yap
Pohnpei
M i c r o n e s
Caroline Islands
M e
Bismarck Sea
New Britain
New Ireland
Bougainville
New Guinea ▲ Mt Wilhelm
Solomon
Solomon Sea
Guadalcanal
Arafura Sea
Torres Strait
Coral Sea
Timor Sea
Gulf of Carpentaria
Great Barrier Reef
Arnhem Land
Kimberley
Great Dividing Range
Pilbara
Australia
INDIAN OCEAN
Gibson Desert
Great Victoria Desert
Lake Eyre
Nullarbor Plain
Darling
Great Australian Bight
Murray
Great Dividing Range
▲ Mt Kosciuszko
Tasmania
Tasman
SOUTHERN OCEAN

CLIMATE AND WEATHER
Papua New Guinea has a hot tropical climate in the lowlands with cooler temperatures in the high mountainous areas in the center of the island. Some of the tallest peaks experience snowfall—a rarity in the tropics. Northern and central Australia has a hot tropical climate with large deserts in the outback and rain forests, grasslands, and mangroves along the coast. Southern Australia, Tasmania, and New Zealand have cooler, temperate climates. The islands of Oceania are mainly tropical with little seasonal variation. They have tropical forests, grasslands, and shrublands.

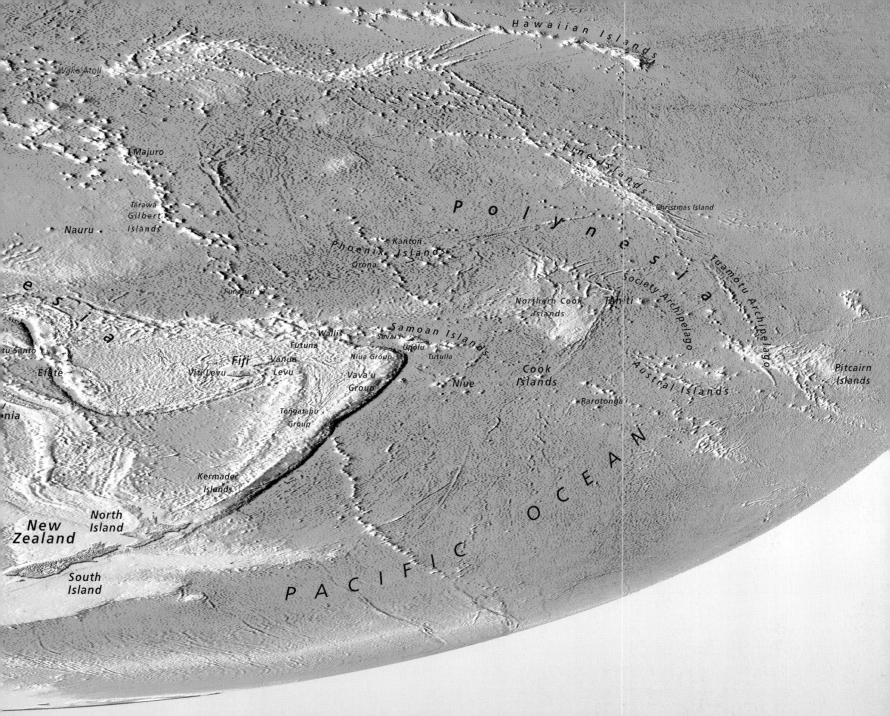

Wake Atoll

Majuro

Tarawa
Gilbert
Islands

Nauru

Phoenix Islands
Kanton
Orona

Funafuti

Polynesia

Christmas Island

Line Islands

Hawaiian Islands

Tuamotu Archipelago

Society Archipelago

Northern Cook
Islands

Tahiti

Samoan Islands
Wallis
Futuna
Savaii
Upolu
Tutuila
Niue Group

Fiji
Vanua
Levu
Viti Levu

Vava'u
Group

Niue

Cook
Islands

Rarotonga

Austral Islands

Pitcairn
Islands

tu Santo
Efate

nia

Tongatapu
Group

Kermadec
Islands

PACIFIC OCEAN

New
Zealand

North
Island

South
Island

PACIFIC OCEAN

Australia is an island and also the world's smallest and flattest continent. Oceania is the name given to the 25,000 tiny volcanic islands and coral atolls sprinkled over the huge expanse of the Pacific Ocean. It is divided into three areas—Micronesia,

AUSTRALIA AND OCEANIA

Melanesia, and Polynesia. Papua New Guinea and the North and South Islands of New Zealand are the largest islands in Oceania. The region stretches northward as far as the Hawaiian Islands, and eastward to Easter Island, where giant stone figures

were carved by an ancient Polynesian civilization. Landscapes here vary from mountainous tropical rain forest to the vast red deserts of central Australia. Many of the Pacific Island fishing and farming communities lie just 15 feet (5 m) above sea level. Australia's Great Barrier Reef, which stretches for 1,200 miles (over 2,000 km) and is the world's longest coral reef, is one of the region's most spectacular natural features. The Mariana Trench in the Pacific Ocean has the Earth's deepest point at 35,817 feet (10,920 m) below sea level (that's deeper than Mount Everest is tall).

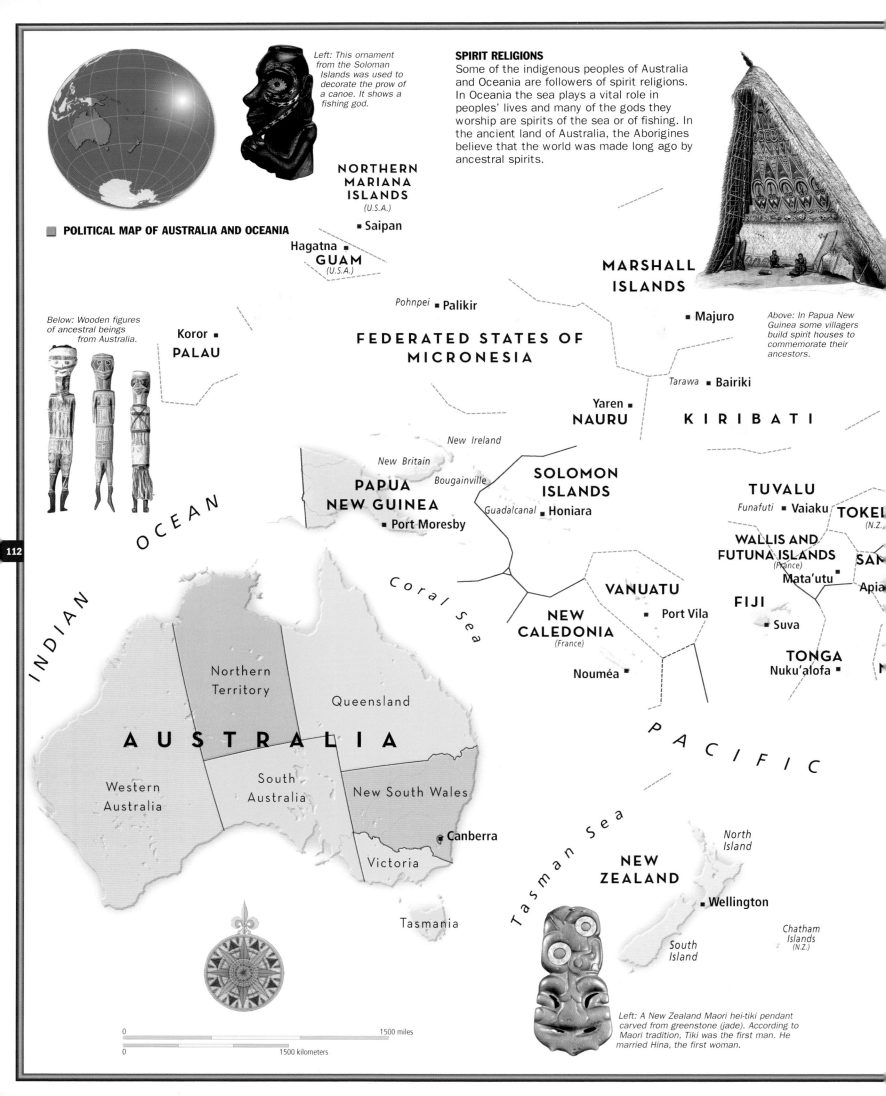

Left: This ornament from the Soloman Islands was used to decorate the prow of a canoe. It shows a fishing god.

SPIRIT RELIGIONS

Some of the indigenous peoples of Australia and Oceania are followers of spirit religions. In Oceania the sea plays a vital role in peoples' lives and many of the gods they worship are spirits of the sea or of fishing. In the ancient land of Australia, the Aborigines believe that the world was made long ago by ancestral spirits.

NORTHERN MARIANA ISLANDS
(U.S.A.)
■ Saipan

Hagatna ■
GUAM
(U.S.A.)

■ **POLITICAL MAP OF AUSTRALIA AND OCEANIA**

Below: Wooden figures of ancestral beings from Australia.

Above: In Papua New Guinea some villagers build spirit houses to commemorate their ancestors.

Pohnpei ■ Palikir

MARSHALL ISLANDS

■ Majuro

Koror ■
PALAU

FEDERATED STATES OF MICRONESIA

Tarawa ■ Bairiki

Yaren ■
NAURU

K I R I B A T I

New Ireland

New Britain

PAPUA NEW GUINEA

Bougainville

SOLOMON ISLANDS

Guadalcanal ■ Honiara

TUVALU
Funafuti ■ Vaiaku

TOKEL
(N.Z.)

WALLIS AND FUTUNA ISLANDS
(France)
Mata'utu ■

SAM

■ Port Moresby

VANUATU

FIJI

Apia

OCEAN

Coral Sea

NEW CALEDONIA
(France)

■ Port Vila

■ Suva

TONGA
Nuku'alofa ■

INDIAN

Nouméa ■

P A C I F I C

Northern Territory

Queensland

A U S T R A L I A

Western Australia

South Australia

New South Wales

■ Canberra

Victoria

North Island

NEW ZEALAND

Tasman Sea

Tasmania

■ Wellington

Chatham Islands
(N.Z.)

South Island

0   1500 miles

0   1500 kilometers

Left: A New Zealand Maori hei-tiki pendant carved from greenstone (jade). According to Maori tradition, Tiki was the first man. He married Hina, the first woman.

Australia and Oceania

Australia and New Zealand are wealthy developed nations with high living standards. Both countries had indigenous populations before European settlement—the Aborigines in Australia and the Maori in New Zealand. Both were colonized by Britain and most people today are descendants of settlers from the United Kingdom and Ireland. More recent immigration from other parts of Europe and Asia is gradually changing this. In contrast to the mainly Western lifestyles of Australians and New Zealanders, the people of Papua New Guinea and the Pacific Islands tend to follow the traditional ways of their forefathers.

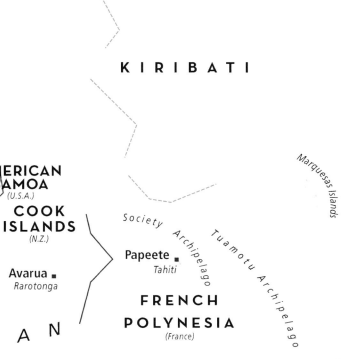

Christmas Island

K I R I B A T I

AMERICAN SAMOA *(U.S.A.)*

COOK ISLANDS *(N.Z.)*

Society Archipelago

Avarua ▪
Rarotonga

Marquesas Islands

Papeete ▪
Tahiti

Tuamotu Archipelago

FRENCH POLYNESIA *(France)*

A N

Pitcairn Island

▪ **Adamstown**
PITCAIRN ISLANDS *(U.K.)*

PAPUA NEW GUINEA

Country name Independent State of Papua New Guinea
Area 178,703 sq mi (462,840 sq km)
Population 5,931,769
Government Parliamentary democracy
Capital Port Moresby
Currency Kina
Languages Melanesian Pidgin, English, Motu, and 800 indigenous languages
Main religions Roman Catholic 22%, Lutheran 16%, indigenous beliefs 34%
Literacy 58%
GDP per capita $2,000 (2007 est.)

FIJI

Country name Republic of the Fiji Islands
Area 7,054 sq mi (18,270 sq km)
Population 931,741
Government Republic
Capital Suva
Currency Fijian dollar
Languages English, Fijian, Hindustani
Main religions Christian 53%, Hindu 34%, Muslim 7%
Literacy 94%
GDP per capita $5,500 (2007 est.)

MICRONESIA

Country name Federated States of Micronesia
Area 271 sq mi (702 sq km)
Population 107,665
Government Republic
Capital Palikir
Currency US dollar
Languages English, Trukese, Pohnpeian, Yapese, Kosrean, Ulithian, Woleaian, Nukuoro, Kapingamarangi
Main religions Roman Catholic 50%, Protestant 47%
Literacy 89%
GDP per capita $2,000 (2007 est.)

VANUATU

Country name Republic of Vanuatu
Area 4,710 sq mi (12,200 sq km)
Population 215,446
Government Parliamentary republic
Capital Port-Vila
Currency Vatu
Languages Bislama, English, French, and over 100 local languages
Main religions Presbyterian 31.4%, Anglican 13.4%, Roman Catholic 13.1%
Literacy 74%
GDP per capita $3,900 (2007 est.)

KIRIBATI

Country name Republic of Kiribati
Area 313 sq mi (811 sq km)
Population 110,356
Government Republic
Capital Tarawa
Currency Australian dollar
Languages I-Kiribati, English
Main religions Roman Catholic 52%, Protestant 40%
Literacy NA
GDP per capita $3,600 (2007 est.)

AUSTRALIA

Country name Commonwealth of Australia
Area 2,967,909 sq mi (7,686,850 sq km)
Population 20,600,856
Government Parliamentary democracy
Capital Canberra
Currency Australian dollar
Languages English, Indigenous languages
Main religions Catholic 26.4%, Anglican 20.5%, other Christian 20.5%
Literacy 99%
GDP per capita $36,300 (2007 est.)

SOLOMON ISLANDS

Country name Solomon Islands
Area 10,985 sq mi (28,450 sq km)
Population 581,318
Government Parliamentary democracy
Capital Honiara
Currency Solomon Islands dollar
Languages Melanesian pidgin, English, 120 indigenous languages
Main religions Church of Melanesia 32.8%, Roman Catholic 19%, South Seas Evangelical 17%
Literacy 76.6%
GDP per capita $1,900 (2007 est.)

NAURU

Country name Republic of Nauru
Area 8 sq mi (21 sq km)
Population 13,770
Government Republic
Capital No official capital (Government offices in Yaren)
Currency Australian dollar
Languages Nauruan, English
Main religions Christian (Protestant 66%, Roman Catholic 33%)
Literacy NA
GDP per capita $5,000 (2007 est.)

TONGA

Country name Kingdom of Tonga
Area 289 sq mi (748 sq km)
Population 119,009
Government Constitutional monarchy
Capital Nuku'alofa
Currency Pa'anga
Languages Tongan, English
Main religions Christian
Literacy 99%
GDP per capita $5,100 (2007 est.)

NEW ZEALAND

Country name New Zealand
Area 103,738 sq mi (268,680 sq km)
Population 4,173,460
Government Parliamentary democracy
Capital Wellington
Currency New Zealand dollar
Languages English, Maori
Main religions Anglican 14.9%, Roman Catholic 12.4%, Presbyterian 10.9%
Literacy 99%
GDP per capita $26,400 (2007 est.)

MARSHALL ISLANDS

Country name Republic of the Marshall Islands
Area 70 sq mi (181 sq km)
Population 63,174
Government Republic
Capital Majuro
Currency US dollar
Languages Marshallese, English
Main religions Protestant 54.8%, Assembly of God 25.8%, Roman Catholic 8.4%
Literacy 94%
GDP per capita $2,900 (2007 est.)

TUVALU

Country name Tuvalu
Area 10 sq mi (26 sq km)
Population 12,177
Government Parliamentary democracy
Capital Funafuti
Currency Australian dollar
Languages Tuvaluan, English, Samoan, Kiribati
Main religions Church of Tuvalu 97%, Seventh-Day Adventist 1.4%
Literacy 55%
GDP per capita $1,600 (2007 est.)

SAMOA

Country name Independent State of Samoa
Area 1,137 sq mi (2,944 sq km)
Population 217,083
Government Parliamentary democracy
Capital Apia
Currency Tala
Languages Samoan, English
Main religions Congregationalist 34.8%, Roman Catholic 19.6%, Methodist 15%
Literacy 99%
GDP per capita $5,400 (2007 est.)

Australia and Papua New Guinea

More than three-quarters of Australia is a parched wilderness, with deserts, scrubby bushland, and arid grasslands dotted with acacia and eucalypt trees. But there is also a lot of good farmland in the south and along the coasts, and meat, wool, wine, and wheat have long been lucrative exports. The country is rich in mineral resources with coal, iron ore, copper, petroleum, and gold among top export products. Japan is Australia's largest trading partner, followed by China, the US, Britain, and Singapore. Australia's population has increased fourfold in the last 90 years. Between 1945 and 2000 Australia welcomed nearly six million immigrants to its shores. About 90 percent of Australians are of European descent, although in recent years many Chinese and Vietnamese people have settled here. Most people live in cities and towns and work in offices. Australia is a wealthy, modern democracy and is usually ranked near the top of quality-of-life indexes. To the northeast of Australia, Papua New Guinea is a much more traditional society, where most people live in the country and work as farmers. The top four exports are coffee, cocoa, palm oil, and coconuts.

RECORDS

World's smallest continent:
AUSTRALIA

World's largest coral reef:
GREAT BARRIER REEF, AUSTRALIA

Country with the largest number of reptile species:
AUSTRALIA. IT HAS 755 SPECIES.

Country with the largest number of ethnic groups:
PAPUA NEW GUINEA

World's most distinctive opera house:
SYDNEY OPERA HOUSE

The first Australians

Australia was first settled about 45,000 years ago by people who sailed from Southeast Asia or walked across land bridges that are thought to have existed at the time. These were the ancestors of the Aborigines, the indigenous peoples who inhabited the land when the first European settlers came in the 18th century. The Aboriginal population declined steeply after the Europeans arrived, mainly because they had no resistance to the diseases the settlers carried, but also as a result of discrimination. The Aboriginal population has increased in recent years and the new 2008 government made a formal apology for past wrongs.

Left: This traditional Aboriginal bark painting illustrates a creation myth.

Australian animals

The Australian landmass has been isolated from other continents for a long time and it has some quite unique animals. There are a lot of marsupials (animals that carry their young in pouches), including kangaroos, possums, koalas, numbats, and bandicoots. Australia and New Guinea are also home to the only three species of egg-laying mammals—platypuses and two species of echidna.

Right: The echidna, or spiny anteater, is one of only three mammals in the world that lays eggs.

Timor Sea

Mildil beach market

Darwin

Arr L

Katherine

Cassowary

Kunnunurra

Rainbow lorikeet

Kimberley

NORTHE
TERRITO

Broome

Grey kangaroo

Didgeridoo player

Devil's marbl

Grey kangaroo

OCEAN

Port Hedland

A U S T

T

Thorny devil

Ayers Rock

Exmouth

Red kangaroo

Newman

WESTERN

Alice Spr

AUSTRALIA

Cathedral anthill

Frilled neck lizar

INDIAN

Platypus

SOUT
AUSTRA

Meekatharra

Australian rules football

Emu

The Pinnacles

Nullarbor Pla

Saltwater crocodi

Geraldton

Swan Bell Towers

Kalgoorlie

Eucla

Koala

Great Australian Bight

Perth

SOUTHERN OCEAN

Albany

| 0 | | | | 500 miles |
| 0 | | 500 kilometers | | |

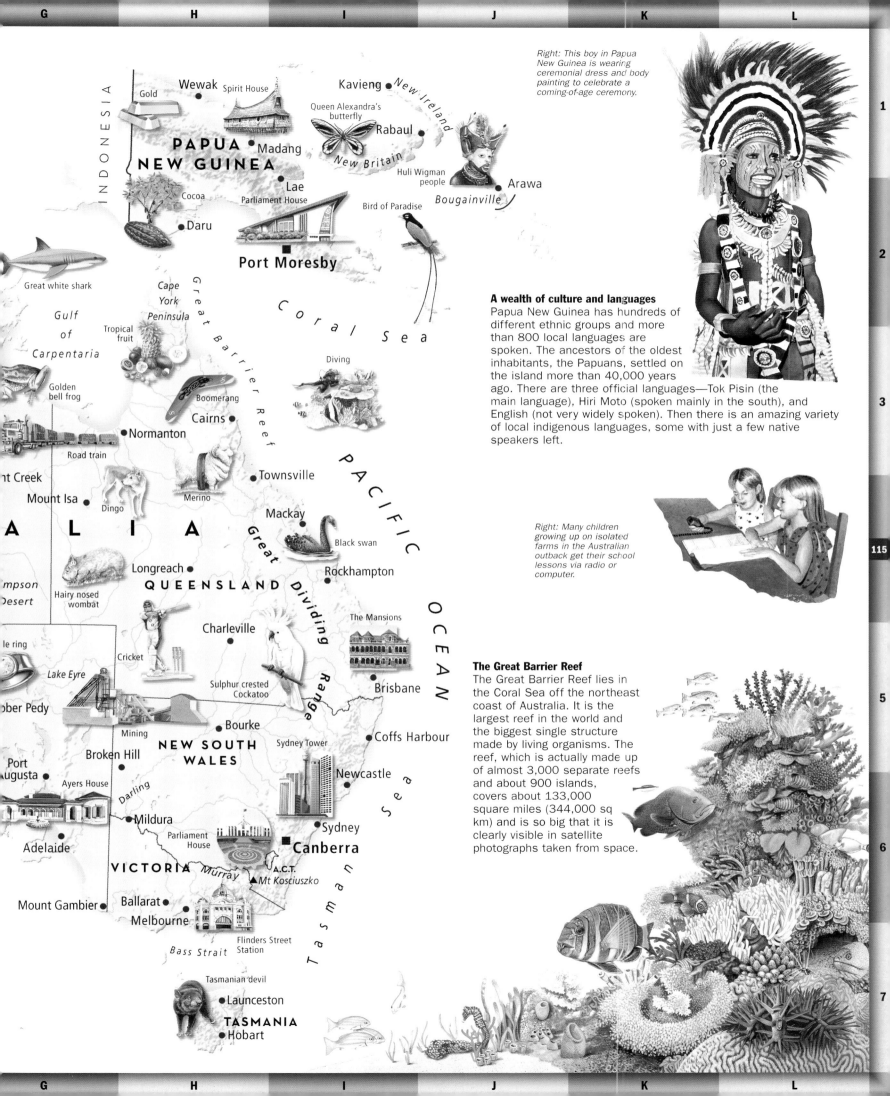

Gold

Wewak · Spirit House

Kavieng · *New Ireland*

Queen Alexandra's butterfly

Rabaul

PAPUA

· Madang

New Britain

NEW GUINEA

Huli Wigman people

· Arawa

Cocoa

· Lae Parliament House

Bougainville

· Daru

Bird of Paradise

Port Moresby

Right: This boy in Papua New Guinea is wearing ceremonial dress and body painting to celebrate a coming-of-age ceremony.

INDONESIA

Great white shark

Cape York Peninsula

Gulf of Carpentaria

Tropical fruit

Great Barrier Reef

Coral Sea

Diving

Golden bell frog

Boomerang

Cairns

· Normanton

Road train

PACIFIC

A wealth of culture and languages

Papua New Guinea has hundreds of different ethnic groups and more than 800 local languages are spoken. The ancestors of the oldest inhabitants, the Papuans, settled on the island more than 40,000 years ago. There are three official languages—Tok Pisin (the main language), Hiri Motu (spoken mainly in the south), and English (not very widely spoken). Then there is an amazing variety of local indigenous languages, some with just a few native speakers left.

t Creek

Mount Isa ·

Dingo

Merino

· Townsville

A L I A

· Mackay

Black swan

Longreach ·

Hairy nosed wombat

Rockhampton ·

mpson Desert

QUEENSLAND

Great Dividing Range

Right: Many children growing up on isolated farms in the Australian outback get their school lessons via radio or computer.

The Mansions

le ring

Charleville ·

Lake Eyre

Cricket

Sulphur crested Cockatoo

· Brisbane

ber Pedy

Mining

· Bourke

· Coffs Harbour

Port ugusta ·

Ayers House

NEW SOUTH WALES

Sydney Tower

· Newcastle

Darling

· Mildura

Parliament House

· Sydney

Adelaide

■ Canberra

Murray

A.C.T.

▲ *Mt Kosciuszko*

VICTORIA

Mount Gambier ·

Ballarat ·

Melbourne

Flinders Street Station

Bass Strait

Tasmanian devil

· Launceston

TASMANIA

· Hobart

The Great Barrier Reef

The Great Barrier Reef lies in the Coral Sea off the northeast coast of Australia. It is the largest reef in the world and the biggest single structure made by living organisms. The reef, which is actually made up of almost 3,000 separate reefs and about 900 islands, covers about 133,000 square miles (344,000 sq km) and is so big that it is clearly visible in satellite photographs taken from space.

Tasman Sea

115

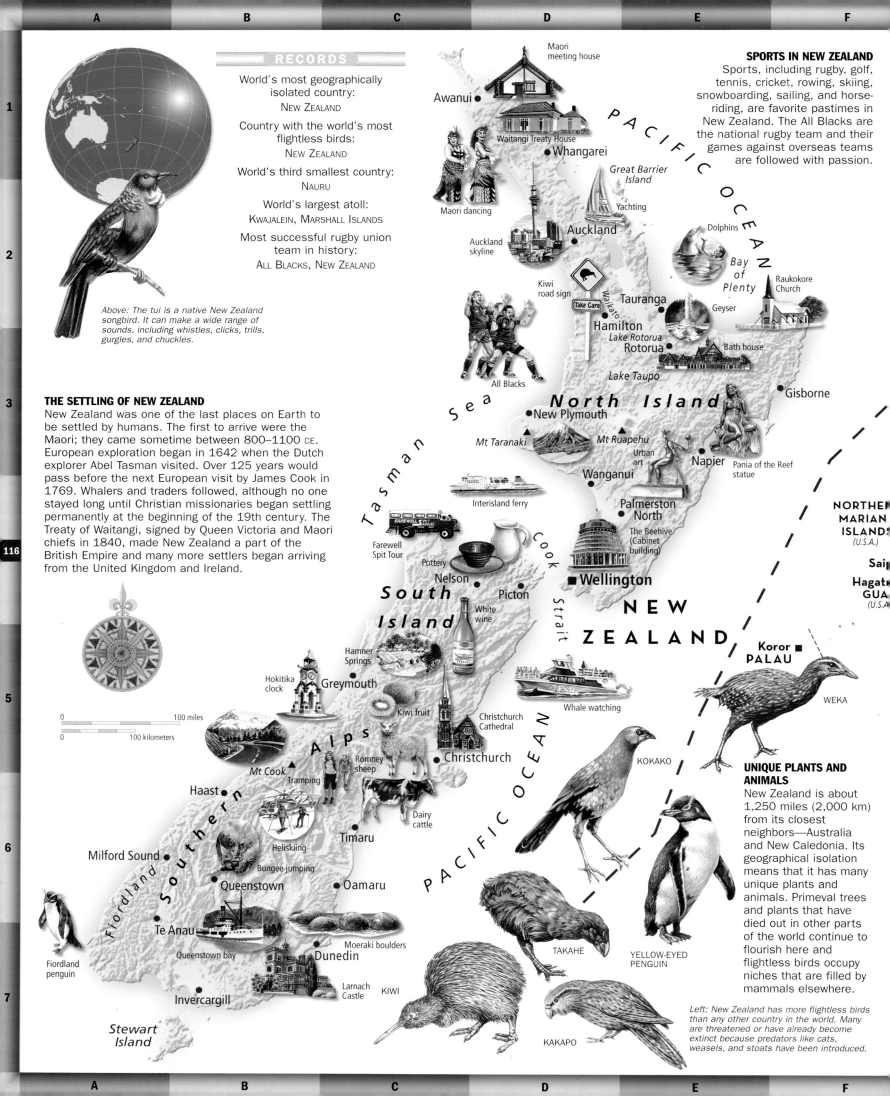

RECORDS

World's most geographically isolated country:
NEW ZEALAND

Country with the world's most flightless birds:
NEW ZEALAND

World's third smallest country:
NAURU

World's largest atoll:
KWAJALEIN, MARSHALL ISLANDS

Most successful rugby union team in history:
ALL BLACKS, NEW ZEALAND

Above: The tui is a native New Zealand songbird. It can make a wide range of sounds, including whistles, clicks, trills, gurgles, and chuckles.

THE SETTLING OF NEW ZEALAND

New Zealand was one of the last places on Earth to be settled by humans. The first to arrive were the Maori; they came sometime between 800–1100 CE. European exploration began in 1642 when the Dutch explorer Abel Tasman visited. Over 125 years would pass before the next European visit by James Cook in 1769. Whalers and traders followed, although no one stayed long until Christian missionaries began settling permanently at the beginning of the 19th century. The Treaty of Waitangi, signed by Queen Victoria and Maori chiefs in 1840, made New Zealand a part of the British Empire and many more settlers began arriving from the United Kingdom and Ireland.

SPORTS IN NEW ZEALAND

Sports, including rugby, golf, tennis, cricket, rowing, skiing, snowboarding, sailing, and horse-riding, are favorite pastimes in New Zealand. The All Blacks are the national rugby team and their games against overseas teams are followed with passion.

UNIQUE PLANTS AND ANIMALS

New Zealand is about 1,250 miles (2,000 km) from its closest neighbors—Australia and New Caledonia. Its geographical isolation means that it has many unique plants and animals. Primeval trees and plants that have died out in other parts of the world continue to flourish here and flightless birds occupy niches that are filled by mammals elsewhere.

Left: New Zealand has more flightless birds than any other country in the world. Many are threatened or have already become extinct because predators like cats, weasels, and stoats have been introduced.

Maori meeting house
Awanui
Waitangi Treaty House
Maori dancing
Whangarei
PACIFIC OCEAN
Great Barrier Island
Yachting
Auckland
Auckland skyline
Dolphins
Bay of Plenty
Raukokore Church
Kiwi road sign
Take Care
Waikato
Tauranga
Geyser
Hamilton
Lake Rotorua
Rotorua
Bath house
Lake Taupo
Gisborne
All Blacks
North Island
New Plymouth
Mt Taranaki
Mt Ruapehu
Urban art
Napier
Pania of the Reef statue
Wanganui
Interisland ferry
Palmerston North
NORTHERN MARIANA ISLANDS (U.S.A.)
Saipan
Hagåtña
GUAM (U.S.A.)
Tasman Sea
FAREWELL SPIT TOUR
Farewell Spit Tour
Pottery
Nelson
White wine
Picton
The Beehive (Cabinet building)
Wellington
NEW ZEALAND
Koror ■
PALAU
South Island
Cook Strait
Hamner Springs
Hokitika clock
Greymouth
Kiwi fruit
Christchurch Cathedral
Whale watching
WEKA
Alps
Mt Cook
Tramping
Romney sheep
Christchurch
KOKAKO
Haast
Dairy cattle
Heliskiing
Timaru
Southern
Milford Sound
Bungee jumping
Queenstown
Oamaru
Fiordland
Te Anau
Moeraki boulders
Fiordland penguin
Queenstown bay
Dunedin
Larnach Castle
KIWI
Invercargill
TAKAHE
YELLOW-EYED PENGUIN
Stewart Island
KAKAPO

0   100 miles
0   100 kilometers

New Zealand and the Pacific Islands

New Zealand is made up of two large islands—the North Island and the South Island—and several smaller ones. It is highly urbanized with more than 85 percent of the people living in towns and more than half of the population concentrated in just four cities—Auckland, Hamilton, Wellington, and Christchurch. Most people are employed in offices or industry. Less than five percent work on the land, although New Zealand is a major exporter of agricultural and forest products. Tourism is also important for the economy. Visitors are drawn to the unspoiled beauty of the landscapes and the opportunities to ski, hike, raft, and relax in the great outdoors. To the north of New Zealand, other major Pacific Island groups include Fiji, Tonga, French Polynesia, Samoa, and the Soloman Islands. Excluding Papua New Guinea and New Zealand, the region has over three million inhabitants. Although most people still live traditional lifestyles, many are moving to the cities. Tourism is widespread and major exports include sugar, coconut, fish, and pearls.

AMAZING JOURNEYS

The early inhabitants of Oceania were skilled boat-builders and navigators. They settled the islands in the vast Pacific Ocean in twin-hulled canoes that were large enough to hold entire families, as well as domestic animals, weapons, and tools. Sailors relied on their knowledge of the night sky, ocean currents, and the flight of birds as navigation aids. Some islanders made ocean charts using sticks bound together to represent currents and shells for the islands.

Right: A "map" made with sticks and shells used by Pacific Island navigators.

Wake Island (U.S.A.)

Above: Sturdy ocean-going canoes were fitted with sails made of matting and attached to upright masts and horizontal booms made from logs.

Right: A giant stone statue from Rapa Nui (Easter Island) in the eastern Pacific. Easter Islanders are a Polynesian people, but the islands are administered from Chile.

117

MARSHALL ISLANDS

Palikir ■

■ Majuro

MICRONESIA

Stone money

Yaren ■
NAURU

Gilbert Islands
■ **Bairiki**

KIRIBATI

Church

Christmas Island

Line

Phoenix Islands

KIRIBATI

SOUTH PACIFIC OCEAN

SOLOMON ISLANDS

Guadalcanal
Honiara ■

TUVALU

Vaiaku ■

Fantail

Tokelau Islands (N.Z.)

Islands

Marquesas Islands

Wallis & Futuna Islands (France)

Mata 'Utu ■

SAMOA
Apia ■ ■ **American Samoa** (U.S.A.)
Pago Pago ■

Traditional house

Coral Sea

VANUATU

■ **Port Vila**

Vanua Levu

Viti Levu ■ **Suva**

FIJI

Vanua Levu

Niue (N.Z.)
■ **Alofi**

Cook Islands (N.Z.)

Society Islands

Tuamotu

Tahiti ■ **Papeete**

Archipelago

New Caledonia ■ Noumea (France)

■ **Nuku'alofa**

TONGA

Avarua ■

French Polynesia (France)

Traffic officer

0 1000 miles
0 1000 kilometres

Tangaroa sea god

Austral Islands

Pitcairn Islands (U.K.)

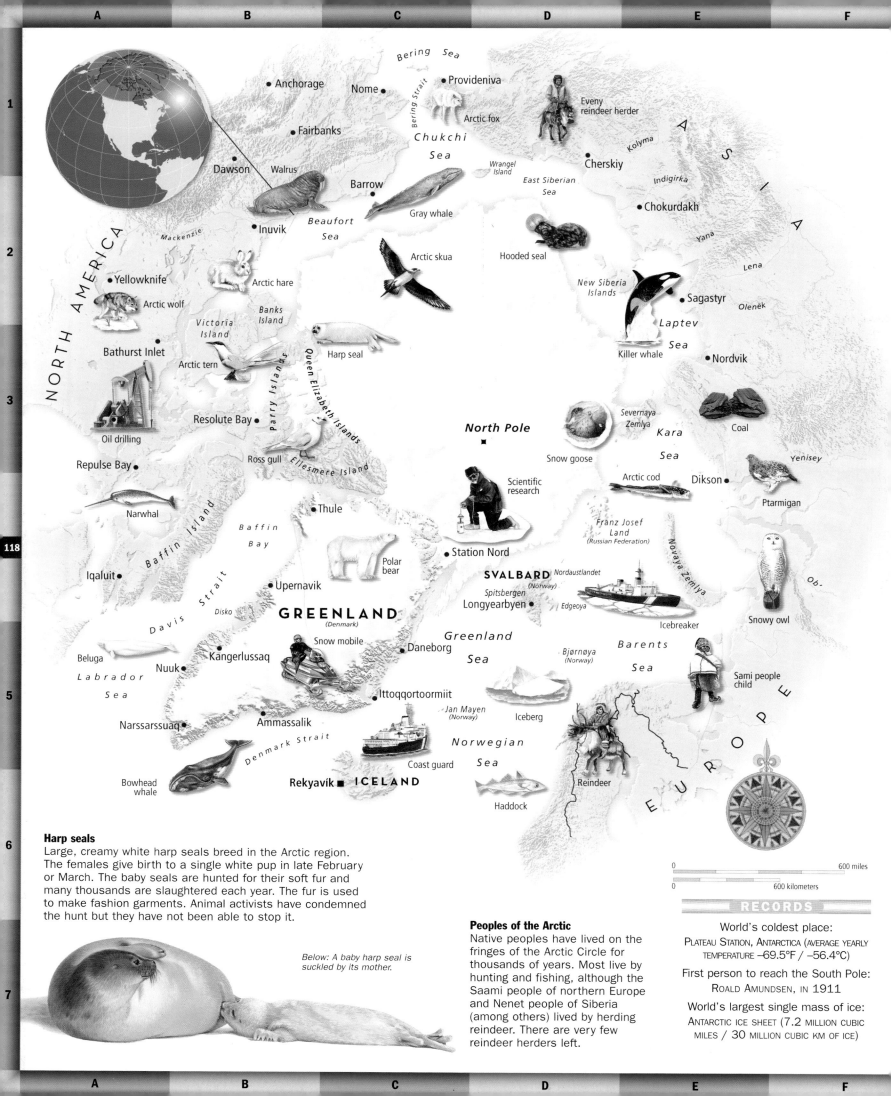

Bering Sea

• Anchorage

Nome

• Provideniva

Arctic fox

Eveny reindeer herder

• Fairbanks

Chukchi Sea

• Dawson

Walrus

• Barrow

Beaufort Sea

• Inuvik

Mackenzie

Gray whale

Wrangel Island

East Siberian Sea

• Cherskiy

Kolyma

ASIA

Indigirka

• Chokurdakh

Yana

Arctic skua

Hooded seal

New Siberia Islands

Lena

• Yellowknife

Arctic hare

• Sagastyr

Oleněk

Arctic wolf

Banks Island

Killer whale

Laptev Sea

NORTH AMERICA

Victoria Island

Harp seal

• Nordvik

• Bathurst Inlet

Arctic tern

Parry Islands

Queen Elizabeth Islands

Severnaya Zemlya

Kara Sea

Coal

• Resolute Bay

Oil drilling

North Pole

Snow goose

Arctic cod

• Dikson

Yenisey

• Repulse Bay

Ross gull

Ellesmere Island

Scientific research

Ptarmigan

Franz Josef Land (Russian Federation)

Narwhal

• Thule

Novaya Zemlya

Baffin Island

Baffin Bay

Polar bear

• Station Nord

SVALBARD

Nordaustlandet

Ob'

• Iqaluit

• Upernavik

Spitsbergen

Longyearbyen

Edgeoya

Snowy owl

Davis Strait

Disko

GREENLAND

(Denmark)

Greenland Sea

Bjørnøya (Norway)

Barents Sea

Icebreaker

Beluga

Labrador Sea

• Nuuk

• Kangerlussaq

Snow mobile

• Daneborg

Sami people child

EUROPE

• Narssarssuaq

• Ammassalik

• Ittoqqortoormiit

Jan Mayen (Norway)

Iceberg

Bowhead whale

Denmark Strait

Coast guard

Norwegian Sea

Reindeer

Rekyavík ■ ICELAND

Haddock

Harp seals

Large, creamy white harp seals breed in the Arctic region. The females give birth to a single white pup in late February or March. The baby seals are hunted for their soft fur and many thousands are slaughtered each year. The fur is used to make fashion garments. Animal activists have condemned the hunt but they have not been able to stop it.

Below: A baby harp seal is suckled by its mother.

Peoples of the Arctic

Native peoples have lived on the fringes of the Arctic Circle for thousands of years. Most live by hunting and fishing, although the Saami people of northern Europe and Nenet people of Siberia (among others) lived by herding reindeer. There are very few reindeer herders left.

0   600 miles
0   600 kilometers

RECORDS

World's coldest place:
PLATEAU STATION, ANTARCTICA (AVERAGE YEARLY TEMPERATURE −69.5°F / −56.4°C)

First person to reach the South Pole:
ROALD AMUNDSEN, IN 1911

World's largest single mass of ice:
ANTARCTIC ICE SHEET (7.2 MILLION CUBIC MILES / 30 MILLION CUBIC KM OF ICE)

The Polar Regions

The North Pole is surrounded by the frozen Arctic Ocean. There is no landmass under the ocean, although in winter the ice sheets spread southward to join the landmasses of Eurasia and North America. The South Pole is located on the continent of Antarctica and is surrounded by the Southern Ocean. Both regions are very cold and windy, although Antarctica is by far the coldest of the two regions. Antarctica is covered by a huge sheet of ice that holds 90 percent of the world's fresh water. If this ice sheet melted due to global warming, it would raise sea levels around the world, flooding many low-lying lands.

Above: A krill. These small animals live in large groups, called swarms.

Amazing krill
Krill are shrimp-like invertebrates that feed on tiny plankton. They are a crucial food source in the Antarctic. Scientists made an amazing discovery in early 2008 when they found krill living at 11,500 feet (3,500 m) in the Antarctic ocean.

0   1000 miles
0   1000 kilometers

Orkney Islands
(U.K.) □ Orcadas (Argentina)
□ Signy
  (U.K.)

Iceberg

Sanae
(South Africa) □
Neumayer □
(Germany)
□ Maitri (India)
□ Novolazarevskaya
  (Russian Federation)

Research vessel

Antarctic fur seal

Elephant Island

Blue whale

South polar skua

Asuka
(Japan) □
Syowa
(Japan) □
Molodezhnaya
□ (Russian Federation)

Esperanza (Argentina)
□ Marambio (Argentina)

Weddell Sea

Queen Maud Land

□ Mizuho
  (Japan)

Crabeater seal

Krill

(U.S.A.)
Vernadsky
(Ukraine)
□ Faraday (U.K.)

Antarctic Peninsula

Tourist flight

Halley
(U.K.)

Explorer

Rescue helicopter

Gentoo penguin

□ Mawson (Australia)

Rothera
(U.K.) □
San Martin
(Argentina)
Alexander Island

□ Belgrano II
  (Argentina)

Berkner Island

King penguin

ANTARCTICA

East Antarctica

□ Zhongshan (China)
□ Davis (Australia)

Jelly fish

Ronne Ice Shelf

Weddell seal

Adeliè penguin

Macaroni penguins

▲ Vinson Massif

Amundsen-Scott station

West Antarctica

South Pole □ Amundsen-Scott
              (U.S.A.)

Mirny □
(Russian Federation)

Leopard seal

Thurston Island

Field camp

Queen Maud Mountains

Vostok
(Russian Federation) □
South Geomagnetic Pole

Amundsen Sea

Chinstrap penguin

Chapel of The Snows

Ross Ice Shelf

Roosevelt Island

Scientific research

□ Casey (Australia)

Below: The hardy Emperor penguin stays year-round in freezing Antarctica.

Russkaya
(Russian Federation)

Minke whale

Scott Base
(New Zealand) □
McMurdo
(U.S.A.)

Giant petrel

Emperor penguin

Ross Sea

Terra Nova Bay □
(Italy)

Cruise ship

The Antarctic winter
Antarctic winter runs from June to August in complete darkness with howling winds and storms. Many of the animals that inhabit the coastal areas during the summer move north for the winter. Emperor penguins are an exception to this; not only do they stay but they actually breed during the winter months, with the male bird incubating a single egg on his feet to keep it warm.

Albatross

Dumont d'Urville
(France)

Leningradskaya
(Russian Federation)

Hourglass dolphin

Balleny Islands

Dumont d'Urville Sea

Davis Sea

119

Territories and Dependencies

Territories and dependencies are regions that are not independent but are governed by other countries. Some are ruled directly by the country to which they belong. Others receive protection and financial aid from their rulers but have their own governments.

Above: The Sikh flag. The Sikhs are one of many groups in India seeking independence.

Left: Hong Kong was returned to China in 1997, after almost 100 years as a British colony. Since 1997 a S.A.R. (Special Administrative Region) of the People Republic of China, Hong Kong remains a center of world trade. After the handover from Portugal to China in 1999, Macau has become the second Chinese S.A.R.

■ SOME ONGOING TERRITORIAL DISPUTES

TERRITORY	CLAIMANT(S)
Aksai Chin	China and India
Gibraltar	United Kingdom and Spain
Golan Heights	Syria and Israel
Hala'ib Triangle	Egypt and Sudan
Isla Perejil	Morocco and Spain
Kashmir	India and Pakistan
Kurile Islands	Japan and Russia
Northern Cyprus	Republic of Cyprus and Turkish Republic of Northern Cyprus
Northern Iraq	Republic of Iraq and the PUK and KDP
South-East Turkey	Republic of Turkey and the Kurdistan Workers Party
Spratly Islands	Various claimants
Taiwan	People's Republic of China and Republic of China
Tibet	People's Republic of China and Government of Tibet in exile
West Bank and Gaza Strip	Israel and the Palestinians
Western Sahara	Morocco and Polisario

■ DEPENDENCIES AND AREAS OF SPECIAL SOVEREIGNTY

TERRITORY	SOVEREIGNTY	TERRITORY	SOVEREIGNTY	TERRITORY	SOVEREIGNTY
Akrotiri	United Kingdom	Greenland	Denmark	Norfolk Island	Australia
American Samoa	United States	Guadeloupe	France	Northern Mariana Islands	United States
Anguilla	United Kingdom	Guam	United States	Palmyra Atoll	United States
Antarctica	None	Guernsey	British Crown Dependency	Pitcairn Islands	United Kingdom
Aruba	Netherlands			Puerto Rico	United States
Ashmore and Cartier Islands	Australia	Heard Island and McDonald Islands	Australia	Reunion	France
Baker Island	United States	Hong Kong	China	Saint Barthelemy	France
Bermuda	United Kingdom	Howland Island	United States	Saint Helena	United Kingdom
Bouvet Island	Norway	Isle of Man	British Crown Dependency	Saint Martin	France
British Indian Ocean Territory	United Kingdom	Jan Mayen	Norway	Saint Pierre and Miquelon	France
Cayman Islands	United Kingdom	Jarvis Island	United States	South Georgia and the South Sandwich Islands	United Kingdom
Christmas Island	Australia	Jersey	British Crown Dependency	Spratly Islands	undetermined
Clipperton Island	France			Svalbard	Norway
Cocos	Australia	Johnston Atoll	United States	Tokelau	New Zealand
Cook Islands	New Zealand	Kingman Reef	United States	Turks and Caicos Islands	United Kingdom
Coral Sea Islands	Australia	Macau	China	Virgin Islands, UK	United Kingdom
Dhekelia	United Kingdom	Martinique	France	Virgin Islands, US	United States
Falkland Islands (Islas Malvinas)	United Kingdom	Mayotte	France	Wake Island	United States
Faroe Islands	Denmark	Midway Islands	United States	Wallis and Futuna	France
French Guiana	France	Montserrat	United Kingdom	Western Sahara	To be determined
French Polynesia	France	Navassa Island	United States		
French Southern and Antarctic Lands	France	Netherlands Antilles	Netherlands		
Gibraltar	United Kingdom	New Caledonia	France		
		Niue	New Zealand		

Glossary

ARID
An area with very low rainfall and little or no vegetation.

ATOLL
A circular or horseshoe-shaped coral reef enclosing a lagoon.

AXIS
An imaginary line running through the center of the Earth around which the planet rotates.

BASIN
An area of land that is drained by a river and its tributaries.

BAY
An area of coastline with headlands that form a halfmoon shape or partly enclose the sea.

BIGHT
A large bay.

CAPITAL CITY
The city where a state or country's government is located. Some countries have more than one capital, usually because they have divided government functions and each one is located in a different city.

CARTOGRAPHER
A person who makes maps.

CIVIL WAR
A war between rival groups within the same country.

CRUST
The rocky upper layer of the Earth's surface. The crust is broken into plates

DECIDUOUS
Trees that lose their leaves in the fall. New leaves grow back again in spring.

DEVELOPING WORLD
Parts of the world that are still becoming industrialized.

DICTATOR
A person who rules over a country with absolute power. A country ruled in this way is called a dictatorship.

ECOSYSTEM
A community of plants and animals and their adaptation to the natural surroundings in which they live.

ENDANGERED
A plant or animal species that is in danger of becoming extinct.

ENVIRONMENT
The non-living setting or natural surroundings of a community of plants and animals.

EQUATOR
An imaginary line that runs around the Earth at an equal distance from both poles.

EXPORTS
Goods that are produced within a country but sold abroad.

FOOD CHAIN
A cyclic pattern of feeding relationships. Plants usually from the basis of the food chain.

HEMISPHERE
One half of the Earth. The Earth is divided at the Equator into the Northern Hemisphere and the Southern Hemisphere.

HIGH-TECH INDUSTRIES
Industries that produce technologically advanced products, including computers, cell phones, and video games.

ICE CAP
A permanent sheet of ice or snow.

INDIGENOUS PEOPLES
A people or ethnic group that has lived in an area for a long time and whose language and culture are strongly identified with it. Usually refers to groups who lived in an area before it was colonized by European peoples.

IRRIGATION
A system for watering dry areas from nearby rivers or underground reserves.

MOLTEN
A hard substance such as iron or rock that has become liquid because exposed to very high temperatures.

PENINSULA
A piece of land surrounded on three sides by water.

POPULOUS
With a high population. China is the most populous country in the world—it has more people than any other country.

PHARMACEUTICALS
Medicinal drugs.

PRINCIPALITY
A country that is ruled by, or whose head of state, is a prince or princess.

RAIN FOREST
A very dense forest located in regions with high rainfall, usually in the tropics or subtropics.

REFUGEE
A person who lives outside of his or her own country because of political, ethnic, or religious persecution.

SAVANNA
An area of tropical grassland with tall grasses and scattered with trees. Mainly associated with Africa, but also occurs elsewhere.

SEA LEVEL
The average height of the sea. It is used as a baseline from which to measure altitude.

STEPPE
A fairly dry and often cold grassland area that covers large parts of eastern Europe, central Asia, and Siberia.

STRAIT
A narrow channel of water that connects two larger bodies of water.

TAIGA
A broad belt of conifer trees that runs across northern Eurasia (Europe and Asia).

TECTONIC PLATE
One of the rocky plates that make up the Earth's crust. The tectonic plates float on the Earth's molten mantle.

TEMPERATE
Regions on Earth that are located about half way between the Equator and the poles.

TEXTILES
Woven or knitted fabrics.

TUNDRA
The cold, barren area just below the Arctic circle. Similar areas are found on high mountains.

URBANIZATION
The process by which people move from the countryside to live in towns and cities.

WETLAND
An area of land covered with water but in which plants also live. It can also be called a swamp or marsh.

WOODLAND
A small area of forest in temperate regions. Usually has mainly deciduous trees.

Index

122

123

124

127

128

North Pole
118

ARCTIC OCEAN

Canada and Alaska
36

NORTH AMERICA
Overview
32

NORTH

Western
United States
40

Eastern
United States
38

PACIFIC

NORTH

OCEAN

ATLANTIC

OCEAN

Mexico, Central America,
and the Caribbean
42

Northern
South America
48

SOUTH AMERICA
Overview
46

SOUTH

SOUTH

PACIFIC

Southern
South America
50

ATLANTIC

OCEAN

OCEAN

SOUTHERN OCEAN